Zerø-Gs

Part I: The Armor Eternal

Joe, "It's better to be a warrior in a garden, than a gardener in a war..."

Thankss Joe!

Darrin Geisinger

Darrin Geisinger

 ALARM
STUDIOS

Cover design and interior formatting by:

King's Custom Covers
www.KingsCustomCovers.com

Zero-Gs Part I: The Armor Eternal
Story, Vehicle and Robot Designs;
Copyright © 2014-2018 4-ALARM STUDIOS

For more information contact:
zerog.darring@gmail.com

Or visit:
www.darringeisinger.com

ISBN-13: 978-1974593002

First Edition: May 2018

10 9 8 7 6 5 4 3 2 1

Acknowledgements

Thank you to my wife and family. I appreciate all your continued support, patience and encouragement.

Thanks to Timothy Alberino for providing the foreword to this book, along with Steve Quayle, Tom Horn, L.A. Marzulli, Derek and Sharon Gilbert, Gonz Shimura, Josh Peck, Justen and Wes Faull, Nick Redfern, Nick Cook and more. You are authors and researchers that both reveal and inspire.

A massive thanks goes out to artist Lucas Marangon for helping me bring to life some of the mechanical designs featured in the illustrative section of this release.

And lastly to all the friends, strangers and innocent bystanders that looked over, read through, and commented on Zero-Gs. *Without you, the project would have never crossed the finish line...*

For Phillip

Can't wait to see you again...

2007-2016

Foreword

by Timothy Alberino

Power suits, aliens, giants, clones, secret underground bases, diminishing gravity… this is just a sampling of the thematic tapestry woven into the extraordinary saga of *Zero-Gs*. As we follow the exhilarating plight of a tight-knit squad of intrepid youths arrayed for battle in armored exo-suits, Geisinger plunges us into the depths of a dark and hidden realm—a top-secret world known to Deep Black Special Operators as "core reality." The substance of this book, though cast in a fictional mold, could not be more pertinent to the time in which we now live.

In *Zero-Gs Part I: The Armor Eternal*, the citizens of earth are reeling in the wake of an extraterrestrial visitation (the "Messengers"). Their arrival has coincided with a new and terrifying predicament for terrestrial life… diminishing gravity. As the people struggle to cope with the bizarre ramifications of the gravitational anomaly, and the volatile repercussions of a global financial collapse and widespread civil unrest, a New World Order is rising from the ashes of chaos. Rumors of wars are growing, and the intentions of the Messengers are still unknown. *Where did they come from? What do they want? What traitorous deals are being made behind closed doors with the leaders of Earth?*

Driven to discover the fate of his missing father, Garret, accompanied by his formidable friends, Jay, Pak, and Beck, decide to investigate the mystery of diminishing *"Gs"* and unravel the conspiracy of the Messengers. They soon find themselves thrust into a world of secret military operators, hostile human factions, and insidious alien beings bent on dominion of the earth. A new religion is emerging, *"The Way"*, which promises to heal the ailments of human society and unite all faiths beneath a banner of universal love and fraternity. Christians, clinging to the doctrines of Scripture and the divisive teachings of Christ, are now rebels and heretics of *The Way*. Their continued existence can no longer be tolerated if global harmony is to be achieved. They must be destroyed. The battle for the soul of the human race has begun.

✶ ✶ ✶

In 1876, eminent theologian George H. Pember wrote that the "unlawful appearance among men of beings from another sphere" was a fearful characteristic of the days of Noah, and that the future recurrence of such an event would herald the End of the Age. As shocking as it may seem, Pember's prophetic forecast is about to be fulfilled.

For decades now, our society has been undergoing a systematic conditioning in anticipation of *Disclosure*—the official unveiling of an extraterrestrial presence on Planet Earth. Religious institutions worldwide, led by the Vatican, are preparing to assimilate the doctrines of an "alien gospel" into the catechisms of their faiths; while Jesuit astronomers are monitoring the approach of something they believe may change the course of human history forever. Before his death in 1999, former Jesuit priest, renowned exorcist, and papal advisor, Father Malachi Martin, made a stunning allusion to the Vatican's knowledge of "what's going on in space, and what's approaching us…" and the impact it was soon to have on human society. Father Martin's veiled hint might suggest that some of the fictional events detailed in this book are already underway. It may be that very soon a declaration of unprecedented magnitude will issue forth from St. Peter's chair in Vatican City, and the "extraterrestrial" presence will be unveiled for all the world to see.

The young protagonists in *Zero-Gs* are forced to contend with an alien adversary armed with a weapon of unimaginable power—*deception.* If they are to overcome the Great Deception beguiling humanity, they must rally what courage and faith can still be found among those who have not forsaken the Gospel of Jesus Christ.

May the story that unfolds in the following pages help to steel your heart and mind against a deception of apocalyptic proportions that is soon to appear in the earth.

Timothy Alberino

Author, *Alien Armageddon*

Zerø-Gs

Part I: The Armor Eternal

Part i: Floating Away
Chapter 1

But Jacob said, "Sell me your birthright as of this day." And Esau said, "Look, I am about to die; so what is a birthright to me?" Then Jacob said, "Swear to me as of this day." So he swore to him, and sold his birthright to Jacob.

—Genesis 25:31–33

October 21, 2045

In dreams, you soar. In nightmares, you plunge—but not always.

Higher and higher, first above our rooftop, and then beyond the trees, I floated skyward until the sight of our entire development overtook me. Roadside lamps were just stirring to life in the evaporating light, sending faint reflections over the black ribbons of winding pavement, damp from an earlier rain. Death stared me in the face—something I had been wishing for, until that horrible night. A sudden and tenacious will to survive had just annihilated that notion. Heroes don't end that way.

Had the planet's gravity at last given out, making me its first victim? Would I be alone, or would I soon see others drifting up to the same height? My neck whipped in every direction at once as

I checked for casualties in nearby yards or distant, panicked specks flailing against the dusky clouds. No one. The utter isolation made the terrible feel even worse, and the taste of dirty pennies poured into my mouth. A runaway heartbeat thundered in my bones and ears.

Stepping out onto the deck with my sandwich, I'd felt the sensational rush that signaled a possible gravitational drop. So I did what all kids did: I jumped to see how high I could get, but this time my feet never touched back down. After confirming that nothing had grabbed me physically, my instincts screamed that this impossible happening felt more…well, *alien* than a result of the gravity crisis, directing my suspicions right to the likely source. Earth was no longer alone in the universe. My father had stood in staunch opposition to the Messengers' arrival, but he was gone and it looked like I was next.

Not a soul in sight as I strayed higher, paralyzed by fear. I knew she wasn't home, but I screamed out for my mother anyway, trying not to wonder if she'd ever return.

The seven houses within Hemlock Hill Estates remained still. Everything below me lay in eerie quiet, as if the resident families had conspired to stay indoors until I floated out of sight.

Through the sensory overload, I witnessed, as if in slow motion, the fantastic effects of the diminishing Gs. Leaves danced in the air, while below, a rake I'd left lying in the grass hovered just above the lawn. Instinctual air-swimming maneuvers and cries for help proved useless and exhausting—and then I scanned the horizon.

My guts nearly heaved. The horrifying beauty of nature's grand theater devoured the last scraps of rational thought. An escalating wind was churning the expanse of the Pend Oreille River, meddling its attempt to mirror the dying sky's wash of pink and orange. The panorama below me was looking more at me than I on it, watching my pitiful plight.

As I ascended further into the great expanse, the evening's frigid air was being siphoned upward, sucked away from my lungs. Now unable to catch a breath worth inhaling, I did the only thing I could: I prayed. More accurately, I let out a panicked screech toward the realm of heaven I was now invading.

It was a mortal cry for help followed by a desperate plea for forgiveness. A recent tantrum pierced my memory like an Olympian's javelin: *If You don't bring my father back I swear I'll kill myself!* The words of an angry seventeen-year-old screamed back at me as if amplified two inches from my thick skull. Foolish words I wished I could retract.

Almost out of air and teetering on the edge of consciousness, I grasped for an appropriate bargain. But what could I offer in exchange for this insignificant life? My heart slid all I had to the center of the table.

It wasn't much.

Blaring sirens shattered the stillness, emanating from a line of red and blue streaming down Highway 2. The procession slowed to veer right onto Ontario Street, then picked up speed again as they headed in my direction. The low groan of a gravity alert sputtered to life and bellowed over the water and jagged pines.

A little late! I thought in angry jubilation, my eyes clouded with moisture. Then Mom's voice invaded my mind, interrupting the joy over a possible rescue: "Why didn't you have your *heavy-wear* on, Garret? We're supposed to be keeping a *low profile!*" My insides groaned deeper than the gravity alert.

Like fireflies frightened aloft, the lights of a flight squad lifted off toward my position. Their shoulder- and hip-mounted anti-gravity packs provided the levitation, while ionic exhaust and mini-puffs of directional thrust looked like cotton candy against the dwindling sun. The sight looked faked, like a stage production of Peter Pan, yet winged men were just one of the many super-technologies that had become commonplace in recent months. Far from the occasional propeller or rocketed oddity, this was the promise of regular, and nearly effortless, human flight. I hugged myself tight against a stabbing chill. Puffs of labored breath rose from my face.

"Seven, eight—no, nine of them," I heaved, counting the air soldiers floating my way.

Videos of the flight squads had done nothing to prepare me for the sight of them up close. Each unit member bore a solitary hose that extended from the snout of a bulbous, black helmet and into swelled chest compartments, like the proboscis of some ominous insect sucking nectar from its own body. Their heads were featureless orbs. Signal lights blinded while the whine of anti-gravity buzzed my ears. The descending swarm was altogether disconcerting, but their presence was better than their absence.

"Don't move," the leader barked synthetically as several of them congregated in a semi-circle. Two bumped into each other, apparently less than competent with their flight systems. The lack of coordination might have been comical if I weren't so petrified. Their primary intention seemed to be to study the event, and several sped off in different directions taking readings, probably to determine how widespread the incident might be. Nevertheless, the two remaining soldiers grabbed me and placed a strap around my waist, fastening our trio together before starting down.

The recovery team maintained a corporate silence—no "okay, son?" Or "let's get you home." Their iciness implied that I was being reprimanded more than rescued, so I remained silent as well. That heavy-breathing air escort would get nothing else from me until I figured out just what was transpiring up there.

As we descended, one of the squad members placed a mask over my mouth and nose and I gasped in several greedy breaths, the oxygen finding its way through my body. The aberration in Gs appeared to be over, with nothing still airborne in sight. By the time we landed in the Flagstones' front yard, I had regained my faculties.

I knew nothing of the Flagstone family except that there was an older son off at college and they had once tried to rename the nearby waterway of Chuck's Slough to something more refined like Charles Creek. *Absurd*, I had decided at the time, picturing the many afternoons I spent getting filthy there.

My attempt to leave the scene, offering some shaken but casual thank yous, was stymied.

"Why aren't you letting me go home?" I asked the officers fervidly. They claimed it was standard procedure to take me downtown for some questions. Nothing about that madness was standard and they couldn't pretend otherwise.

Mrs. Flagstone opened her front door to greet the agents, and I could see her scan for a point of interest. She found none in the chaotic mix of people running here and there. Her enormous brick-and-block home was bathed in flashing light, like an eyewitness to some strange and terrible crime.

With a blanket draped over my trembling shoulders, I sat on the back of an ambulance while several paramedics checked my vitals and asked some forgettable health and state-of-mind questions. My own rambling questions about what was going on fell on deaf ears. No one offered an opinion on the matter, let alone an answer. Looking up at the now-peaceful sky, I wandered off in thought, trying to reconcile the bizarre incident with the sobering view around me. Despite the prevalence of freak happenings, that yanking of my metaphorical hair went far beyond anything I'd heard about so far.

"Artificial induction of a gravity crisis," suggested my father's voice from somewhere in the ether. Dad had suspected that someone was lessening the planet's pull, or was at least trying to experiment with how. *But why here, and why so severe?* I thought. Nothing I'd learned so far about the Earth's dropping Gs could explain why one street might suffer such an attack. After all, as far as we could tell, the four-letter agency had backed off on its surveillance of our family some time ago.

Could someone have been onto us anyway, sending a coincidental glitch right toward our house? And if the so-called alien saviors had caused the strange happening, why had they let me survive? I hoped the local authorities would allow me to make the news. If they didn't, Jay would never believe it.

It's been a decade in dog years since that fantastic event unfolded. The day I floated away still stands out as the most bizarre and vivid, despite many close competitors. The choice of where to begin this narrative was obvious, but the time ahead feels short. I may not have enough of it left to explain how I became such a large fly in the universal ointment. The destruction that's always meant to have me inches closer. I've made my last daring escape.

Exhausting my final days relaying some grand campaign would be satisfying, but the truth stands in the way. So I will go ahead with it as it happened, translating my own scribbles, notes, quotes, sketches, and collected letters—one more tale for the drowning sea that so many have filled before me.

The air in this room has turned from a hint of smoke into something more threatening and my pen moves faster.

Part 1: Floating Away
Chapter 2

"While rumors about our gravity sporadically plummeting are becoming more widespread, public coverage of the growing phenomenon remains vague at best. The big three channels have all but ceased broadcasting the tragic accidents that are occurring as a result, and with the Internet still down, it's problematic for the average citizen to determine just how many of our Gs have already been lost. Something sinister seems to be soft pedaling Earth's most recent, and most monumental, catastrophe."

—Piper Corcoran, *Can Things Get Any Stranger? Volume I*

This is the story of a boy's journey from nothingness to somethingness and back to nothingness again, finally embracing all that broke him along the way. Like an insensitive butcher carving meat until he reaches bone, the past, or destroyer as I came to call it, stripped away all the unnecessary. Was it fate's way of keeping this rich man smaller than the eye of a needle? If so, I'll be eternally grateful.

I'd like to say it was a simple journey, but the odds were too often defied to say so. More than that, the odds were slapped about like a stunned child. That I still have breath is a testament to the miracles that have safeguarded me so far.

If my archaic writing style curdles your ears, please forgive me. Like most, I suffer from the influence of Golden Speech with every stroke. You, my reader, may be battling this tendency as well. It's been difficult to resist the impulse to artificially elevate one's self. When the gods again decided to mingle with man, we puffed ourselves out any way we could. Some called the attempted sophistication "Florid Tongue," but whatever title you give this convoluted grammar, it sent us backward, just where they wanted it all to go.

While the urge to write this tale has been undeniable, its intent is unknown. Will any flesh be left alive to read it? If you've happened upon these words and they have not been consumed by fire, ask for what purpose. Then move toward that purpose straightaway. Your time is even shorter than mine. Let's waste no more of it.

I had floated away and returned, or so it seemed. Baffled, I strained to decipher the cause, or if events had actually happened as my panicked memory recalled them. Inside a traditional cruiser, I sat in startled silence for the short drive to downtown Sandpoint. I guess they figured I'd had enough of flying for the night and avoided sending me down in one of the hover-types.

When we arrived at Central Station, the parking lot was crawling with agents carrying out some kind of drill. If I wasn't already shaken to the core, this sudden rush of activity finished the job. A large transport screeched to a stop, and the rear of the hauler groaned and tilted skyward. Its steel panels slid open to reveal a massive, civil defense exo-suit. A big toy for a small town, maybe, but places like Sandpoint, in what used to be known as Idaho, had gotten a lot bigger.

Nestled within mountains and endless waterways, the area had dodged much of the destruction that had trampled the world. When the calamities unleashed, our evergreen hills and crystal streams drew a much higher population as masses of people fled California, the Southwest, and other water-starved or war-torn areas for greener, wetter, more peaceful pastures. Our town was far from a bustling metropolis, but then again, hardly anyplace was anymore.

As an officer used my elbow to guide me toward the station's front entry, a loud beeping, accompanied by whirling lights of red and yellow, caught my attention. The squad shouted to each other as the single-pilot armor looked ready to step its massive alloy foot out onto the pavement. Lumbering and impractical, yes, but made simply because we could. However, if the exercise was a rapid deployment drill, it was hardly a success. The men scrambled to figure out why the giant hulk remained motionless inside its truck-based cocoon.

At an absurd rate, our society was rebuilding from the ashes. But in those days, it felt like our phoenix was floundering, rather than soaring.

Moods didn't improve much inside the station when I refused to take a blood test. It was family policy to treat the authorities—and what they might do with one's DNA—with a healthy dose of suspicion, so the situation soon grew into a standoff. Most blood specimen requests were mandatory, but since I was not being accused of anything they weren't justified to push it.

Still shaking a little, I kept expecting them to show some concern. The "Cooperative Force of Peace and Order," or CFPO, was presented by the media as an improved and enlightened body of justice. In reality, however, it seemed that there was a lot of force behind "peace and order."

After ushering me into the most featureless room I'd ever seen, several plainclothes officers left me sitting there alone for an indeterminable length of time. If these civil servants intended to agitate me, they were succeeding. From what I could see on my way in, I was the only person in Central who had been caught up in the phenomenon, confirming that my experience was isolated.

The lone table and chair I occupied were nearly the same shade of beige as the walls, floors, and ceiling. Like many structures, Central Station was newly built and fit the current style of lacking style. The smell of new paint was refreshing at first, but had turned quickly nauseating.

My knee pounded against the underside of the table with increasing force. It was downright excruciating to be stuck without my earphone, unable to call the team and relay the surreal scenario of being sucked up into the clouds. My iBud was at home on the kitchen counter along with an assortment of sandwich-making ingredients. No doubt Mom had walked in the door by now, aghast at the mess left on her immaculate counter tops, wondering why the culprit was not around to clean it up. One of the agents had promised twenty minutes before that I could make a call, but no one had provided the means.

I considered some inappropriate gestures I might offer those behind the large rectangular mirror on the wall, actions that might alleviate the boredom, when an agent entered.

"Can I call my mom now?" I asked before he was fully in the room.

The agent paused and grimaced at the sight of me. A very large man in a black uniform, with a tie of the same color, walked in and leaned against the wall opposite the mirror. His appearance was without wrinkle or defect, as if he had just stepped off the factory floor where they make stereotypical, square-jawed police characters. The sudden mixture of too much cologne and paint fumes made me ache for air.

"She's on her way," the flawless agent replied, opening a red folder to grumble through its contents. He continued, not bothering to look up. "So you're Evan Philmore's son. My name is Chamberlain Maddox. I wasn't here when your father went missing in…" he kept scanning, "in May of this year? I transferred in shortly after." His left eyebrow rose as he stared at the file and continued grumbling. "Your mother may have had a hand in replacing my predecessor..."

That was likely true. The chamberlain went on. "Are you aware of any new developments in his case?"

"Aren't *you* the one with the update?" I sniped, eager to see where provocation might lead. Chamberlain Maddox looked up at me with an expression that said he was already fed up with Central's new visitor. Like every other adult, he did not appreciate my arrogant approach. I thought he might bite and get right to straightening me out, but instead, he sighed and went back to looking through his notes.

"Incredible..." he dangled with nothing more. I didn't bite either. Finally, the dramatic pause ended. "Filthy rich: filthy—filthy—filthy. It says here your family hardly felt any economic hardship during the crunch. I've never seen that notation before..." He shook his head and feigned some more reading until: "Tell me, what was it like to have so much when so many had so little?"

The tapping of a manicured finger against his pursed lips suggested he'd just said something profound. The kinder, gentler Garret would have to wait. This guy was pushing all the right buttons.

"It was great, actually. I used to throw rocks at all the poor kids when they came up to beg." My hands praised the ceiling before finding the back of my head, showing how absurd I thought the exchange had become. "If that folder of yours is any good, it'll have my parents' foundation in there. My family gave away a ton, and they always wished it had been more. Can I see your account statements and find out what you were—"

Feeling an urgent heat flush my face, I cut myself off. Not only were account statements non-existent during the era in question, I was giving Maddox just the reaction he wanted.

I shifted gears to get us back on the topic that should have been dominant. When I asked if *we* knew why the Gs had given out completely, suggesting *we* were all on the same team, the chamberlain ignored my sudden rationality. He insisted he'd get to all that in a moment and kept to his script.

"...I mean it's no wonder your family ran into trouble. Those posh houses scream of the old regime, of entitlement and comfort. I'm surprised any of you survived. It says here that your mother actually purchased a custom six-person transport with only two citizens in your home. The resources that must have wasted! Why own anything anymore? Isn't *free* good enough?" The thick-jawed chamberlain locked his eyes on me, asserting his will to crumble mine. When it didn't, he softened, intrigued over my self-control. Then, suddenly seized by boredom, the folder closed with finality. The chamberlain let out a long, exaggerated sigh.

"We made some calls and there's a difference of opinion. One department wants to take that blood sample of yours, with or without your permission, and run some tests. I ruled against it. There's nothing extraordinary about you. They needn't waste their time..."

Chamberlain Maddox paused on his way toward the door. "By the way," he added, his tone dripping with disdain, "how *did* you like being dangled up there, helpless for the world to see?"

A grinchy smile curled the corners of his mouth while mine fell open, stupefied by the insinuation. Had this man just suggested he was party to the incident—or even the source?

I fumbled to formulate a clarifying question but he was already out the door.

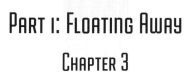

Part 1: Floating Away
Chapter 3

"First came the earthquakes in the U.S. and Japan, then reactor meltdowns, Pulse Attacks, the total unraveling of European society over ethnic and religious strife. Then a global economic collapse, food and water shortages, rampant disease, civil and international war. Christians everywhere thought the Great Tribulation had begun, but instead of a rescuing rapture, 'they' came on the scene to save us. Not much is known about the 'Messengers' as many call them, except that our circumstances became dire enough to trigger an intervention clause in their 'intergalactic rules of engagement.' Thank goodness it did, as they have already done more than offer assistance. They've given us back our humanity."

—Warner Roxwell, *Our Backs Against the Wall*

'm okay, Mom," I offered, as she released her firm grip on me. There was an almost-palpable relief in her eyes, but I knew that from this moment on, no matter what had happened, it would somehow be all my fault. As she handed me a duffle bag, her look of concern gave way to one of suspicion.

"You were testing something for *him* weren't you? Some kind of super-secret-stupid stuff?" I was glad the waiting area was empty, otherwise everyone would now be aware that I was into *super-secret-stupid stuff.*

Mom's excited whisper could be heard over the inspiring Song of Unity, an anonymously-composed choral arrangement playing from somewhere above our heads. I cut her off and pushed us toward the farthest seats in the lobby before relaying any more of the inexplicable episode. We sat under a sign that read, "Stand and Build a Dream-Worthy Future"—an ironic slogan, I thought, to place behind a row of chairs.

After I conveyed a brief summary of my flight, neither of us could dismiss the event as part of the larger gravity crisis. It was purposeful. It was almost diabolical. More than anything else, it left us mystified. When I started in about how the chamberlain implied he was in on it, she silenced me with a wave of her hand. Even I had to admit that sounded ridiculous, and it was a darn foolish place to discuss the possibility anyway.

"Garret, where did you find those clothes? You can't be outside in just that." Dad's T-shirt and khaki pants were still too big for me. She sighed and looked me over, not expecting a response.

"I just wanted to see if they fit. They don't I guess," I said, plucking at the excess fabric. A few months ago, I'd found a chest of Dad's old things. Sad at the initial discovery, it eventually felt better to wear his clothes around, as if I were keeping them warm until he returned.

"Okay, THIS might explain why you lifted off so quickly—"

I was ready for that. "But mom, this wasn't just a dip in the Gs. It was bizarre! This was nothing a weight belt or heavywear would've helped with!"

She took a deep breath and stared off into the distance for a moment before offering me the bag as a first step towards making things up to her. The way she carried on, someone observing us might think that I was guilty of committing some major violation of the Philmore family rules, rather than escaping a near-death experience. But this was Mom's normal demeanor. She was always at the end of herself: the circumstances hardly mattered. Any deviation from "a smooth life" could set her off. It was just the way she functioned.

With a hushed promise to discuss the details later, I stood and searched for the rest room. When the door closed behind me, I found the only dry spot on the long, metal sink to set the bag down. Unzipping it, I picked through the contents, noticing Mom had taken the opportunity to include some of the things she felt I ought to be wearing more often.

I undressed and packed the soft cotton clothes back in the tote, letting my eyes linger on Dad's old T-shirt now laying within it. As I zipped the duffle closed, I saw my father wearing the shirt, lounging on our couch at home.

It was time to hide his things in my room, and hide the memories that endured with them. Everything must be hidden from a world growing ever more intolerant of me.

Part 2: Sandpoint

Chapter 1

"Even before rudimentary weight belts, panicked communities began erecting 'travel-lines;' Metal posts set lengths apart would connect by rope or chord. Children on their way to school or residents walking to their mailboxes would affix themselves to these lines. The limitations of this kind of precaution were obvious. The means for overcoming fluctuating gravity varied from the rich to the poor, but fears subsided once the ETs arrived, bringing with them the promise of technological safeguards previously beyond our ability."

—Warner Roxwell, *Our Backs Against the Wall*

Our beige brick house with its light gray roof stood beyond several security gates at the center of an exclusive, heavily treed development. Gone were the machine gun nests and barbed wire that had once decorated the stately exterior. Now, its three noble stories could announce privilege without fear, windows perpetually lit as if anticipating the arrival of an event-worthy dignitary. I thought I might hear mom declare its imminent sale for the fortieth time, but she remained quiet and troubled as we crossed the slough into Dover and pulled into the west entrance of our circular drive.

Tall white cabinets, nickel hardware and stone floors were a welcome sight when I walked through the back door into the kitchen. The sprawling granite breakfast bar sat covered with grocery sacks. This indicated Mom must have gotten the call from Central right there in the middle of unloading, because the perishables were just sitting there, perishing.

Seeing the room again halted my mother's frenetic pace. She froze, torn between anguish and gratitude that I'd survived the day. After a moment she expanded her chest, inhaling deeply. I knew that posture well and hid behind the wall of brown bags as a shield.

"Mom, I think that was just a freak, one-time—" I attempted, but she squawked and closed her eyes as if gripped by a seizure. There would be no down playing this bizarre episode, and I was not about to get out of hearing her evaluation.

"I don't have to remind you who is the prince and power of the air, Garret. I doubt tonight was a satanic attack, but we need to figure what really happened! We can't just shrug the whole thing off and move on to the next big thing, you know."

I nodded in silence knowing anything I offered verbally would escalate this sermon, even if I agreed with her. Despite Mom's delicate looks, she was leather-tough. She probably viewed my lingering sentimentality about Dad as a weakness, a hindrance to my life. Her calendar practically had a day marked for when I should be officially done grieving over his disappearance. She tended to come across as overly rigid, even abrasive, but I adored the steel of her inner strength, a strength that had carried us through some perilous times.

In truth, though, describing those times as perilous is a gross understatement. A glittering civilization, once flush with electrical power, buffets and bottomless ATMs lost its luxuries and hurtled downward into a dark and murderous nightmare. Men became monsters and neighbors turned on one another after the first week of terror and hunger. Humanity was not prepared for the bloody contest that played out in every corner of the Earth. Like a well-seasoned naval crew sent naked and adrift who morph into the unspeakable, people soon discovered what lurked just below their surface nature. A devil's card—a black club—was pulled from the teetering house above and down it went.

Though too sheltered to recall much of the *Meltdown*, as it later came to be known, my limited perspective saw Mom as the one who got us through in one piece. I supposed that's why everything was a crisis to her. The trauma of it had left an indelible mark.

After wrapping up her dissertation about the unseen forces of evil at work in the world, Mom gathered herself and came to embrace me with a comforting, if brief, hug. Mission complete, she threw off any persisting anxiety and turned her attention elsewhere.

"Display on." She barked the command for a floating screen to come to life and it materialized, growing rapidly from a small white dot into a large monitor broadcasting Channel 2. The TV hung in mid-air a few feet from the kitchen where she'd last placed it, but a wave of her hand coaxed it slightly left for just the right angle. With that, she zeroed in on her one and only indulgence.

Mom had gone from watching no television to being glued to it. Following the Meltdown, programming had been reduced to a mere three channels, with one solely dedicated to what our alien benefactors were sharing with mankind, and how we must implement their advice with urgency. She was instantly engrossed in tonight's coverage, shaking her head with audible protests as a way to deal with the shock and disgust. It would now be hard to get her attention, but I would also enjoy a respite from constant commentary and frequent scolding.

I let out a discreet sigh of relief and scooped my iBud off the counter where I'd left it. *Yep,* I thought, *seven missed calls.* Placing the inch-long, banana-shaped device atop my ear, I was now re-armed with the multitasking, multimedia extravaganza that had replaced cell phones in the late twenties. iBuds, or just "buds," empowered the user with floating, virtual screens activated on demand, and had the power to change your entire world into an augmented reality.

As if attention spans hadn't dwindled enough from the mobile phone revolution, now nearly every aspect of life could be spiced up with a constant flow of colors and information. Of course, Mom restricted my interface to all the least fun settings. She maintained complete control over which virtual neighborhoods I visited, if you know what I mean.

Surgically-implanted buds were becoming the rage before the Meltdown, and that trend had resumed. The number of people resisting that kind of robotic integration into their bodies was fewer than you'd think, but the Philmores were among them. I think Mom's exact words were: "Over my dead body."

Pausing for a moment to watch the TV display, I decided to suffer through the overly-familiar voice of Chandra Keegan. Channel 2 was the local station, so I was curious about a possible gloss on my crazy flight, even from her. The gravitational anomaly ended without tragedy, so maybe the news would let the story slip through for a change. Her unnecessarily complex sentences made it difficult to focus on the substance, if there was any. She droned on about the Council's position on some edict or other and I didn't have the patience for it.

"The census? It's taking forever. Any news on that?" I thought about asking our newly delivered Auto-Maton, but Mom was defying the law and leaving it powerless.

"Nothing official. Just rumors still. Looks like we're down by half since '35."

If the Messengers didn't come through with the much-anticipated solution for aggressive blood cancer, the remaining half of us would soon follow suit. Not many were escaping that end. I shook my head and risked bringing the lack-of-gravity incident up again.

"Do you think they'll report on what happened tonight?"

"I doubt it," Mom replied, not bothering to look my way. "They're letting it out now that the Vatican had contact with the ETs for years before they showed themselves to the rest of us. Everyone is falling over each other to get every last detail about where and when." She rolled her eyes so severely I thought she might dislocate one. "Heavens, the old devil is more popular now than before he shut everything down. He probably dissolved the Papacy to prevent anyone else from ever hogging his spotlight. But at least for tonight, I'm glad the news won't find the time to show my son floating down the street like some kind of parade balloon."

"Oh. Okay. Well, let me know if you see anything." Failing to hide my disappointment, I set about putting some of the groceries away and assembling a fresh sandwich, since everything was still out. Now that Mom was busy, it was an opportune time to conclude our family meeting and get to the good stuff.

"I'm going to catch up with the team. Mind if I have them over?" I asked, unsure of how many times I'd have to repeat it. "We'll just hang out in the study for a bit."

Mom fumbled with a net of green that looked like avocados, not managing to open it while fixated on Ms. Keegan's every word. Several seconds into the process, she abandoned the attempt and tossed the whole thing in a bowl, equally repulsed by it as by the latest reports. It was still comforting though to see a regular flow of fresh fruits and vegetables coming back into the house. A nod and beleaguered grin gave me her blessing.

On my way to Dad's study, I used the bud's phone-only feature to ring the team, getting Beck's recorded response first.

"This is Rebecca. The Queen O'Hearts is out—try me back later!" Then Jay clicked in.

"Jay here. All right, you've been MIA. Is Beck with you? I couldn't reach her either. What's up, G? Spill it."

Before I could answer Jay, Pak came on the line, grunting to formulate his words.

"Man, I thought I wouldn't hear back from you guys tonight. What's going on?"

"Sorry, Sleeping Beauty," I shot back. "Listen, can you guys hit the books over here? I'm behind, and so are you, *for sure.*"

Jay chirped out his signature whistle that meant he'd head straight over. Pak, on the other hand, needed some convincing.

"I'm a growing boy. I gotta sleep."

"Come on Pak, you're a dumb jock, and a big one at that," I pushed. "If you grow any more, someone is going to use you as a houseboat! Now get over here. We can avoid strenuous mental exercise tonight,"—my code for avoiding training since *ears* could be listening—"but let's not get too behind, ya know?"

With an exhale, grunt, and an elongated "fiiiiine," Pak agreed to leave his couch and put most of the team together to hear my wild tale.

"Pak, where's Beck? Have you talked to her?"

"Huh-uh, no. Not since school. See you in a minute—*out.*"

What was up? Beck had made just one attempt to reach me all evening and now no answer? After a few more tries, I headed for the study to gobble down my sandwich before the guys got there.

A mouthful of wheat bread and salami inhibited my voice command of the room's main light so I navigated the familiar clutter and sat inside the study's nook. The nook was an inlet set back inside the room's far wall that featured twin vinyl covered benches with a center table, not unlike a booth at an all-night diner. The décor was obviously Dad's handiwork, done without consulting his better half.

I sat and scooted to the center of one of the benches. Gulping hard, I called for the nook's small, overhead lamp to illuminate the table's faux-wood surface. The rest of the room was left nearly black, its landscape dotted with hills of papers and mountains of boxes; booby traps for my arriving guests.

As much as I wanted to decompress and enjoy being safe at home, the memory of what had taken place returned like a sudden sucker punch. The sensation of floating echoed through my body, seizing my throat, and I sat there choked in disbelief.

Staring down at the sandwich, now missing a single bite, I decided I'd lost my appetite.

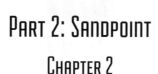

PART 2: SANDPOINT
CHAPTER 2

"Shortly before the UN, fronted by the former Pontiff himself, announced the ETs' arrival, the Earth's gravity began to fluctuate—and drop with little warning. This crisis generated renewed fear and panic in a surviving population that had thought they'd seen it all. Once the initial hysteria had passed, once every household became equipped with G-Indicators and even some with Gravity Enhancers, humanity soon adapted to living with the daily threat. With so many other amazing breakthroughs to focus on, this crisis, no matter how dire, was destined for the back burner. Nothing short of aliens from outer space could have distracted us from losing our precious gravity—and it was doing just that."

—Piper Corcoran, *Can Things Get Any Stranger? Volume I*

Jaxon Green found me at our usual meeting spot in Dad's study and immediately requested that the sandwich remains be transferred to his care. Jay was my partner in crime, my Tonto, my Robin, and we found adventure even in the most mundane.

Standing a little shorter than I, Jay's skin tone made his ethnicity hard to identify. When asked about his race, he would answer "everything and nothing," in a "what's-it-to-ya-punk?" sort of tone. His goatee was already thick and his black, curly hair sat on his head in a tower shape, lightened blonde at the summit. He magnified his look even more by wearing a headband around the base of his 'fro and teasing the rest out the top, making the whole thing look like some kind of potted plant.

Jay thrived on provoking negative reactions, and exaggerating his appearance was one of his favorite ways to do that. One minute he would appear normal, and in the next his hair would be all inflated, with a colorful rubber band or two strangling his goatee. It was hilarious to us, but to few others.

Occasionally, I would feel more like his sidekick than the other way around, but I figured it was my rightful place, since I usually took the lead—and therefore most of the blame—in our mishaps. So, it came as no surprise that he could do little more than lament missing out on *all the fun* as I relayed the still-jarring story. After he got over his initial disbelief that such a thing was even possible, I could see that he was disturbed beneath his cool exterior.

By the time Pak sat down with us, Jay had heard enough that he decided to preempt my account with his own hysterical version.

"… then the chamberlain told Garret they were planning to hit your house with the G-Zapper, Pak, but changed their minds because they couldn't muster enough power to get you off the ground!" He laughed too hard at his own joke while Pak let forth a monster yawn, ignoring Jay's buffoonery.

Knowing the two of us to be a couple of selfish so-and-sos, Pak took note of the empty plate and simply shook his head. He had a steadiness about him that I envied and he got straight to figuring out what might have happened to me. Big Pak took a moment to consider his words before relaying them, which was beyond Jay's ability.

"So, they gave no explanation at all for what caused it? How could it only affect your block? That's just *weird*, man. This goes to show you they have no idea of what's going on with the gravity thing."

"Not only was there no explanation, I'm pretty sure Maddox knew about it." I proceeded to quote the sinister chamberlain word for word, and relay how he'd alluded to being a part of the plot to pull me airborne. The strangeness of it contorted my friends' faces.

"This guy is a piece of work, dude. You can't trust anybody or anything." Pak's volume increased as he rubbed his clenched fists. As the eternal protector of the weak, he was prepping himself to knock some heads together.

Pak Pateras was a natural in that role. After Jay, Beck, and I were forced to attend public school, a group of thugs caught Jay alone in the gym and would have pulverized him until a large Greek linebacker jumped in to the rescue, and that was our well-timed introduction. As a senior, and a grade ahead of us, he was a hulking, teddy-bear type—the mascot we never knew we needed. He bordered on massive, with muscles-on-his-muscles, slicked black hair, always sporting T-shirts several sizes too small for his frame.

The awkward tension created by my narrative must have gotten to the guys as they had found the only open area on the floor to try out some wrestling holds—in the dark. Pak, twice our size, was about to finish what Jay had started. Just before the finale, I decided to join in and try a sleeper hold on Pak that proved ineffective. Before long, Mom called for the main light and stood over our heap with her hands glued to her hips.

"Sorry, Mrs. Philmore." Pak spoke up first, knowing he was her favorite. He loosened the double headlocks holding Jay and I and offered us up for the imminent rebuke.

"How old are you boys anyway?" She tried to look mad but she couldn't hide her affection.

"Seventeen!" Jay exclaimed, having recovered both his voice and his face's natural color. "I'm sorry too, Mrs. Philmore, but I was defending your honor. If you'll just hear me out..." He didn't wait before continuing. "Big Pak here was just saying he thought you were thirty years old, and I just couldn't let him get away with that. I insisted you weren't a day over twenty-nine and I'd have to take him down for hurling such an insult..."

Mom bit her tongue and managed a smile before walking away. "Okay, then—but I'm sure your mothers are expecting you back soon. Better hurry home."

"Yes, Mrs. Philmore," they said in unison. I tried to catch her with a long-distance "I love you," but she was gone. Jay sat up and rubbed his neck, sending me a grin that said he'd gotten his jollies.

After showing the guys out, I checked the covert signal on our coffee maker. A green light meant a training session was possible, a red light meant it wasn't. I grabbed a tall glass of milk and headed back toward the study.

The light was bright green.

Part 2: Sandpoint
Chapter 3

"Jay came with us to Oregon to visit Uncle Scott over the weekend. He and I capped one of our woodland adventures by covering ourselves in war paint, and then we launched a surprise attack on my Uncle's house. When Mom realized the purple designs we'd decorated our chests and faces with was the juice from poisonous pokeweed berries, she almost fainted. We didn't get sick, but the stains are just now fading. We've started calling our duo the Pokeberry Boys, despite Mom's disapproval."

—Garret Philmore, *Letters on the Lamb: A Collected Journal*

Dad's study was a fascinating exhibit. Its strange mixture of high and low tech appeared to be tangling in a fight to win the room. Lately, a third candidate—dust—looked like it was gaining a strong foothold.

Tall mahogany bookcases lined the dark green walls on every side, stuffed with books ranging from the ancient Sanskrit texts of the *Ramayana* and *Mahabharata* to Einstein's *The Evolution of Physics*, and the latest volumes by Dr. T.R. Hornbrook on *Mercury Magnetic Vortex Propulsion*.

An enormous wooden desk dominated the center of the room, piled high with folders and a wide variety of mechanical components that overflowed into the remaining spaces. Tentacles of multi-colored wire made it look as though a troop of sea urchins had roamed an ocean of loose paper before settling down there.

Sitting perpendicular to the desk, Dad's drafting table was draped in grid paper displaying intricate pencil sketches of complex widgetry. Like ants leaving a conquered picnic, his many scribbled notes wound away from the drawings in every direction.

Mom had declared the room my responsibility after Dad died, so I kept the piles of metal boxes, wires, files, and loose papers just how he left them. She never pestered me to straighten it up. Either she sensed how important they might be to my grieving process or she hoped Dad would reappear someday and be obligated to clean it himself. Besides my bedroom, the study was the last holdout in Mom's war of cleanliness and order.

But it was the little diner nook in the study's corner that had distracted me from my sorrow. It was far more than a simple alcove for doing homework. It was in fact, a fireman's pole to our secret lab.

The ceiling was low and the space tight, forcing you to duck and choose one side or the other of its bench-style seating. Upon entering, hidden electronic eyes identified me and began a program to simulate me remaining there while the entire booth lowered into the floor.

The first step in activating the lab elevator was to leave your bud on the slight shelf that ran along the compartment's interior. This allowed hidden sensors to identify who was there and create the appropriate impression of you—an impression that would simulate your presence in the nook even after you yourself had gone.

Placing my bud on the ledge, a faint beep signaled the all clear and the floor rumbled to life. The whole table, benches and all, began its semi-smooth descent.

Watching the large metal bulkheads close above me was both comforting and unnerving. Taking the plunge gave me a sense of belonging, as if underground was more my natural habitat than above. My heart began its usual palpitations, my senses becoming knife-sharp. Dropping into a secret lair when secrets about anything were in short supply—was thrilling.

Sudden jolts, retinal scans, and other safety checks made it a fifteen-minute process to get to the final stop, where Newt, the team's obligatory mad scientist and mentor, would need to identify newcomers to allow entry. Sometimes he would be distracted or indifferent to my arrival, and on those occasions, it took even longer. But at last, the machinery stopped and the hatch gave way.

My imagination longed for something more refined about our subterranean complex. I wanted to see squads of white-coated technicians bustling about a bright, high-energy environment. The atmosphere would crackle with tension as I merged myself with the commotion, learning of the latest news or mission.

As the door opened, it was anything but refined. It looked more like a training area for has-been wrestlers—and smelled about as good. Every color was a variant on gray, with a little rust thrown in. Jumbles of cables and wires hung low, as if the herniated ceiling lacked the strength to contain them all.

The gloomy murk hid just how large the space really was. With most of the lights off, I could only see a narrow path through the clutter that led toward a dark, windowless room in the far corner. Although it lacked the cool factor I wanted, I still felt a thrill as I stepped off the lift. The strong hum of gravity control, air vents, and massive amounts of electronic jamming equipment gave the impression you'd just entered the belly of a living, breathing beast.

An act once born out of anxiety was now a habitual routine. I walked straight for the nearest bank of lights to brighten the area and, if I was honest, my mood. Among the few things that were not voice controlled, the large, old school light switches clacked on with a series of satisfying snaps.

As the first row came up, I scanned over to the expansive training arena. The place was gigantic, a cavern the size of an average high school football field. Most of the area was roped off with what looked like a huge boxing ring, complete with its own obstacle course. It stretched far into the darkness, and only the next four or five sets of lights could fully illuminate it. The whole facility lacked even a hint of thoughtful arrangement, appearing almost bombed out. I wondered sometimes if we'd ever clean up the piles of twisted metal parts. But the junk inside the ring provided a challenging landscape in which to train.

I took a deep breath and began to wend my way up the aisle towards Newt and the control room. It was time to get serious. I put my psyche on alert. Dad ingrained in me from the beginning that this facility did not exist to alleviate boredom. He said more than once that just going down there put all our lives in jeopardy. His incessant words rang in my ears as I took my last few steps towards the control room door: "Make it count, son. We don't have much time. They're more talented, they're better equipped, and they're just plain better than us."

I shouldn't have let myself get annoyed with his repetition. He was right, and realized I wouldn't have internalized the lesson unless I'd heard it over and over. Anger coursed through me when I pictured his smile and wondered who might have taken him. I struggled with why God would let such a thing happen. Dad was one of the good guys. I forced myself to cut those thoughts short and redirected all my anger towards those in the shadows; toward the men who took my father.

The main control room was an unimaginative mass of blackened steel we affectionately called "the box." Though it appeared well worn and ragged, the gleaming identification panel affixed to the box's doorway looked lifted from something else and grafted onto the makeshift construction. I raised my index finger to the panel for biometric verification, leaving it there long enough for the machine to read my vital signs, anxiety levels, and who knows what else. The door groaned aside, in no rush to perform its only job. Inside was a mess of cables like the rest, but at least there were areas that flashed and beeped, giving some impression of low-tech activity.

Seeing Newt's back against the wall of monitors was a relief that further pushed the night's bizarre happening behind me. I decided at that moment to withhold the details of the floating event, even though I was dying to get his take on it. Newt was quite jittery then about our situation, and I wasn't ready to bug out. Depending on his mood, bugging out might be just what he'd declare.

"Newt!" I let out with cheerful gusto. "Newton?"

Ears blocked by his signature headphones, he was scribbling away on his scrap paper and didn't respond—but I could tell by the way he was shifting in his seat that he was preparing a greeting. He spun around in his chair and put his fingers together.

"Gaaah-rret." His voice trailed higher and so did one of his eyebrows. The look on his face said he was up to something clever.

Dr. Newton Bigsby was the guy you wanted in charge of all your important gizmos. In his mid-fifties with curly, graying ringlets, he looked every bit the crazy professor, always absorbed with his next invention. His curls frizzed out around the back, accenting a large balding dome up front. He wore glasses in a time when almost no one did, and he had nice teeth for an Englishman. I insisted he wear a white lab coat to help with my fanciful illusions of a techy environment. His coat was not especially white anymore, and it had rips down the back of the sleeves and tatters around the edges. He had embraced wearing the costume despite the memories it held for him.

"Newt," I cocked my head to the side, joining the game, "you've cooked up something cool down here, haven't you? I've had one heck of a crappy day so far so I hope it's something to make me forget all about it."

"*Crappy?*" he said, raising his left eyebrow to join the right. Even *that* word sounded smart under his pronunciation.

"Yes, crappy." I did my best to match his accent but with my usual comedic twist. I divulged no more details and hoped he wouldn't ask for any. He was entrusting me with great responsibility and tales of being hauled to Central would not only delay getting to the drills, but inspire him to cancel the training in favor of some cautionary lecture.

"Well speaking of that, you might want to give B1 a good wiping out before you leave tonight. He doesn't smell very *fresh*. Haven't you noticed? I had the unfortunate experience of trying to upgrade some hardware in there and I was nearly overcome."

Newt knew I relished his accent and he exaggerated it, adding extra flare for my sake. It was common for me to repeat my favorite words after he spoke them, adding in my own ill-fitting colloquialisms, like "tally-ho, my bloke," and the decidedly antipodean "g'day mate." It didn't have to be English to be part of my own amusement. If only to me, it was quite funny to add in the occasional "down-under" bits and kangaroo jokes, as if I had no idea the difference between England and Australia. Although they were soon to give up their status as sovereign countries, their clichés lived on and I mixed them together as sport. Newt didn't react to any of it, but my continued gratification wasn't dependent on anyone noticing.

But overall, Newt provided little comic relief. He had a calming voice and a gentle, guiding presence; my "Houston" if I had a problem. Stressed, tired, confused, or in trouble, I could call out to Newt in training sessions and he would be there. I referred to him as "Control" over the Com, but he did little in the way of controlling things. "Garret, simply do A, B, and C..."—and his suggestions would be right on and save the day. While our hole in the ground didn't live up to my spy fantasies, Newt exceeded them.

The brains every movie-hero needs backing him up, Newt tolerated my antics, and in my saddest moments had provided essential strength for me to carry on. Still, he reminded me that he could be taken away at any time—killed or worse. As much as I tried to put that reality out of my mind, our crisis-reaction drills made it impossible to forget how precarious the situation was.

I pulled myself away from my private thoughts to hear him rambling about something he'd stumbled upon, and how it was going to be all this and that.

"Newt—I think YOU'RE not smelling fresh!" I interjected out of nowhere with a spirited smile.

"Am I?" He made a half-hearted gesture to lift his arm and sniff, smiling back at me. "That could be a distinct possibility. No team tonight?"

I sighed and made up something. "No. Mom and I got into it. Friends were out of the question."

Newt looked puzzled, but resisted asking anything else. Picturing Beck, I could feel my hands start to tremble again. Something wasn't right. Once a bud was placed in the nook, the black box control room automatically tracked its incoming calls. I hesitated to ask.

"Newt, has anyone try to reach me in the last...while?"

He spun back around in his chair and shook his head no, and I experienced the same horrible sinking feeling as when I'd heard Beck's stupid recording.

I wanted to send out a prayer for her, but it would have been the same, desperate, last-resort type stuff that people engage in more for themselves than anything else.

After my own outlandish event, I feared the worst.

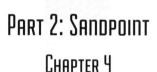

Part 2: Sandpoint
Chapter 4

"It's one of those things your parents talk about that you're certain you'll never see happen—until it does. Only days after the start of the Meltdown, Sandpoint's City Council ordered the iconic two mile Long Bridge spanning the mouth of the Pend Oreille River, blown. This drastic action was meant to keep desperate marauders, no doubt flooding Highway 95, to the South of our once, 'Most Beautiful Small Town in America.' It appeared to work, as the mercenary force charged to guard our gated community encountered very few bandits, and spent most of their time helping Mom and Dad with charitable handouts. The town as a whole managed to keep order throughout the Meltdown's most chaotic stretch, even after they tried to take all the guns."

—Garret Philmore, *Letters on the Lamb: A Collected Journal*

N ewt's singular focus was coming in handy, allowing my flustered demeanor to escape his notice. He was engulfed in the last stages of his newest training program, alternating between humming and mumbling to bring it across the finish line. My impatient protests were met with a raised index finger to signal that he needed a few minutes more, so I took a seat on a rusted and wobbly chair in the corner. As I waited for Newt to complete his final preparations, I remember staring intensely at the crooked photo pinned to the wall of Jay, Beck and Pak hanging on each other's necks. Getting lost in it enticed me to relive yet again the most nerve-wracking day I'd spent in our lab, almost six months prior. Even now, the revealing of our underground complex to the team is nearly as vivid as the night I floated away.

In an unrelenting display of determination, I had convinced Dad and Newt to allow my friends into the lair to train with me. From the moment they'd let me see the facility, I agonized to tell the gang until the obsession bordered on mania. The secret's weight was suffocating me and nothing else mattered.

It took several months of continual protest before Mom finally weighed in on my side and said it was Dad's fault for getting me started in "all that robot stuff" in the first place. The tension around the house got so bad that she even left for a few days. "You boys and your toys. Just seal the whole thing off down there before we all regret it."

Dad resisted until Newt assured him that it was almost impossible for any of my companions to pass the stringent mental and physical requirements. From his days training in the military, he knew that being an exo-suit pilot took uncommon talents and tolerance, with most tryouts failing within the first hour. Once my triad of friends proved unfit, we would tell them there was a secret hideout we could all escape to in case of emergency and leave it at that.

Dad gave in and began interviewing the three, including administering lie-detector tests. Electrified by the intrigue, my friends went on the attack with a barrage of questions they assumed would break me, but my resolute silence left them stumped. I objected to Dad's endless interrogation, but he made it clear that patience was my only option. So I waited—waited and prayed that my companions would break into the ethereal world that was fast absorbing me. I hardly ate or slept for weeks.

Dad let Newt, who made a few rare above-ground appearances, take their examination to the next level, running the team through a battery of physical and mental trials to reveal their limit. I was shocked to overhear what Newt had planned: testing their underwater skills, challenging them to solve complex math problems with little sleep, and even asking them to repair or assemble exo-suit components in extreme temperatures.

I felt so guilty that I hadn't endured all of that myself that I volunteered to go through the testing as well. This threw gasoline on their curiosity, causing the three candidates to act out a short-lived protest before agreeing to go on—and I mean *short*. They lasted about five minutes and then resolved to see it through. Like me, my friends were not satisfied with the life they'd been handed, and this mystery had already elevated them beyond the routine. My ambiguously tantalizing promise of a huge payoff renewed their determination, and going through the tests with them sure beat sitting idly by, wringing my hands to see if they passed. The weeks of fun and stress made us zombies at school, stoking our reputation as weirdos.

When the decisive moment arrived, Newt called Dad and me down to the lab, amazed at his findings.

"Evan, I'm stunned," he said as he removed his glasses and laid them down on the table. "They're all good candidates, even Rebecca. No signs of claustrophobia, high anxiety disorders, or significant weaknesses." It took a moment for the information to travel from my brain to my heart as he went on. "We have the extra prototypes to try them out on, and our concept for the larger C-Type unit might be perfect for Phillip..."

Unable to contain myself, I leapt from the table with a victory dance. It was a brief one, however, because Dad caught me by the front of my shirt, wadding the fabric up in white-knuckled hands as he shouted in my face. "This is life and death, Garret!"

That was the last of my inappropriate enthusiasm.

Though fatherless families were more the norm than ever before, Dad sure had a lot on his hands with the four of us. With Pak's estranged home situation, Jay's father having been killed by secessionists when he was nine, and Beck's real father gone long ago, Dad carried that responsibility for the whole team. But opening the door to our clandestine underworld would break hard from his role as surrogate parent. This divergence had the chance to both save— and take—their lives.

"This is war, not a game," he said as he left the room. How little had I known then the prophetic truth in those words…

When the climactic day arrived, the four us crammed into the study nook with my father. The team leaned close, beyond ready to find out what the weeks of strenuous buildup were all about. The air was packed with expectation, becoming even more so when I asked them to place their buds on the shelf behind them and remain quiet. Their eyes nearly popped from their heads as the booth shuddered to life and dropped into the floor.

As we descended down the rabbit hole, Jay and Beck spun in every direction, looking for an explanatory clue. The goofs saw none, and began jiggling and jabbing each other with nervous energy. They were unable to contain themselves despite seeing my finger pressed hard against my mouth. Pak made up for their juvenile behavior somewhat by remaining calm, nodding as though he'd known all along about the hidden lift.

When the doors slid opened, Dad gave the all clear to speak but no one took him up on it. The foreboding darkness and acrid smell had stolen their words. I stepped out first and snapped on a few rows of lights to reveal the space's enormous size, juggling both apprehension and pride over the impending revelation. I made sure to leave the lights off overhead to help hide the grime and disorder piled high just outside the elevator.

Pak had time to let out a quick, "this place is huuuge," before I was assaulted by the flabbergasted tour group. Twenty simultaneous questions flew at me as arm-grabs and pressing bodies demanded to know how I could keep such a secret. Dad raised his voice and ended their melee by calling them what they were.

"Kids – kids – please! Garret IS showing you. Look..." His outstretched finger pointed to the massive training area and suggested they advance in that direction. Jay, Pak and Beck fell silent again, embarrassed by the verbal slap. Dad motioned them ahead and quirked his lips in a failed smile. Awestruck, Jay took the lead and walked out into the lair, stuttering something about having his own bat-cave at last.

Pak followed and Beck held onto his arm. I shrugged off a jolt of possessiveness and noticed her wide-eyed but pleasant smirk. She was wearing her long, ash-blonde hair in its usual style: pulled back in a ponytail, with an additional sports band around her hairline. Having played volleyball for a few years, she decided to adopt that athletic look permanently, and it suited her. I watched a few salty expressions flicker over her face, as though she had expected something better than a cluttered cavern, but she couldn't disguise her wonder.

As the five of us wound our way down the narrow aisle snaking left of the training area, the air's thick mechanical hum drowned out their muffled commentary. When our single-file group fanned out in the twenty-by-twenty space at the arena's half-crumbled concrete stairs, I cleared my throat for a speech that would never happen.

Through the dim light, Jay had caught sight of three strange-looking vehicles parked along the wall, in front of a row of battered lockers. He dashed over the haphazard dirt and metal flooring and began stroking their irresistible metallic surfaces.

"Hey-heeyy…what are these?" Jay practically swooned, angling his head to drink in every detail. "It's like a super-bike or something." Then he noticed lights beginning to glow inside my Brawler unit —the one I'd decorated a glossy blue with white stripes. Newt was powering it up remotely from the control room but it looked as though Jay's continued caress was responsible for bringing it to life.

The Brawler bike was double the length of a normal motorcycle, with twin rear wheels fully concealed underneath its armored frame. At the midsection, two arm-like cowlings extended on either side of an enclosed cockpit, reaching up to hold onto both sides of a large front wheel. Seeing the growing illumination within the canopy elicited a cascade of *oohs* and *ahhs* as the rest gathered for a better look.

At first unnoticed, I'd dug into one of the pale-green lockers and undressed down to my boxer shorts. As I began stepping into the skin-tight black body suit we called *mecha underwear,* Beck cocked her head and shot me a look like I should get a room. She resisted saying anything out loud, however, and I was grateful for her restraint. The orderly orientation I had imagined a thousand times was now out of control and going where it wanted. A frustrated exclamation rose up in my throat, but I talked myself out of it and heaved a prolonged sigh instead. Why was I so jumpy? I longed to be cool under pressure, but I never seemed to have it in me.

Jay kept right on speculating. "They're secret weapons—are they? Oh man, these are like top-secret weapons? Super vehicles? What are these things?"

I put my hands out towards him in a calming gesture, ignoring the churning of my stomach. "I'll show you. Hatch," I commanded.

At my voice, the translucent windshield slid backward, hiding itself within the roof. Stepping up on one of the blue arm cowlings, I crawled in, donning the flexible helmet we called the Control Hat. When I ordered the yellow-tinted windshield to close over me, it forced three, heavy-breathing faces to remove themselves from gawking around the cockpit. Newt's voice was waiting for me inside my Hat.

"Relax, Garret."

"Nervous," I said into the mouthpiece.

"Don't be," he said, "You'll do fine. You've impressed me over these last few months. You're going to be quite a leader."

Newt's words struck a comforting chord as I waited for the systems to cycle up. I looked out at my friends and shook my head in disbelief. They were at last coming on the adventure with me. I archived the moment.

"All set. The external speakers are on, Garret. You can talk to them now."

"Make some room, guys," I said, as Dad motioned the watching assembly back a few yards. Beck crossed her arms and tapped her foot in an exaggerated, comical way, while Jay flailed his hands about the air as if to conjure some patience.

I thumbed the accelerator to move into the open and as my momentum slowed, I hit the selector to Brawler mode and let the magic unfold.

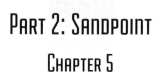

Part 2: Sandpoint

Chapter 5

"Their fantastical gifts already include a new, dynamic power grid providing free energy for the masses (mothballing our old electrical lines), assistance in decommissioning our remaining nuclear facilities, and a method to safely clean up their waste and radiation in planet-wide locations. The Pacific Ocean is said to be almost safe to swim in again! The Council, which has been hard-pressing the Messengers about disease, is claiming forthcoming cures—even for cancer, which is affecting over 80% of us now. In just a little over two years, our civilization will rise from ruin and catapult half a-millennia into the future, with limitless possibilities at our fingertips. So what's the catch?"

—Warner Roxwell, *Our Backs Against the Wall*

The three-wheeled, blue and white craft stood up before their eyes, its front wheel splitting, the cowlings becoming mechanized arms. The windscreen again retracted, only this time a robotic head emerged, bristling with sophisticated cameras that synched with my own vision via the Control Hat. In two seconds, I stood eleven feet tall. Towering above my astonished friends, I stepped forward and flexed the suit to provoke a full reaction. Jay jumped up and down like a kid on Christmas morning.

"Dude, you're a Transformer! A transforming exo-suit! You're a real Transformer guy! I can't believe it." He moved in for a closer look as Pak remained rooted in place, nodding his head. It was hard not to sound dramatic, but darn it, that's what the spectacle called for.

"Transformers are make-believe, my friend. You're looking at real, military-grade hardware. It's called Variable-Power Armor. Dad and Newt invented it down here."

Though teens in the forties were now nearing the summit of the fourth industrial revolution, this masterpiece of engineering was enough to send even this jaded crew into shock. But Beck's reaction stood out. She howled laughing, like this was the funniest thing she'd ever seen. Doubling over, she placed both hands on her knees, pointing and laughing at the phenomenon I'd become. After a moment, I could tell it was a good kind of laugh, one of delight, and I enjoyed watching her give in to it.

When Jay walked up close to touch the armor, I put on a show by flexing the arms, rotating the wrists, and *thinking* the mechanical hands through a series of movements. The suit's head unit turned with mine and I looked down to see Jay jump back in amazement.

The mecha was capped with a more realistic head than the suits designed for construction and police duty. Dad wanted to have fun with the designs and fulfill some childhood dreams, and it showed. The face bore a jester-like grin that made you feel like the joke was on you, and the customized blue and white racing theme looked almost recreational.

"So, what do ya think?" I stepped back and placed the massive fists on the suit's hips. My father started toward Newt and the control room and I hoped I was handling everything the right way.

Beck, exhausted from her reaction, stopped laughing long enough to walk closer. She folded her arms across her chest and looked the suit up and down, nodding with approval.

"Well, Beck, I didn't know you cared." The external speakers broadcast my voice with deep, processed effect, adding to the spectacular show. Beck said nothing as she continued her inspection with a long smile.

Jay grabbed Pak to pull him nearer, pounding on his arm and pointing at the mechanized armor as if he could not see what was in front of him. "You need a serious license for that, don't you?" Pak let out, breaking his silence.

"Uhhh, yes, we do," I answered. "But we don't have one, and that's why this is all such a tight secret, you big dope." He nodded some more while Beck remained in place looking me over, searching out every detail. Somehow, I'd gained a greater devotion from her that day, in ways that were hard to identify.

Since then, we'd grown closer, and spent most nights talking for at least an hour. So along with feeling rattled by the floating incident, my "Beck Withdrawal" was making it hard to focus on anything down there. As much as I relished that memory, dwelling on it too long left me melancholy. Maybe it was because Beck's admiration had yet to grow beyond that day.

I remember Newt blurting out something from his chair that detoured me from memory lane. As the vision faded, my bouncing, nervous knee signaled I'd again joined the present and was ready for some action. What little distraction remained was zapped away by an uproarious clearing of Newt's throat. He slapped his pen down on the counter, spun around in my direction and called my attention to his notebook.

"Look, you're going to love this," Newt exclaimed with unusual gusto. "I've programmed in a bomb-defusing mission and a new set of enemy combatant reactions..." He trailed off and stopped short when he realized I wasn't hanging on every word.

"Newt, I'm pretty stressed out. I think I just need to blow off some steam."

"So you want to try these new programs or run through existing exercises?"

I shook my head from side to side, surrendering to the laziness that often resisted fumbling through anything unfamiliar.

"Existing."

"Fine. Allow me a few minutes to get everything running and you'll be ready to *rock and roll*." He tried to drop his accent for the "rock and roll" part knowing that change of speech pattern made me happy.

"Just give me the all-clear when you're ready." I grabbed the starter fob for my Brawler 1, or B1 for short, and pushed the exit button to get out of the box.

"Oh, Garret, before I forget—don't go outside tonight, at least not until morning. I've been picking up some very strange gravitational readings in the area, real bizarre stuff. Just wanted to give you the heads up."

I pointed my finger back at him, shot him a wry wink, and wondered how mad he was going to be when he found out about my adventure in levitation.

Part 2: Sandpoint

Chapter 6

"And following this latest wave of violent break-ins, many are asking themselves if these giant robotic devices are a benefit or a detriment to our reemerging society. With how easily this technology can be misused and become another tool in the hands of criminals, will we be forced to ban them outright, or, despite their drawbacks, embrace the idea we might all be wearing one someday?"

—Chandra Keegan, *True News 2, Evening Anchor*

My machine *was* ripe; in fact, the whole place down there was stale. Mom had tried to straighten it up once but any progress she managed was undone in rapid fashion. She once put it that cleaning a pit conducting war games was like trying to brush your teeth while eating OREOs, and she eventually avoided going down at all. Our situation felt very temporary, so organization seemed beside the point.

The arena stirred to life as the training program booted up, illuminating our secret complex in its lengthy entirety. A few overhead lights resisted turning on and flickered above our row of variable armor vehicles parked just outside the roped enclosure.

As I walked up to B1 in its bike mode, I tried to stop myself from smiling, but couldn't. In my eyes, this machine was the *baddest* personal craft ever invented, and I wanted more than anything to show up at school and watch the kids react.

"Hatch," I commanded, and the composite windshield slid backward. I stood and admired the three-wheeled work of art as I finished putting on the one-piece body suit.

Dad had let me add a custom blue theme with a few crude white stripes, though many of the exotic materials had to remain unpainted. The Brawler's waist and legs reacted like rubber under intense weight or pressure. They had the strength of tungsten, yet could bend and return to their original shape.

Newt called these alien metals, but Dad always challenged that assertion. "They're not *aliens*," he would shoot back. Newt would nod to avoid another debate on *who* or *what* we were facing. All the materials were classified above top-secret, but Newt had gained access to them with his high-level clearances. These suits had gotten the best of everything he'd ever come in contact with.

Lights glowed in the interior as the boot-up process ran its course, and subtle flickering danced across the instrument panels as fresh programs finished downloading and the systems check completed its run.

I stepped up onto one of the forearms and lowered myself in to get comfortable. Lying on his stomach, the pilot assumed a dynamic flying position: legs back, arms forward to grasp twin drive controls, or Control Sticks, that were loaded with triggers and buttons. The black Control Hats were more elastic and formfitting than a rigid motorcycle helmet. The rim that ran around the helmet's interior blended man and machine by translating thoughts into mechanical action. Newt referred to this tech as a "non-invasive brain control interface," or NIBCI. I just called it robotic telepathy.

Helmet use rules were stringent, and Newt bombarded me with them daily. When I asked what would happen if one was broken (the rule or the helmet), Newt said to consider them irreplaceable, because their source wouldn't be handing out any more. The advanced NIBCI helmet was learning me as the suit adapted to my DNA, increasing my fluidity and reaction time. Dad described it in terms of having to break in a wild horse all over again if we ever had to replace my Hat. We would lose all the progress I had gained through months of training. My questions kept flying and when I pushed him to find out why the data couldn't be saved or backed up, I pushed too far. He raised his hands in the air and shouted something about "living data," spouting off a lot of technical gobbledygook until I regretted wanting to know anything about them at all.

I slipped my Control Hat on and wriggled down inside B1. Together again. Its cockpit: a driving pod. I: the living seed it both protected and confined. The surrounding Brawler unit bucked with intense energy to carry out its occupant's bidding. Every thought, every twitch made the contraption jerk and flutter, like a thoroughbred anxious to breach the starting gate while high-voltage wires brushed against its skin.

The purr of the windshield closing over me added to the hum filling the cabin. B1's "bike mode" mimicked a conventional driving experience, with a view of its glowing dash light already seeping into my helmet. That convention would be eclipsed the instant I stood up into Brawler form as my Hat connected with the cameras on B1's grinning face for a complete view of the outside world.

Systems scrolled through their final checks as Newt's voice streamed across the Com.

"Almost there…okay, all set. Change modes and head to the training area. I'll brief you on your mission parameters in a moment. Oh, and please go easy on the stairs until we can get metal replacements."

After a controlled exhalation, I ordered the restless machine through its metamorphosis into Brawler mode. In a flash, the sleeves containing my legs found grip against the ground, and lifted the rest of the craft into a standing sentinel. Waist and lower body functions were obedient to my own movements, only magnified.

B1's arms, *on the other hand,* operate through telepathic interface. By gripping the twin Control Sticks in the cabin, thought projection and electrical stimuli are interpreted directly to the Brawler system. It's necessary at first to strap your wrists to the controllers until it's second nature, because your first impulse is to let go of the Sticks and uselessly flail your own arms and hands around the cockpit. This technique took months for me to get down, and moving your real appendages again after long training sessions felt darn peculiar, to say the least.

Stepping up into the training arena as my exotic robotic alter ego, I could hear Newt's voice giving me the all clear. Show time.

"I call this one 'On the Waterfront,'" he said proudly. "You will have to penetrate a warehouse under heavy guard, rescue three hostages and diffuse a bomb, all within forty-five minutes. There are enemy J-22 and X-7A combat suits, as well as terrorists with armor piercing rifles. You'll encounter some other surprises as well."

"What happened to the training sessions we agreed on?" I complained.

"Naaahh. Told you, you're going to like this."

"Do I get some guns?" I mused, knowing the answer.

"Guns? You're just a kid. Ten seconds…"

Having no weapons, I was left with only agility and smarts to complete the mission. Newt said that I wasn't ready for real firepower, and frequently reminded me that if I could accomplish the mission without weapons, imagine what I would be able to do once I had them. I tried to enjoy the challenge of always being outgunned.

The training programs converted the arena into a digital world with enough twists and turns to keep me well inside the ropes. There were plenty of junk piles that the mission program converted into virtual items to navigate around, such as parked cars, a hotdog stand or park bench.

"Program up," I directed, and the new scenario, *On the Waterfront*, filled my view. Near the ocean, I could see a few large buildings just beyond a parking lot surrounded by an array of docks and ships ready to be loaded. The program was using numerous water inlets as the edges of the ring to keep the action confined.

"Seagulls. Nice touch," I noted, but Newt didn't respond. His lingering silence was there to remind me that it was time to embrace illusion as reality. Accepting what my eyes were telling me, I needed to believe actual lives were hanging in the balance.

Displays and sensor readings could be added to the peripheral view just by thinking about them, while a few other commands still relied on voice activation. I wanted more information, so it came. The heads-up display sprang to life with distance measurements, heat signatures, power sources, and threat warnings.

Moving with B1 was fluid, and maneuvers like squatting and body rolls were within its range of action. The super alloys had an amazing bend-but-not-break quality to make such dexterity possible. Advanced gyros and gravity controls forced you back into a stable position, so staying upright was hard to avoid.

A bus was parked along a dock not far from my position, and I decided to move in behind it and see if anyone would notice. The program offered extensive detail, with changing weather patterns, civilians running in terror, and others yelling and throwing objects.

Activating all sensors, I could see through the bus to the target building on the other side. Multiple power sources in the warehouse closest to me were coming alive and moving about within the structure. I gripped the Control Sticks tighter in anticipation.

Then an alarm blared through the Com and adrenaline gushed into my body. This was not a training alert but a facilities alarm. The complex's detection suppression barrier was having a fault, leaving our subterranean lair vulnerable to surveillance.

We were almost certainly being watched.

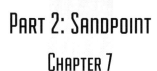

Part 2: Sandpoint

Chapter 7

"Evan, with this design, Garret's field of view will come via the helmet type we've been discussing (if we can get our hands on one). He will be restricted to seeing the Brawler's robotic arms and the outside world, nothing of the cabin's interior, making him forget he has any real arms at all. The experience will be not one of driving something, but more like having his teenage consciousness transferred inside a larger, more powerful body. The longer the training session continues, the stranger it will feel when he reacquaints himself to his fleshly counterpart, or "real-self" outside the suit. Please note: a syndrome can occur where mecha pilots no longer want to exist outside their robotic identities, and it's not as rare as you might hope."

—Dr. Newton Bigsby, *Notes from Beyond the Edge*

In a flash, I hunched B1 over and took myself, and the combat suit, down to our knees. My finger rose to the main power switch, but Newt had beat me to it. The cabin went black, and the low whine of power ebbing away trailed off in my ears. The head unit hatch popped above me to let in air as my mechanical body slumped motionless in the dark.

The lab was silent. I could see out of the hatch just enough to notice a yellow flashing across the ceiling. That meant the electronic counter-measures device (or ECM) was experiencing a perimeter fault warning. Yellow lights meant "warning"; red would have meant a total fault, a problem I wasn't sure we had a solution for. Dad and Newt had fortified the complex with a vast amount of jamming equipment to prevent detection. They also had government contacts on the inside that kept a close eye on us and let us know if anything looked suspicious, but the system wasn't immune to problems.

With the elevation of power-suit development from basic to super advanced within a few years, it hadn't taken long for the technology to be abused. Now you couldn't own or operate a powered exo-suit without very expensive licensing, leaving them for military, construction labor, or off-world uses. Big Brother gained a very sensitive means of detection for anything resembling a power suit signature. A few moments exposed without cloaking or countermeasures, and the lab—along with the Brawler units—might be visible.

I was relieved that this alert didn't come at the end of an exhausting training session. Even still, it was hot and getting hotter by the moment. I tried to ignore the sweat running down my forehead before giving in and removing my helmet to wipe the moisture away. Looking down at my hands, I valued having them in there with me. Newt often contended that we needed to appreciate this design during power-down drills because most other suits required your arms encased as well. "There's nothing like a nose itch you can't scratch," he'd say.

The verifications necessary to return to an all-clear status were extensive and could take some time. So as the temperature built, so did my anxiety—and I knew better than to let it get out of control. Wigging out during any prolonged confinement, especially a powered-down exo-suit, was a distinct possibility. Intense training reminded me how vital my thoughts were to survival. Dad had created this Brawler mechanism as my source of protection, not a death trap. I needed to envision myself protected, not confined, within it.

From imagining swirls of poisonous gas flowing over the motionless armor, to hungry monsters lurking just outside—I tried to content myself with the idea that I was sheltered within this now-sweltering body sleeve. As I strained to keep my thoughts distracted, the throbbing in my legs pulsed on.

Deep breaths, deep breaths. Sweating, feeling sick. Had it been an hour?

"Newt!" I half-yelled, half-whispered with little hope of a response. "Newwwt!!" Time ticked and ticked. "Newton!" To my relief, I heard a faint call come from the far side of the training area.

"Hang on, Garret. Hang on!"

A few moments later, Newt's face filled the small opening in the suit's top port. An intense ray from his penlight caught my right eye and I winced from the beam.

"How are you holding up in there?" He whispered and clicked off his penlight, not waiting for an answer. "Let me run back to the box and do a last check. I think we're almost in the clear."

He turned to go, but I called him back. "Newt!"

"Yes, what? Please be quiet. What?" He strained his face against the metal frame to see me in the darkened cabin.

"You're right. It is smelly in here," I deadpanned.

Newt didn't smile. "Hang on a minute more, and I'll give you the okay."

He disappeared into the darkness while I fought back frantic screams of protest. Finally, the word came over the Com.

"All clear, Garret. Phew. Power should be coming back up now.

Had a bit of a scare there. A failure threat along the east wall. Surge of some kind."

Opening my eyes to see the pleasant glow of orange filling my view, I counted the seconds before I could stand up. "Three, two, one…" I stood up inside the robot and it obeyed me. Jogging in place brought no relief so I stepped down out of the arena and came back to vehicle mode. "HA-A-ATCH, please…"

Dragging myself up and out of the cockpit was harder than I thought, and I managed to catch my foot during dismount on the front arm. I plowed headlong into B2 parked alongside and everything went dark.

"Garret! Garret! Hang on, lad!" I felt Newt turn me over and cradle my head. A warm trickle over my lips begged me to raise my hand to my mouth to inspect the flow.

"Nice." I looked at the blood running down my wrist. The day wasn't getting any less miserable.

"Well, you've done it now," Newt said, which meant it was bad, I looked a mess, and Mom was going to be upset.

I lay there motionless for a few moments until a jolt of electric determination shot through me. *Stop this!* I screamed at myself. *You're embracing defeat! What if this was a life-and-death situation and others were depending on you? What if you had to run across an open field under heavy fire and save someone, with ten times the pain you're in now?*

I forced myself up and shook away from Newt. The locker door took a quick punch before I opened it and grabbed out a stiff towel, long overdue for a wash. I rubbed it over my aching face until the cloth looked like a bloody Rorschach test. I blew my nose in a clear spot and threw the towel behind some metal containers.

Newt stood watching me in silence for a moment before turning to look over B1, its hatch still ajar. I panted in simultaneous relief and pain, trying some levity for comfort.

"If it was bad in there before, it's really bad now. I know you'll scrub my Brawler out for me, Newt."

"I can't do that," he monotoned. "Your mother said to make you clean up after yourself down here."

With a sniff and sigh I got the lucid picture of Mom instructing Newt on "Garret Management." "He's not your butler of sci-fi!" she once shouted, shaking a pointed finger. I probed my injured face and tried to rectify the situation with my mentor, mumbling humbly, a sore tail between my legs.

"I know, I know. I'll wipe it out tomorrow. Sheesh. I was going to." Feeling a little more blood run down my cheek, I wished I had my towel back. "I might as well take my jumpsuit up and wash it, too," I griped, as I began removing my sweat-soaked body suit in defeat. Then Newt added insult to injury.

"Clean the team's while you're at it. I gathered them over by the lift. If you can manage, that is?" He spoke with a hint of compassion, but a double hint of sarcasm.

I nodded and sniffed another long sniff, deciding not to say anything except "Good night Newt," as I passed him.

"Oh, and take your pill, please." He then handed me the pill that I, as well as the rest of the team, took every night before leaving training. The tall glass of water was a relief.

At first I thought the pills were vitamin supplements, but Newt said they promoted healthy sleep and made our dreams more "productive." It often felt like I trained all through the night after taking them, in vivid and startling ways.

At times, I could recall the dreams so well that I would suggest ideas for our missions based on them. Oddly enough, I almost always had weapons in my imagination, with super-powers far beyond anything he allowed in his scenarios. This made normal sessions feel a little drab by comparison. My head was starting to pound as I shook it in disappointment. I moaned.

"Hopefully, I'll have a better training session in bed..."

Newt smiled a wan smile.

"Good night, Garret."

Part 2: Sandpoint
Chapter 8

"If the Earth is not losing mass, how can it be losing gravity? Is the emperor of theories shedding his clothes? If we do not put aside long held 'certainties,' and soon discover urgent new truth, our apples are about to start falling upward."

—Piper Corcoran, *Can Things Get Any Stranger? Volume I*

The following morning my normally violent, hair-trigger reaction to the blaring alarm was absent, replaced by an unusual contentment to coexist with it. A long series of groans escaped my chest as I tried for twenty minutes to push out of the comfortable covers.

As always, Popo and Gigio, my energetic zebra finches, chirped and fluttered noisily. While their calls were never loud, a persistent honking sound flowed from them to welcome each day. They buzzed over me, all around between their two cages, which were open on opposite sides of the room.

Their messes and the occasional loose feather flew in direct defiance of every other tidy thing my mom kept throughout the house, except the aforementioned study. I protested that a normal boy needed something messy, or else he might just go crazy. Besides, I couldn't stand the thought of caging the birds up and locking the door. Mom conceded, but she harbored an open desire for their premature death.

To my disgust, my head wound had dried to the pillow during the night, making it impossible to move my face without a new round of sharp pain and fresh blood as I pulled it free.

Mom had been in her room reading for the night when I'd come up from the lab. It hadn't seemed worth it to bother her for medical attention. I'd opted to lie low and keep bleeding rather than risk worrying her into an impromptu safety lecture, but she would have fixed me up a sight better than that mess.

"Oh, *that* looks lovely." I grimaced into the bathroom mirror and touched my fingers along the three-inch cut across my forehead. The bandage was half as large as was needed for the job, hanging on more from the wound itself than the now drenched and useless adhesive. Pulling the tape-tangled gauze free, I watched chunks of dried and bright-red blood swirl down the drain until the water ran clear.

"Oh man—what is this?" I noticed a nasty scrape on the tip of my nose that looked like it would hang around, getting attention for all the wrong reasons. "Great. Just call me Rudolph. How come I can't get a scar somewhere cool?" I touched an index finger to my sensitive nose in disbelief, hoping it was only a mirage. It wasn't. I stepped back and flexed in the mirror, showing a growling under-bite in an attempt to lift my spirits.

Between martial arts training and home workouts, my frame was bulking up nicely. Jay, Beck, and Pak had enrolled in the classes with me and we'd become a force to be reckoned with, no longer needing protection at school. Though the sad sacks who make up a percentage of every class did plenty of jeering—"There go the karate kids" and such—but at least they stopped calling us the "homeschoolers." Well, except for one individual that is.

I admired some new lines of muscle rippling along my shoulders until a jolt of pain extinguished the under-smile. My tongue had found an excruciating puncture through the back of my lip, courtesy of my jagged bottom teeth. Tugging the lip down to take a look caused spit-laden blood to spill out into the running water.

Ugh. I resolved to stop looking before I found more stuff broken and grabbed some toilet paper to wipe my mouth. Bits of the fragile tissue broke free and remained on my lips, and I bent close to the sink as one hand splashed water over my face and the other fished for replacement bandage materials in a cluttered drawer.

My closet held two sets of school uniforms, white shirts and dark gray pants. The shirts were government-issued; given out the previous year, they featured a new, high-tech fabric everyone called *heavy-wear.* The material was a composite mesh that could realign its molecular density and more than quadruple its weight on demand. Along the right seam toward the waist, a small, touch-activated gauge could slide up and down to increase or decrease the weight.

Although inadequate to resist any serious gravitational drop, it was still startling to behold and much better than tying rocks to oneself with rope like I'd heard of people from poorer regions doing. No matter what device they issued to cope with the Gs, though, kids always pushed the limits to see how high they could jump. Whenever a gravity alert sounded, foolish children everywhere shed their weights for liftoff, often resulting in injury.

Starting down the stairs, I realized just how sore my legs had become from being confined the night before. The day was feeling wretched until I smelled the sweet smell of cinnamon toast guiding me down to the kitchen. I heard the next batch pop up for buttering as I walked over to Mom and presented my face.

"Pretty," she said with a startled expression. "Something I should know about?"

"No. Nothing, except that your son likes to smash his head against things." Making quick light of injuries usually kept my activities below from scrutiny. The tactic appeared to work again as she returned to buttering another piece of toast, being careful not to get any on her glimmering silver suit.

Marcee Rae Philmore, better known to me as "Mom," was the kind of woman you rarely see in what the rest of us would call street clothes. That day, like most days, she wore boardroom attire; like all days, her straight, dark bob was perfectly coiffed, and it looked freshly dyed. She might not have had an office job since before I was born, but that didn't keep her from looking like she did.

One thing that betrayed her armor-plated disposition was a small vase that sat above the kitchen sink she would often fill with wildflowers. I tried to notice them whenever possible and commented on how nice they looked.

"I picked those this morning," she said. "It's just trefoil. Last of the year, I think. It's supposed to get much colder this week."

I nodded and slipped away from Mom's watchful eye toward a plate holding a small stack of toast, buttered and glistening with cinnamon sugar. About to grab and dash, she followed me there, still staring at my forehead.

"I see you've done a thorough job bandaging…" Words spoken to herself as she tried to pat down my bed-head.

"Can I take this one?" I asked, levitating one piece of toast above the others, knowing they were all fair game.

"Yes," she said, and I made a lateral move, veering a few feet closer to the news on the display, taking a large bite on the way. Time to distract her.

"What's going on? The Council?"

There on the monitor was a slow pan of their iconic amphitheater, gigantic enough to hold the many thousands in attendance. At the front was a long stage where the three hundred members of the Council of Resplendent Light, or CRL, sat facing the audience. Multiple microphones sprouted before each representative. The hall was buzzing with activity of all kinds, with people walking up and down the aisles amidst flashing cameras and television crews.

The Council was made up of individuals chosen from every walk of life and region on earth. They were the point of contact with the new Messengers, passing on their secret knowledge to our world. The Council also passed our most crucial questions back to these enlightened ETs, and their answers inevitably became the latest headline until something more intriguing or controversial replaced them. What our alien saviors looked like was an airtight secret and an inexhaustible topic of conversation. The Council was supposedly sworn to secrecy, or maybe they simply didn't know.

CRL councilors were not model politicians, or even what you might imagine to be Earth's best and brightest. Most were common people—nurses, plumbers, and teachers—and they were humbled by their own selection. The makeup of the Council appeared the only rational choice since nearly all politicians, royalty, movie stars, and the ultra-rich were villainized the world over for their part in the global Meltdown.

A napkin and plate came into view and I swiped them away to catch my falling crumbs. About to give Mom a sugary kiss goodbye, I saw Jay's face at the kitchen door and stopped short. Glued to the broadcast, she didn't see my attempt at affection, so I gathered up my lunch and school things and headed out. I checked the gravity indicator on the wall and all read normal. Not a perfect technology, the indicators were there mostly to help fight "G-Anxiety," but after last night's flight, nothing was going to make me feel better.

"Bye, Mom. Do you have a meeting or anything today?" She spun herself out of a stare and fumbled to straighten something.

"I'm going to the *interfaith* temple for a last protest," she answered, "although we both know how that will go. Then I'm having lunch with Angie. Have a good day." She didn't look my direction. I opened the door and Jay shook his head at me, wearing a perplexed expression that bordered on anger.

"What happened to you?"

"That noticeable, huh?" I appreciated honesty, but not the brutal kind he was best at. I tried to divert him from my appearance by asking how the gravity was feeling out there. Mistake.

"Garret, I've said it a million times: it's not the gravity we have to worry about, it's those dang aliens. They were trying to abduct you because they know we're onto them. People report being pulled into the air all the time. You're lucky you came back at all."

I took a deep breath. Particularly this early in the day, I didn't have the energy for a verbal sparring match. Unlike me, Jay was a morning person and ever ready to tangle over the alien question. His opinion on the Messengers went far beyond distrust and into open contempt. His aunt was convinced that she had been abducted and experimented on over many years and had some pretty strong proof to back up her claim. The word coming from the CRL was that the entities responsible for those abductions were now eradicated from Earthspace.

Now Jay felt more than justified by his suspicions, and trusted these Messengers about as much as the evil Vril, our accused abductors. He changed gears away from the intergalactic alien invasion to increase my insecurity.

"Hey, you've got blood on your shirt too. What's up?" He asked with slight smile even as my frown grew. I hadn't noticed the blood on my collar, but I looked down and shrugged it off, pretending I had.

"The day didn't get any better after you and Pak left last night. I should have gone straight to bed."

Suddenly an aircraft ripped through the overhead sky and disappeared out of sight. Its blinding speed made even its large size indiscernible. The cracking sound came from tearing the atmosphere, not from its nearly silent engines, if it had any engines. My heart thumped.

"More testing…" I said, guessing like I knew, hiding some sudden fright.

"They look ready to me!"

"No thanks," I scoffed, like a codger longing for the good ol' days. It had been nearly ten years since "the planes fell," when almost half the world's airborne fleet became pulsed out of the air. Even with most electronics becoming instantly defunct, the bits of footage that captured the happening were enough to keep me grounded—forever. The Meltdown made it impossible to get anything reliable back in the air, at least not pulse-proof. And then there was the issue of who was going to pay for them to be built, or pay to fly in them. Nearly a decade later civilian flight was just getting ready to come back online, but it wouldn't be planes this time.

"Wait, where's the rest of the team? Beck?" I asked, shaking myself from the vision of jumbo jets splatting to their fiery deaths.

"She said she was going right to school," Jay answered, turning to walk away, "And I haven't heard from the big man…" I stood there bewildered.

"Why didn't Beck tell me?" I wondered aloud as I slung my bag over my shoulder, scarfing down the last bite of toast. "I've had my bud on." Beck always had us on group-call in the mornings. Why had she cut me out?

"Just go," I told Jay. "I'll be right behind you. How are the Gs doing out there?"

"Fine. All fine here." Jay looked around, did some jumping in place, and threw me a look that said I was a loon. I waved him on and shut the door.

For a moment I considered bagging the whole day and crawling back under the covers. Placing my pack on the counter, I couldn't manage to let go of the strap. Beck always dropped by the house first and then we all went down together. I resolved to make sure she was safe.

Mom was standing close to the display, biting her fingernail over the threatening information she was subjecting herself to. "They're going to call our whole region the New Atlantis," I heard her mutter. "I know that's what it'll be…" I shrugged and thought Atlantis sounded cool. She hadn't turned around to see the exchange between Jay and me, so with a long sigh I dragged my bag off the counter and left before she noticed.

The garage door opened to Jay's capsule-shaped vehicle zipping out of our drive toward the estate's armored gate. Velops, one-man "pills on wheels," streamed obediently within the controlled Automated Highway System, or AHS. Self-driving and self-flying copter cars were just getting their bugs worked out when the Meltdown struck. Velops were the eventual culmination of those efforts, but with unprecedented tech and power sources. Granted, they were safe, but that made it impossible to break the law, crash— or especially have fun. Hover-mode models were already in the testing phase.

Manual driving capabilities weren't available during school or business hours except for police and other authorized vehicles. You were supposed to just punch in your destination and let the velop do the rest. Most everyone looked at this in a positive light. You could finish your make-up, eat breakfast, or cram for that morning's English test. I found it maddening and longed to take my Brawler down those streets at combat speed, knocking all the flimsy conformists off the road in my wake.

Nearly all models were sterile in color: cream, beige, gray, silver, with an occasional black. This fit well with the increasingly popular ideals of unity, community and all that. I'd unaffectionately called my glossy vanilla model; Bean.

"Morning, Bean. Door," I demanded, edgy. Her left scissor panel obeyed and swung open. I sat inside the tan cabin as the radio, by default, stirred to life with a Song of Unity in midstream:

"Stand up, survivors of Earth, stand up, prisoners of starvation.

Reason resounds like a volcano, celebrate the erupting sensation.

Wipe clean the slate of our past, stand up, stand up, you freed masses.

The world's foundation is changing at last..."

Despite the catchiness of our main anthem, I called for silence and ordered the door closed. I tried the team again on group call, afraid that Beck wouldn't accept. My fears were realized.

"Yep. This is Jay. Don't tell me you're not coming in after all."

Pak cut him off. "Morning. Slept late. Getting my stuff ready now. I'll make it in on time, *out.*" Pak wasn't an early riser and took considerable time in the morning just to get cognizant.

"Beck? Beck?..." After two more seconds her recorded response clicked on. I threw my pack onto the dash in frustration. "Out. School, please."

Bean's female voice confirmed; "SANDPOINT JUNIOR AND SENIOR HIGH SCHOOL, PLOTTING COURSE. PLEASE BUCKLE UP SO WE CAN BEGIN." And just like that, my capsule-car pulled away to join the "freed masses" starting their day.

I looked down and realized I had forgotten to change my bloody shirt, and then decided I didn't care.

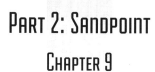

Part 2: Sandpoint
Chapter 9

"Since much of the world had to live without motorized vehicles during the Meltdown, the push to revive some semblance of what everyone loved about fossil-fueled or electric cars and trucks promised great payoff for the corporations that could reemerge and provide the next generation of transit. One company soon dominated the market with its clinical-looking, capsule-shaped enVelop. Others joined in with their own versions but thereafter they all became commonly known as 'velops.' Their gravity stabilization, coupled with total immunity from pathogens and pollution, suited the need for safety—while the new government subsidized their production to make sure every Global Citizen got one. Like Hitler's Beetle, the velop became cheap transportation for the rebuilding masses."

—Prescott Hamilton, *From Pandemics to Paradise & Back Again*

With an uncertain future facing us, Dad and Newt had taken their best ideas and cooked up the Brawler exo-suit design as something they hoped could change modes and disguise itself into a velop-like vehicle. Traveling undetected on the AHS, my secret variable-mode armor would protect me wherever I went.

They both relished the challenge once the project got underway, and Dad said it helped Newt put his tumultuous past behind him. Long-divorced and childless, Newt developed a great deal of parental protectiveness towards me. Creating a radical new defensive armor gave him an outlet for it.

Once complete, the Brawler suits outperformed their expectations, but the bike mode would never pass for an average velop. Not only would they be obvious on the AHS, the attention on our family would be worse than not having the super-machines at all.

Mom took one look at the Brawler bike and refused to let me go anywhere in it, asserting that it would be confiscated inside of a day. No one could disagree. Robotic exo-suits were strictly controlled, with licenses available only to those in a select few industries, such as construction and civil enforcement. If the authorities discovered one in unlicensed hands, it meant prison.

Although Dad and Newt had failed to make the bike mode look ordinary, Newt asserted that they'd created something better, something far more capable of safeguarding me. I wished I were in my Brawler that morning, heading off for some noble mission. Instead, my plodding velop delivered me to the place I'd least like to spend the day.

After a ten-minute ride, I arrived at the temporary home of Sandpoint Public School. It had been converted from an abandoned hospital several years ago as a holdover until a new, state-of-the-art learning center was completed, which was promised within the year. Until then, the interim "mortuary" sat waiting for me. It crouched well off the main road and up a steep, wooded incline.

Maybe all public schools exuded a creepy feeling, but this one was downright menacing, looming over us students as we approached. Many healthcare facilities had been abandoned during the pandemics, and this one was no exception. Dad said that those fomenting depopulation let hospitals everywhere—to say nothing of nursing homes—fill up and then withheld needed medicines and supplies, leaving the poor souls in there to perish. The building's gruesome history made it hard to imagine a sanitation method thorough enough to make it safe for us kids, but the lingering smell of antiseptic was at least some comfort.

It was well known that the moment we moved to the new school, this haunted mansion would be demolished—adding to the notion it wasn't fit for anything else. The dirty, war-torn, insane-asylum appearance made it impossible to forget that people had died in the same place where we were learning about split infinitives and the Pythagorean theorem. Everyone was impatient for the new facility to be built, counting the days to be free of the place despite rumors it would contain co-ed bathrooms. That trend, like many others staved off by the Meltdown, was now the new normal.

Rows of velops lined up to enter the parking garage and find parking spots, like so many eggs in a giant carton. The garage towered six stories high with more than enough space for all the velops, since they were automated to pack themselves in.

"You have arrived. You may now exit the vehicle." The door swung open with just enough clearance between units to allow you to pry yourself out. A windy chill was flowing through the garage, so I slung my pack over one shoulder and picked up the pace.

Flying down the crowded stairs several flights, I dashed towards my locker on the second floor. I needed to find Beck as soon as possible.

Up ahead, I could see her closing her locker door and heading off towards her first class, which happened to be in my direction. Realizing I was in an all out run, I slowed to a walk and tried to conceal my jitters.

She was anything but fragile, and I had a habit of rubbing her the wrong way at the worst times. But she had a soft side too—I'd seen it come out for a few months around her father's death. Those moments when she cried on my shoulder were painful yet treasured experiences. I wanted that part of her again, but she had packed all of her softness away and locked it up tight. She looked intense that morning, which stoked my panic over the imminent exchange.

"Hey, what's up Beck? Blowin' us off this morning, huh?" I stopped close to my locker and reached for the handle, assuming her pace would slow. It didn't.

"No, not at all. I had something to do before school—everything's fine." Not even turning to look my way, she intended to glide by. I found myself striking out with my pack to make contact with her shoulder. It worked. She halted with an impatient huff, her face scrunched up in a "this-better-be-good" expression.

"What's your hurry? Don't I look awesome?" I held out my hands and turned my face side to side so she could get a look at the battle damage. "Nice, huh?" I smiled and pointed out the ridiculous scrape on my nose.

"What happened?" she asked robotically. Something in my chest sank at her lack of enthusiasm.

"I, uh, fell—bad. But it's all right now. Why are you acting so weird? Are you mad about something?" I took a step in her direction but she turned from me as if repulsed, looking far away at nothing.

"Wait," I warned. She remained frozen as I walked close enough to see the tears welling up in her eyes. There was a sizable bruise on her left cheek.

"Kyle? KYLE! That bastard!" I said in a hushed roar. She didn't protest. "That's *it*. We're telling my mom, or we're telling CFPO, or we're telling...we're telling *someone,* okay? That's the last time, Beck—no more." I was shaking with anger, yet feeling a strange relief that I wasn't the source of her ire.

"I wouldn't go to the authorities. Kyle just got a promotion with the City." Beck avoided looking at me, as if not making eye contact might somehow hold back the tears. "I don't remember everything. I'm not sure what happened. I think he's putting something in my water or something." She bowed her head and moisture pooled in her eyes, a few drops cresting her lashes to rain down on the floor.

I knew better than to bring up telling Beck's mom. We'd already been down that road. After her father's sudden illness and death, her mom had grown emotionally frayed, suffering a series of severe breakdowns. It had taken a few years before she would even talk much with Beck or hold down a job. Ms. Sprankle snapped out of it when she had met and married Kyle Caster, getting her life back on track. But when confronted with the notion that her new husband was abusive or worse, she had reverted back to some of the same neurotic behaviors.

Now Kyle hated Beck for accusing him and inciting a new collapse. He detested us by association, and we avoided him whenever possible. I refused to call her mom, Eleanor, "Mrs. Caster," even to her face. Kyle loved that, too. Beck was petrified of bringing anything else up for fear of sending her mom to the mental ward and ending up at home alone with a monster.

"I gotta go." She swiped at her watering eyes and moved away. I grabbed for her arm with no objective in mind. She looked at me, expecting me to speak up, but I hadn't the words.

Suddenly a large figure loomed into our space, with a few more following close behind.

It was Timmy Gorgola and his gang of goons.

Part 2: Sandpoint
Chapter 10

"It is particularly coincidental that our Junior/Senior High School is a converted hospital: The original school was put to use as an emergency triage center shortly before it was destroyed by local terrorists. These crazed activists, paranoid over the pandemic vaccines being distributed there, chose the dead of night to blow away half the school's historical structure. With the lack of sense in these parts, it's no wonder these medicines soon became mandatory."

—Daphne Fletcher, *Managing Editor, Bonner County Daily Bee*

He became known as "Terrible Timmy" following our legendary blood-fest, which some people, in hushed tones, still referred to as "the showdown." The after-school mayhem looked and felt like a tie—and felt pretty horrible too. My right ear still aches when I sleep on that side. Far from glamorous, the carnage ended in a dusty, exhausted pile. There was no applause.

Timmy's Uncle Boris had worked with Dad at AnEvo Corporation back in the day, and it seemed the entire Gorgola family came to obsess upon the Philmore's prosperity and conservative views. Well, loathe us really. Per Mom's orders, I did my best to steer clear of Timmy, his relatives, and his friends whenever possible.

Red-haired and freckled, Terrible Tim was wearing his ragged orange and blue sweater (the one pilling up with fabric balls the size of peas) over a sullied school uniform. It featured a chest-mounted food stain that I could have sworn was there three weeks ago. In his mouth sat a lone metal bar guarding yellowing front teeth, which gleamed as he sneered down on me. He glanced over his shoulder to verify that his goon squad was close in tow and then started yapping.

"Looks like you two got in a fist fight last night and you lost, Garret," Timmy slimed, his clowns chortling behind him. I avoided his eyes and focused on Beck instead. She looked at me as if I'd just made matters worse.

"We'll figure it out later," she said, pulling free of my hold. I watched her slip away and disappear into the tide of gray and white, a sea of half-asleep kids, oblivious to her pain.

"So what happened, Numb-Nuts? You and your girlfriend using *karate* to beat each other up now?" The cackling grew louder and I turned to Timmy without saying a word.

In most of our run-ins, I could send back a sly comment that would turn the laughter of Timmy's goons in my favor, defusing the situation. Today, finding myself too rattled for quick wit, I imagined myself punching his throat to watch him thrash on the floor in the puddle of Beck's tears. My fist began to clench of its own volition.

"What's going on?" Pak pushed through the mouth breathers to arrive inches from Timmy. "Anything I should know about?"

"Hey, it's Lard Boy, your bodyguard." Timmy seethed. "Don't let me stop you from baby sitting your little homeschoolers, *Phil*." Pak put on a large, cunning smile as Timmy backed away, unable to mask his trepidation.

"Well, hang on a second, let's not mix subjects here. Do I need to hurt you or not? That's what I'm asking," as Pak's shirtsleeves nearly burst at the seams to contain the enormous arms inside them. The awkward group knew the battle had already been won.

"Am I too late?" Pak whispered in my direction, looking bewildered at my scuffed-up mug. "You're a mess." I shut my eyes for a moment and tried to shake off the emotional hangover Beck had left me.

"No, you're just in time to save him," I responded, snarling in Tim's direction. A tense moment passed before Jay joined the growing congregation.

"Yeah, you need to hurt him," Jay said, shooting the group of thugs his best threatening stare. Timmy decided to push his luck.

"Garret, did I ever tell you that my uncle used to talk about your old man? Said how your dad and his buddy would run gambling rings to bet on fights in those power suits. They'd have 'em fight down in the mines and let 'em tear each other up for jollies. Maybe your dad had some bad debts, huh? Maybe they came to collect and sent him swimming away in a pair of concrete overshoes…"

I didn't know that Cheshire cats always grinned. "They all can," said the Duchess to Alice, "and most of 'em do." Timmy knew the kind of blow he'd delivered. His smile grew even wider and he watched it wound me. There were twenty sets of eyes on us.

"Yeah, you told me, and it was just as pointless the first hundred times you said it. You know, I think we should just…" I started to move towards Timmy with vicious intent, out of control, until Pak intervened and drew our attention to a group of teachers moving our way.

No one said another word as we dispersed. I managed to bump Timmy on the way to my locker. He tried to shove me back, but missed awkwardly.

"Idiot," I huffed, throwing my backpack in the locker and slamming the door, wishing I could slam Timmy's face instead. Leaning against the wall, I clutched my throbbing forehead.

"What's his problem?" Jay asked. He and Pak stuck around to get caught up.

"Who cares? We've got bigger issues. Beck's got, uhh...*family problems* again. Not sure what to do. Can't think right now."

I should have stayed in bed.

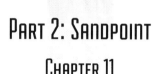

Part 2: Sandpoint
Chapter 11

"If anyone scans the house for heat signatures, they'll see me and the team working away in the study like we're really there! Dad says to keep sessions below ground to less than two hours to make sure the amount of time spent in the nook doesn't seem too unrealistic. I just watched it play back. If spies are watching the house, it will show us coughing, switching sides of the table, and even gesturing to each other. Knowing myself though, it's difficult to believe that anyone will buy that I'm doing that many hours of homework."

—Garret Philmore, *Letters on the Lamb: A Collected Journal*

By the end of third period, Beck and my headache had gotten the best of me. With blood dribbling out of the bandage, it wasn't hard to convince Mrs. Bradworth that I should call it a day. Besides, I needed to concentrate on important matters and I considered their "false history" class foolish at best, and at worst, propaganda.

Once I got into the hallway, I called Mom for the release clearance with the history teacher standing close by. The bud's phone function didn't operate inside of the classrooms, but Newt had programmed the team's with a working channel in case of emergency.

My bud produced a floating screen and Mom's face flickered to life in front of me. She was at her luncheon, but she spared me a moment of her time and a comforting expression. As usual, she was trying to lean closer to the screen, which was pointless since the view maintains a constant distance from the user.

"What is it, Garret? Is everything all right?"

"I shouldn't have come in today Mom, sorry. I feel terrible."

"I'm sorry, too. I'll send the okay for you to come home now, and I'm on my way. Anything else?"

I shook my head no and she asked for a console screen. A second, barely-visible monitor joined the other. With a tap of her finger in midair, I was cleared to go. She also unlocked my velop and authorized its early departure. Velops gave parents total control and tracking ability, making it impossible for kids to make unauthorized trips, stops, or joyrides. The thought of teenagers racing all over in their hot rods fifty years ago was hard to imagine. Rebellious independence had gone the way of the dodo.

I said goodbye to Mrs. Bradworth and she nodded at me before heading back to her class. Walking down the silent hallway towards my locker, I was hit with a sudden and massive wave of relief. The only time I was comfortable there was when everyone else was absent. Like a beached whale, I just didn't belong in that environment. Even the thought of a sparkling new learning center, bristling with the latest tech, wasn't enough to make the prospect of senior year appealing.

Realizing the period was ending in a few minutes, I got a move on. Grabbing my pack, I stopped to stare at Beck's locker.

Should I leave her a note? I thought. *What would I write?* I shook my aching head and resumed my brisk walk towards the stairwell. The parking garage felt even more frigid now, strangely empty, and a chill crept over me, running down my back. I paused, wondering if I was coming down with some kind of flu, but then the back of my neck began to prickle.

All of a sudden, the parking garage didn't feel so empty.

Like a hunter trapped within his own forest; dark and craggy trees seemed to close around me. Escape was impossible as something large and hungry rustled in the underbrush. I closed my eyes and shook myself. The garage reeked of sulfur.

As a habit, I called up a pop-up screen from my bud that overlay the forty velops in front of me. It mapped them in green, highlighting mine with flashing red. This technique could be used in numerous ways, from finding a person in a crowd to locating an elusive product on a grocery shelf. As part of its function, the locator feature also zoomed in on your target before zooming back out, helping you gauge relative distance and position.

The sight of something frightening in the enlarged view jolted my senses. A dark figure, absent of color or detail, appeared to be standing behind my velop. By the time the screen dissolved, the shape was slinking fast through the maze of parked vehicles.

When it reached the concrete barrier, it disappeared.

Part 2: Sandpoint
Chapter 12

"When 'disclosure,' or the revelation that man was not alone, struck, it burst forth declaring not just one type of extraterrestrial among us, but also multiple types. The epiphany that we'd gone from an isolated position at the top of the food chain to being surrounded by hungry space critters sent much of the surviving human population into stammering disbelief. The Messengers quickly positioned themselves as a galactic pest control, painting several species as the cockroaches they were eradicating on our behalf. And with the monstrous appearance of these deadly pests, it was hard not to agree. The Vril, apparently from the Reticulum Constellation, have long been enemies of the Messengers. These long-necked, putty-colored reptilian creatures match the classic large-eyed alien 'Grays' featured in countless movies long before disclosure. Witnessing them as a special effect on the big screen did little to brace humanity for their horrifying reality. Many people refused to believe the Tall Grays actually existed until the World Court tried, convicted, and executed thousands of them."

—Piper Corcoran, *Can Things Get Any Stranger? Volume I*

"**H**ey! Hello? Heelloooo?" Heartbeats hammered in my throat, strangling the faint calls I tried to send through the parking deck. "What the heck was that?" I hissed to myself several times, terrified. My feet resisted their orders to move forward until some long breaths subdued the panic.

"Anyone there?" I was whispering now, not quite sure what I'd do if something replied from the cold walls and rusty girders.

Shuffling stiffly toward my velop, I ordered it to open its scissor door on the near side. A quick scan of the interior neither revealed anything unusual nor provided any reassurance. Walking around the perimeter and doing a belly flop to check underneath proved just as useless. I rocked it a bit for lack of a more sophisticated test and surveyed the parking garage once more. My mind raced for answers.

Who or what was that? Did they bug this thing, or plant a bomb? Could it be one of Timmy's goons playing a joke? I thought of the emergency channel and fought the urge to call Newt. He emphasized that if we ever broke that seal it might mean bug-out time. It could be traced to him and to our facility. Just where we would bug out *to* was a constant source of curiosity, but today was not the day I wanted to find out.

I settled myself inside and ordered the door closed, squeezing my lower lip into a fold to help me think. A Song of Unity spat to life and I erupted in a furious shout: "Shut *up!*" This failed to end the chorus until I asked for the radio to be OFF. The velop appeared unoffended by my temper. A soft, feminine voice purred from the dash, unaware of my cold sweat and shakes.

"Please choose an authorized destination."

"Bean, when was your last repair session?" I wanted to ask if she knew what kind of monster was prowling around just outside her doors.

"My last maintenance was performed on 7-16-45. Please choose an authorized destination."

"HOME, where else would I go? Blown—up—maybe…" I cringed and could come up with no other plan than to cross my fingers and get back to Newt.

"PLOTTING COURSE FOR #5 HEMLOCK HILL. PLEASE BUCKLE UP SO WE CAN BEGIN."

Hopeless and vulnerable. I shook my head at my lack of options.

"What a puny insect, so easily squashed," I complained out loud. The picture of being in my Brawler felt far different, invigorating and powerful. That dark thing would not have just oozed away. I would have caught it and demanded to know where my father was, and something deep inside me knew, as certainly as I knew my own name, that it could have told me. As the velop whooshed back and then forward to head out of the garage, my eyes darted to locate any source of movement. I continued to murmur through the fear, gritting my teeth, resolving to not be caught so naked in the future.

"Most kids can only *dream* of a weapon like that, but I've *got* one. I can do it. I can put my full armor on…"

I felt myself spoiling for a fight, spewing anger as my capsule whirred down Highway 2 into Dover. But the silent backdrop of the Selkirk mountain range began to soften my rage and a thin strand of cloud caught my eye. It wove itself in between several snow-capped peaks, and the scene put me in mind of a group of ladies sharing a long white scarf. A sudden ache for the safety of home and my mother subdued me all the more as I crested the last hill.

"YOU HAVE ARRIVED," the velop cooed.

"Stop here. Stop in the drive please." If it was going to blow up, a little distance seemed better than none. Half-expecting a sudden drop in Gs to carry me away, I pumped up my shirt gauge to its max density and sprinted for our garage. I opened the side door to the pleasant sight of Mom's black transport and skittered into the kitchen like a petrified five year old.

"Mom, something super freaky just happened!" She didn't turn from the floating TV monitor so I put a shaking hand on her arm. "Mom!"

"Yes, yes," she said, a kid caught in the cookie jar.

"Something was waiting by my velop when I went to come home just now. *Lurking.*"

"Something? Like what?" She blurted back, matching my intensity.

I babbled out a scattered description of the event. She blinked rapidly and nodded, turning me this way and that. I guess she was looking me over for those dreaded things moms always look you over for.

"Okay, calm down. How's your head? Maybe we should have Doctor Takari take a look at this..." She inspected the loosening gauze and tape for stability.

"My head is fine, but I'd better *do some homework in the nook* so that I don't get behind. I think we'd better *let someone know* about my velop and maybe have it checked out."

An exaggerated expression indicated I wanted to tell Newt right away, if he was in. I nodded for confirmation and she nodded back, signaling that he was. My sprint from the kitchen had the feel of cross-country skiing as I swept my stocking feet over the slick tile landscape. Mom wasn't finished, though.

"This sounds strange, Garret! What do you think it could have been? Did you pray?"

"I have no idea, and *no*, I didn't pray!" I shouted back from the hall and then stopped abruptly to walk back to the kitchen. A sour expression had replaced my frightened one. "Oh, but Mom..."

It seemed strange that the Beck situation would rise to the forefront of my mind, displacing the disturbance from the shadow creature, but it did. They no longer felt like separate issues, but parts of the same tangled mess. I thought of Kyle and shook my head in disgust, feeling part of the bandage adhesive lose its grip. The dressing flapped free for a moment before my hand shot up to re-secure it. I waited for Mom to spring into instinctual action and reach for me but she held back.

"I have to talk to you about Beck. She's in a bad way. Something's going on, and we're all worried." My mother's eyes grew round and white, panicked over the possibilities.

"It's about her step dad," I clarified hastily. "Girls are so confusing," I added, my face growing all the more sour. And this is when I should have sounded the alarm, told mom everything, and gotten Beck out of her house. I should have, and if I'd known then what was coming, I would have.

But I didn't.

Mom observed me for a moment before offering a smooth reply.

"Yes, we can be." Her smile teased out my own, despite my considerable efforts to hold it back. I held the bandage in place as I nodded, and then turned to leave. Mom darted her eyes to a heaping plate of fresh baked cookies on the counter and their aroma struck my nose. She raised both eyebrows.

"Oooh—oatmeal raisin?" I wondered aloud, forgetting about the garage monster.

"No, oatmeal chocolate chip."

"Even better. Did you save any dough?"

Like a punctured inner tube, she deflated with an audible wheeze. I regretted asking and then said "maybe later" as I dashed away again. She yelled after me, each sentiment louder than the last as I ran through the house. It was her way of getting those last vital points across without the threat of rebuttal.

"Tell me how your *studies* go!" She bellowed. "I don't think we should take what you saw lightly. Take authority over it, Garret! Remember who you are in Christ: 'No weapon formed against you will prosper'—and let me know about Rebecca, how I can help!"

Part 2: Sandpoint
Chapter 13

"What infuriates me more than anything else is their promoters calling it the The Way, or New Gospel. Based on the wisdom of the recent alien presence, this movement is making traditional religion seem archaic at best, at worst a threat to the entire rebuilding process. Many churches have already been converted to 'interfaith temples,' where they say traditional beliefs will be "preserved" instead of lost, but counselors are always on hand to point out just how antiquated the good ol' religions are. If it's found out you're part of a common Christian bible study, they will likely call in 'enlightenment councilors' to help bring you into our modern era. To me, this has nothing to do with 'good news.'"

—Marcee Philmore, *Director, The Philmore Hands Foundation*

Newt took an extra fifteen minutes to okay my trip below; an agonizing wait. He seemed overly agitated that I was "skiving off," so I was glad I didn't take my bud below and break procedure, agitating him all the more—but I wanted to see if any images of the shadow creature could be retrieved from it. When I relayed that idea to Newt, he said he doubted he could get the screen grabs, but that somebody could: namely, whoever or whatever had been prowling around the parking deck.

"Odds are, they've pulled up the images from your bud," Newt declared. "They know they've been seen, unless it's not a government agent at all. Perhaps it was some kind of entity that doesn't care if it was observed…" His voice trailed off.

"Well, it sure seemed to care, because it ran away *fast*." I looked at the floor until Newt had sucked in enough air to respond.

"I'll see if I can pull up the images myself—but not from your bud. I can't get them that way. I'll have to hack in somewhere. Maybe I'll track you and get some readings on anything that might be following along. Sound good?"

His request was kind and gentle, as if he was offering me a piece of candy, rather than what amounted to a digital security detail. When he patted my leg, I exhaled. Knowing that someone as brilliant as Newt was on the case felt like hearing "don't worry" from a doctor who's seen your condition a million times.

Newt was an invaluable security blanket, and I shuddered at the thought of being without him. The top-secret government projects he'd worked on were so deep, so dark, that they were like a black hole ever lusting to drag him back in.

Prior to his time in the land of top-secret, Newt had worked with my father at AnEvo Corporation. He was Dad's right-hand man in all his important robotic breakthroughs, and they had grown famous and wealthy together, to say nothing of the trouble they'd gotten themselves into on the way.

They were the pioneers of the big-boy bots, the heavy-duty construction and mining suits that revolutionized resource extraction with striking precision. When stocks, crypto and fiat currencies became worthless overnight, precious metals and a host of commodities were seen as the only lifeline to save our dying world. Dad and Newt's inventions helped propel AnEvo to the top of the heap as the largest and fastest growing company to come out of the Meltdown.

It didn't take long for the military to take an interest on their exo-suit systems, hoping to add the tech to their burgeoning array of combat armor. The army made Newt an offer he couldn't refuse and he left AnEvo for their R&D department against Dad's advice, spending a decade in weapons development.

They kept in discreet contact during those years, but Dad and Newt knew that their days were numbered as against-the-grain conservatives who were not on board with the new order. There was no way to hide Christian ideals in a world that was fast embracing godlessness and super transhumanism. So preparations were made for a time when they would no longer be allowed to refuse orders.

Using their mining and military resources, and with the aid of other mysterious allies, they constructed our covert lair in complete secrecy. To say it had been an ambitious project was a laughable understatement, and they'd needed access to outrageous tools to pull it off; fortunately, they had that access. Large tunnel boring machines, whose hyper-drillers melt through miles of solid earth, were used to "deflagrate" the rock walls into a glossy surface with no debris. I pleaded to see one of these contraptions in action, but never got the chance.

When Newt "disappeared" from government ops, the bloodhounds pounced on us in a fevered rush to find him. Even the Men in Black paid us a creepy call. Dad had to use up his remaining favors to get the heat off of our family and then retired from AnEvo, claiming an emotional breakdown. I later learned he wasn't acting. He and Newt were working at all hours perfecting the underground lab, keeping it undetected throughout the investigation.

When Dad came clean to Mom and me, she was furious and

I was elated. I vowed that someday I would be that tough and courageous. Life went from a casual experience to an intense new reality as I wandered, mouth agape, around our hidden underworld. Dad warned me that our lives would never be the same, but at the time, I'd had no concept of what that really meant.

Newt was now an endless resource of amazing tales about escaping the black projects and their early days at AnEvo. Whenever I stirred the pot, he would stare off into an imaginary place and thrill me with another adventure.

I considered conjuring up one of those stories when suddenly the image of the shadow-being raced across my imagination. It hid away in a dark fissure, waiting to be called out again, perhaps in a distant nightmare. A fresh wave of chills ran over me, unnoticed by Newt, who was mumbling about something when I cut him off.

"Do you think these things got Dad?" I asked, startling him.

He looked away for a moment, removed his glasses and stared into the distance. At first Newt shook his head, feigning indecision, but changed his mind.

"Yes."

Part 2: Sandpoint
Chapter 14

"Evan, my boy, if you thought we had great stuff at the company, you wouldn't believe what I can get my hands on here. The military's TBMs can do up to twenty miles of smooth-coated tunnels a day, and the Magneto-Leviton trains they're running through there are now going well above Mach 2.

L.A. to the Big Apple in a half an hour. I'll see if I can get you a ride!"

—Dr. Newton Bigsby, *Notes from Beyond the Edge*

mom kept me home for a week, foiling Newt's plans to track my shadowy stalker. I was relieved to be away from the morgue they called a school, and away from that ominous parking garage, but I hated missing any action, good or bad. The guys had been calling me between classes, but there wasn't much to tell—no sudden drops in Gs, no troubles with Terrible Tim.

I wanted to protect Beck, but it wasn't at school where she needed the protection. The sense of relief I felt over not being in her doghouse was in sharp decline. Her problems felt like my own and I needed to look her in the eye and offer some ideas that might solve this dilemma. But without a solution, I dreaded facing her again.

Rebecca Lynn Sprankle. It was hard to interpret my fickle affections then. We were both only children with a long history as friends, waffling conversely from being each other's strongest allies to each other's stiffest competitors.

When Beck took over her prototype Brawler suit, her first order of business was to accent it candy-apple red to counter my blue. Once training started, she took to it faster than I did, and her progress amazed everyone. I felt satisfaction in her success, but my pride took a huge blow when she rejected the mentor role I was expecting to fulfill in favor of mastering every aspect possible without my input. She began besting me at every turn—and I sometimes wanted to throttle her for it.

Jay's Brawler had gone down with repairs and it was suggested that he and Beck trade off units to keep the training even. Beck would have none of it. Her red battle suit had become the Mr. Hyde to her Dr. Jekyll, her new identity and place of refuge. She had painted a heart on her Brawler's left shoulder, with a playing card's capital Q intersecting it. Proclaiming herself the Queen of Hearts, she warned us not to "play around with her." This drew uncomfortable laughs from us boys, who saw her as a tough little sister, an object to tease at will. But something pointed toward a fiercely independent, feminine side emerging (well, as feminine as a girl can get in a combat suit, I guess) that we weren't ready for.

Ms. Sprankle said it was obvious early on that she was a play-in-the-dirt type of girl and that she would have no problem keeping up with us. We'd spent the best parts of life's first decade together, building forts and collecting salamanders. Then Beck broke our masculine context one day by wearing a bracelet loaded with pastel charms; it was a defining moment. Even at the age of ten, I remember thinking we'd hit a crossroad. My plan for us to be lifelong buddies had been foiled. Her biological father, taken by the cancer claiming so many, had given the bracelet to her before he died and it remained on her arm as a prized possession.

I would often see Beck toying with the charms, lost in them when I was trying to get her attention. Reaching out for the bracelet resulted in an unpleasant surprise as she jerked it clear of my grasp.

"*Sheesh.* Can't I see it?" I asked, shocked by the rejection.

"From a distance…" she said, displaying her wrist to spin the silver loop holding the delicate trinkets. "My dad said that these charms were for all the loves I would have in my life, and that before I could take one off and give it away, I had to be able to say to that boy that I loved him and mean it."

A missile of extreme discomfort, shot without warning. I wanted to crawl in a hole and never bring up the subject again. And I didn't.

As the years crept by, I sometimes caught myself staring at those charms, wishing they would go away or get lost on laundry day. But they remained, and often felt like a whiny neighborhood kid who kept showing up just when you started to have fun. That jangling bangle was a burr of frustration, an irritating passenger on our journey of friendship. I felt angry for giving it so much thought. The longer the hoop kept its original number of charms, the more valuable it became: a brave knight's frustrating quest, I supposed. Whoever that poor sap turned out to be.

"That darn bracelet!" I shouted to no one. My sudden outburst made Popo and Gigio shake loose a feather or two as they dashed for their respective cages. I looked at them, oddly envious.

"Sorry guys. Didn't mean to scare you. Hope you appreciate how good you have it." I gave them each a small broccoli top and decided to head downstairs for a treat of my own.

Mom was sitting at the breakfast bar, eating some scrambled eggs and reviewing a pop-up from her bud. There was a covered pot sitting on a hot pad next to my empty plate, along with my journal and favorite pen. Mom often placed the pair in various spots throughout the house to encourage my writing. The journal's binding was Kelly green, its cover pistachio. An elastic strap the same shade as the binding held the cover closed, a cover bearing an embossed image of two antique fish swimming in tandem. The pair was drawn in that "early explorer cataloguing the species" style. This may have been the morning I started calling the first entry of the day "Scrambled Eggs & Notes," but I can't recall.

"Principal Morag phoned me earlier," Mom said as a substitute for "good morning." The name *Morag* was not the first thing I wanted to hear.

Principle Byron Morag was an oil slick of a man, cantankerous to a fault. He'd made it known when all the private- and home-school kids were forced to go public that he didn't mind the private students because they were applying themselves and not dodging hard work. He didn't say anything about homeschoolers, but he didn't have to.

Whenever he engaged in conversation, he had a habit of taking his pinky finger and using it to drag his greasy bangs to the side away from his forehead, exposing the shiny skin underneath. In a few seconds, the hair would fall back down and he would repeat the tick, made all the worse by a jagged fingernail twice the length of most other men's. I stuttered out a "good morning" and sat down.

"That guy is something else. It was him in the school's garage— that must be what he looks like without his artificial skin," I joked. Mom closed her eyes and shook her head.

"He wanted to know the reason for your absence, and to make sure I wasn't doing any 'unnecessary teaching' at home."

I looked up, amazed at my principal's audacity. Mom was still stirring her coffee, but she sensed my stare and opened her eyes with a gleam, confirming she knew what a tool he was. Just then, cheers erupted from the TV monitor as a loud applause sounded out for the Council of Resplendent Light. Mom closed her pop-up, picked up her cup, and walked closer to investigate.

"What have they been saying?" I asked, bracing for the long answer.

"The Council is outlining all the mistakes we human beings have made, illustrating how Hollywood has brainwashed us to fear the unknown. Apparently, that's why the Messengers have to reveal themselves to us slowly and methodically."

"What about our darn *gravity?*" I demanded. "How are they answering the fact that all the weirdness started happening just before disclosure?"

"The Council claims that the Messengers are concerned and they're monitoring it, but they deny any connection. They're saying that our Mother Earth is beginning to heal, and it's birth pangs before something beautiful, or some garbage like that. You don't hear anything anymore about the gravity problem, except on the forecasts. I don't think they want to talk about it. The CRL did confirm we're having forty percent fewer sunny days than five years ago, and that 'Gaia is once again draping herself' to protect us from cosmic radiation." Mom shook her head at her own words.

Other reports claimed that our electromagnetic field was strengthening and our atmospheric pressure increasing, with both oxygen and carbon dioxide on the rise—at micro levels, of course. Plants were even growing at accelerated rates. My head was shaking back and forth too.

"But wasn't this caused by all the spraying and geo-engineering Dad always talked about? They shut all that down when they closed the FEMA camps and stuff, right?"

"I don't know. With fewer people and cars and less industry now, there was bound to be an effect on the environment. It does seem cloudy almost all the time, though, doesn't it?"

Confused, I remained silent and wished my father was watching that infernal broadcast with us. He had a way of cutting through the deception to reveal the truth, stilling my uncertainty. I questioned everything the Council was saying, but unlike him, I couldn't articulate why. Mom turned up the volume, and with it, my feeling of turmoil.

An unkempt-looking woman in her forties with long, frizzy hair stood up and prepared to speak from the gigantic stage. With it now illegal to alter or enhance photos and video, the world wanted the "plain truth," no matter how it appeared. By the time the Meltdown struck, nothing could be trusted in print, online or on TV. Regardless of how jarring the story, people's emotional responses had dwindled to nothing, eroded by years of fake internet news. With no more Photoshop and no more beauty filters, this makeup-free councilwoman was doing the best with what she had, tossing one side of her mane dramatically over one shoulder. She struck a commanding pose and called to the audience.

"What they are conveying is the awareness of our physical and spiritual brokenness, the injustice done to man's genotype and mental eyesight over millennia. We have the ability to correct this and be what we were meant to be: whole…" The woman's nameplate gleamed: *Olivia Barton, Homemaker*. The audience shot back question after question while Mom stared unblinking at the monitor. Olivia continued.

"Doesn't everything we've ever known feel flawed, containing a critical defect that runs through its entirety? It's as if someone threw a wrench into the blueprint of my life, my friends' lives, and the lives of everyone I know."

The speaker's inflated Golden Speech and sincere demeanor drew waves of concession from the crowd. It was brilliant and difficult to resist. Gone were the polished, perfect faces of the politicians and "banksters" we distrusted, replaced by the common clay of man. Our brothers and sisters were now pulling aside the curtain to reveal the wizard that had been keeping us from going home. Mom shook herself free of the display.

"You need to do a journal entry and then some homework. I don't want you getting behind," she barked. "Because when you stress, I suffer for it. And no sketching in your journal today, just writing!" She instructed me to have some eggs and get right to it.

So she'd seen the drawings of Bean and the Brawler Bots. I'd even included some little Garrets for scale, practicing to get the likenesses right before transferring them into my journal (plus the occasional projection from my bud, shhh). The result had turned out better than expected and I was already finding it more enjoyable to sketch than to struggle with words. Mom must have sensed that, and was now redirecting my efforts where she thought they belonged.

"Fine," I said with finality, wanting to be away from the TV, away from the Council of Resplendent Light and the angst they created. The idea of schoolwork didn't sit well either, but it was too early to go below for training. I wanted my next session to be with the rest of the squad, anyway. Jay, Beck, and Pak had agreed to miss martial arts this week so I wouldn't go berserk stuck there by myself. They were skipping class and coming over.

The anticipation was unbearable.

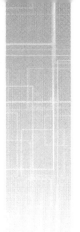

Part 3: Training

Chapter 1

"If ever there was a drastic turn in human hero-worship, it was with the sudden popularity of the un-famous. The less glamorous, the less flamboyant the personality, the more likely you were to be chosen as an icon of the New World Order. Anything that even hints at the old high rolling, 'lifestyles of the rich and famous' could cost you your societal standing, and possibly your life."

—Kelley Fenella, *The Death of Hollywood*

"I'm hit!" I heard Beck yelp out over the Com.

"That is correct, Rebecca, direct hit to your left arm. It looks like the front wheel coupling is unaffected; however, that arm will be useless when you change to Brawler mode. You *should* be able to run that diagnostic yourself, even during combat maneuvers."

"I'm busy with all these plasma beams, Newt! That's why I have you!" She shot back the retort like a true swashbuckler.

"You may have to lock that arm in place," Newt replied. "Otherwise it could flop around and cause additional damage."

Glancing in various locations within your field of view accessed the Brawler's complex system menus. You selected your desired option by *thinking* your choice, and it could be done in milliseconds with the right amount of practice.

To put it mildly, we were still practicing.

"I suppose I should know how to do that too, huh? YIKE!" She squealed as another beam missed her crimson bike. It felt great to have her back training with the team, enjoying herself and allaying some of my fears about the Kyle situation.

We were all dodging incoming fire as we zipped around inside one of Newt's virtual exercises. Called "Dodge & Weave," this program created a racetrack environment within an area that matched the training arena, but added a much more fun and futuristic landscape, along with sudden obstacles and enemy projectiles. It also simulated battle damage you carried for the rest of the session.

"That's okay," Beck announced. "I can fight the bad guys with one arm tied behind my back. If I can just get through this course and dodge all these lasers…"

"I'm not dodging much in this thing," Pak called in, short of breath. Whereas our B-Type Brawler vehicles looked like streamlined street trikes, Pak's massive C-Type, or Caliber, was a four-wheeled monster that looked like it had been birthed straight from Army R&D. The custom camouflage and sergeant's stripes he added only enhanced its menacing look. The Caliber was a variable armor as well, with its robot, exo-suit mode looking something like an irate twelve-foot ape in fatigues. Like Pak himself, it was intimidating enough to stop a fight before it even began.

Since the three Brawler units were initially claimed, Pak was forced to wait an extra four months for Newt to complete the Caliber prototype. Newt said the Caliber design was so revolutionary that he might just be able to save our skins with it if the agencies ever caught us.

He'd hand over the secret plans in exchange for our freedom, but he admitted that plan was far-fetched, as they would more than likely take the suit, slit his throat, and call it a day. But he claimed he was keeping all the schematics encrypted and the designs difficult to duplicate.

"You're doing fine, Pak," Newt encouraged over the Com. "Your vehicle is much more heavily armored, but remember, it's more maneuverable than it looks. Two more laps to go, team. In fact, change modes at full speed and run those."

A collective groan rose up over the airwaves as we catapulted into suit mode and tried to control our driving inertia into all-out robotic sprints.

"Move it, fat boy!" Jay was trying to shove aside Pak's bulky suit.

"Get away, you bug. HEE-YAHHH!" Pak belted back. He was using the Caliber's large arm to block the next lane, keeping Jay's smaller Brawler trailing.

"Watch the fancy equipment, big fella, you mess those up and I won't be able to get a decent station in here." Jay's Brawler, which we called B2, featured double pairs of shoulder-mounted antennae. Their full capabilities were yet unknown—even to him—but they sure looked cool. B2 bore the appropriate shades of green, and it was half holding onto the Caliber's giant armored forearm, half trying to wrestle past it into the lead. Newt was sending out his usual exhortation, for us to keep our spacing to limit unnecessary repairs, when Jay suffered a setback.

"Hey! They're still firing at us!" Jay hollered, noticing a second too late as a shot impacted his exo-suit's customized shoulder. At the same time, he also failed to get around Pak's Caliber. "Aw, man— running analysis…"

Jay had accented B2's now virtually damaged shoulder with a cluster of cartoonish, alien-gray faces, representing imaginary kills. "The only good alien is a dead alien," he'd say, his gleeful words defying the growing affection for all things ET.

The primary colors of our suits, or "rides," as we liked to call them, made us look like superheroes, each with our own identity and special powers. Most piloted exo-suit designs didn't feature actual necks with turning heads. Until now, it had been deemed too complex or impractical, but Dad had gone all out with ours, mostly for the fun of it, giving them distinct head units with unique faces and features. He said they were trying out variations to perfect the best head design, but the result was even more personification for each suit.

"I win," Beck panted joyfully, "and B3's arm is locked in position!"

As Beck enjoyed her victory celebration, I agonized over the rest of the team finishing ahead of me. How would I ever be viewed as a leader if I kept coming in last? Dad had said a number of times that the best way to gain respect is to say as little as possible and prove yourself on the field, but I wasn't exactly known for keeping my mouth shut, and I couldn't even manage to prove myself within my own pack. Just then, Newt rattled in with an announcement.

"Sorry, Garret. A transport is pulling into your driveway. Marcee thinks it might be for Rebecca."

A fresh rush of adrenaline coursed through me as I changed to bike mode and sped off towards the arena's entrance. Vaulting over the stairs, I changed back to Brawler to slide all the way to the lockers before changing back to bike mode. Without even looking, I knew Beck was right behind me.

A command to the rest of the team to hurry up lingered on the tip of my tongue, but embarrassment held it back. Despite training for several months longer than them, my progress was lagging. Who was I to call out orders when they'd already surpassed me?

"Newt, we'll change in the lift. Bring the elevator back down for Jay and Pak," I shouted into my helmet as I yanked it off and dismounted. Beck tore into her locker for her street clothes. I did the same and dashed for the elevator, navigating over and around the clutter in between. Reaching the lift doors first, I looked for Beck, but she had stopped to change behind her makeshift privacy wall. A ratty piece of corrugated sheet metal, buckled and rusty, she had fancied it up with a coat of red and called it her *diviseur de pièce*, which she informed us was French for "room divider".

I growled at the inconvenience, but she was every bit as resolute as I was during crunch time. The study nook was already at the basement level, its doors open. I hopped inside and resolved to be changed by the time she caught up.

It was a painful fourteen minutes to the surface. We didn't speak to each other on the way up, incessant finger tapping and long sighs replacing open speculation. Breaking into the topic of Kyle, and whether he was with her mother, would open up a can of worms I wasn't ready for.

Beck and I attempted a casual stride to the front door, but there was an unmistakable air of panic between us. I'd hoped to see both moms chatting in the sitting room, but instead, Ms. Sprankle remained standing at the front door, her rain-spattered jacket still buttoned. Beck cleared her throat.

"Sorry, Mom, we had to finish up a big problem. I have to be Garret's tutor, you know, with him missing so much time." Beck avoided looking at our mothers and grabbed for her jacket and the pack that should have been with us in the study area. Neither parent offered comment. Beck approached her mother and risked some eye contact at close-range.

"Why didn't you call? What's up?" Beck asked, trying to seem relaxed.

"We decided to go out and had the crazy idea that it would be nice to have you with us," Ms. Sprankle said, as she turned toward Mom. "We'll stop back by on our way home and get Rebecca's velop then, if that's okay." She put up Beck's hood and looked over the rest of us for approval. Mom nodded back and I saw them catch each other in a stare that spoke of silent dread. The bleak expression on Eleanor's face revealed a hidden terror, telling my mother more than I could have ever conveyed.

With the door closed, Mom walked out without a word, leaving me alone. That was her way of saying, "Thanks for putting me through that with your silly games down there." I didn't try to apologize, and took comfort in the fact that I would have much less convincing to do now that she'd seen the issue face to face.

The morning's headache had returned.

Finding a chair in the darkened room I sat to collect myself, heaving a sigh of relief that our secret training sessions appeared to have stayed that way: a secret. The relief disintegrated as I pictured Kyle's sneering face, impatiently waiting for Beck in our rain-soaked drive.

The Kyle Problem was about to reach critical mass.

Part 3: Training
Chapter 2

"Jay is very frustrated with his family, but mainly with his aunt, who once claimed to share his opinion on the 'alien agenda.' She is now convinced that the new ETs have brought to justice her former alien abductors, something the local authorities, and even her prayers, failed to accomplish."

—Garret Philmore, *Letters on the Lamb: A Collected Journal*

"They were *huge*, Marcee! I mean huge—maybe ten feet tall. There was a total lockdown as soon as word got out we'd found something." I had never heard my father in such a state of fear, and it shook me to my core.

Risking a glance, I peered out of the darkness at the top of the stairs. Dad was pacing, pleading with Mom to hear him out. It was rare for them to cancel our Bible study, and even rarer for me to be sent to my room. My parents never argued, so I was unprepared for the sudden upheaval in our living room. Ten-year-old fingers fidgeted with the carpeting as I lay there in my pajamas, listening.

"There were troops with guns, and a few agents from who knows where. One was from the Smithsonian, I think." After a few more jumbled sentences Dad began to calm down and he sat to rub his head with both hands.

As much as I wanted to wander down the stairs, fear held my trembling frame to the floor. I was frozen. Eventually, though, Mom soothed the two of them into a long, quiet conversation, and they sat talking for the rest of the night.

So terrifying was the memory that it took me several years to muster the courage to ask my father about it. On the night when I finally broached the subject, he took on a serious air and walked us back to the study. Anxiety mounted as the desk drawer opened and he began digging through his files.

A yellow envelope emerged, the kind with the long, blood-red string that loops around the seal. I watched as his fingers unwound the string, and time faltered into slow motion. What horrors could lie within the packet? I cowered as if something would bite him.

Taking out several prints, he fanned them out on the desk before my bulging eyes. A mining expedition had stumbled upon an ancient tomb nearly a mile underground. The team, testing AnEvo's latest platinum mining techniques, had radioed in the finding. Dad was one of the first on the scene.

Grainy photographs showed several rows of skeletons resting on stone slabs within the preserved chamber, every one was more than twice the miners' size. These were the remains of ancient warriors, adorned with elaborate copper armor over decorative burial garments. A few of the figures clutched stone tablets bearing hieroglyphic symbols. A few others held giant weapons. Dad had taken the photos, printed them, and deleted the files before the arriving agents started their all-out interrogation of everyone who had seen the crypt.

"Each tooth was as big as your fist, Garret!" Dad looked at me, and then back at the prints, suggesting that I do the same. "The agents took everything and told us not to breathe a word or we'd be fired. The miners were scared to death, and no one ever talked about it again." Dad went on to explain that this had been a turning point for him. Afterward, he began questioning everything, right down to Sunday morning sermons.

I sat speechless, staring at my own fist and then back at the images. Since then, I've tried to forget the photos, but the sight of those giant bones and armored plates often haunts me. Even now, the memory is close, well within arm's reach, like a horror waiting for me on a nearby shelf. If I try to bury it, turn it under the dirt in some secret place, it appears back on its shelf the following day. Waiting there, it knows I'll come back to pick it up again.

When left alone in our Dover house, I never failed to reach out for that envelope full of giant skeletons. Whether with my hand or mind, the effect was the same. I remember fighting the urge to locate those prints shortly after Mom left for the day, despite the fluctuating Gs in our area. Between my aching head and the garage monster, she was not about to let me go back to school, so I busied myself rummaging for other treasures and avoided terrorizing myself with those dreaded photos.

Taking one of Dad's shirts from the old chest, I noticed a small jewelry box tucked in the corner under a weathered jacket. I opened it and found a few of his watches lined up, wrapped in some Christmas tissue paper. The first one I unwrapped was running, but an hour slow. My heart gave a hopeful *thump*, as if somewhere out there my father was still ticking as well. I put the watch on and adjusted its metal shell around my wrist. This was his bulky, nickel-plated outdoors one, with the olive green canvas strap. It featured a world map splayed behind nickel hour and minute hands—but it was the smooth-rolling orange second hand that always drew my eye. The timepiece was clearly too big, but I doubted it would ever make it back into the chest.

Making my way to Dad's dusty book collection, I hoped a random grab would strike something interesting. That technique had worked on more than a few occasions. My index finger bumped along a row of bindings before running into one not pushed in as far as the rest. I tucked the worn paperback under my arm along with my journal and my favorite pen, carrying the stack up to our cushioned bay window (after a slight detour to the kitchen for a capacious glass of orange juice).

Skimming through the pages, I noticed a particular section decorated with multiple shades of fluorescent highlighter. Wild scribbles filled the margin. *"But like the days of Noah, so will it be at the end,"* Dad's hand-written note shouted out to me in his voice. *"Just like before the Flood when the fallen ones came down and corrupted all flesh, that's what's going to happen again. They'll promise immortality, but it's the same old trick."*

"Corrupted flesh." Boy, now *that* brought back the memories.

There was a particular backyard talk that disturbed me nearly as much as that envelope stuffed with bones. It was the day that Dad told me sinister forces might inject "alien or snake junk" into people; a nightmarish phrase forever burned into my mind.

His talks (or "lectures," when I was old enough to realize what they were) would start off by saying "the main thing was to keep the main thing the main thing," which was to keep my focus on Christ, but that the times we lived in demanded that he teach me about a lot more. Mom didn't care much for his concentration on "obscure, conspiracy-based nonsense," as she called it, so Dad would wait until we were alone to spring it on me. The Frisbee we were tossing back and forth had gone over the fence into the Voegle's back yard, giving us an unplanned break. My father wasted no time.

"Listen Garret, I'm worried that during your life you may have to face some decisions that no one else has ever faced. Well, not for ages, anyway."

He looked off at the distant, pine-covered hills and struggled to make it simple. He never succeeded, though the talk had started off innocently enough.

"It has a lot to do with Noah—you know, Noah and the ark?" Wide-eyed, I nodded, and thought he might be making our chat a little *too* simple. I bragged about Sunday school and the multitude of two-by-two coloring pages I'd completed there. When Dad asked if I knew what the story was about, I said it was when all the people were really bad, and everyone was mean to each other. This he politely acknowledged, but insisted it wasn't the main reason for the Flood.

He went on to mention Genesis 6:9, a verse stating that Noah "was just a man, perfect in his generations." My simple mind grappled with why anyone would point out that Noah was just a man. I mean, what else would he have been? Then my father conveyed how vital the scripture was because it revealed how all flesh had become corrupt.

I asked what "corrupt" meant.

"Good question. It means flawed, not as it was meant to be. Like if Mom was making you a birthday cake and instead of sugar and sweet stuff, someone snuck in and put salt in the mixing bowl. Can you imagine how bad it would taste? It wouldn't be a cake. So somehow, something snuck in and changed how things were being made, or born, and altered their genetics. Genetics is the way we're formed in our moms—what makes us have brown hair, or light skin, or even what makes us human or a dog a dog, and a cat a cat."

"So during Noah's time, people and cats and dogs were messed up?"

"Yes. I'm not sure how they did it back then, but I know how they can do it now. In fact, they *are* doing it now. It's being done in secret places. Very powerful people are figuring out ways to change everything. You know how Mom won't buy genetically modified food? Big companies used to modify or changed the food so that corn wasn't natural corn—it looked the same, but it had become something different. Bad people can do that with us, too. Change folks. It's being done in secret, and they might try to change everyone someday."

"Why?"

"Another great question—boy, you're smart!" He had smiled then, a genuine smile that I now missed terribly. "This is why I love talking to you. Most of the regular workers on these projects think it's for good, but I've been studying and I suspect that the higher-ups want the same thing that happened back with Noah. They want to corrupt everything. They hate God and they hate what He's made." He checked to see if I was still listening and continued.

"Remember how Mom and I say that Jesus dying for us is the most important thing that ever happened? He was born of Mary, and He was fully God and fully human, so He could die for us and pay our sin debt so we don't have to pay the penalty when we die? That's so we can go into a perfect place like heaven, even though we're not perfect."

I nodded at the easy parts, so Dad went on to say something about Jesus being a real man, pure as a human, and how that was critical, but my focus must have faded because his words get hazy from there. At some point I picked up a dandelion and began to blow off the wispy seeds, attempting to get a few as possible to fly off with each puff. It was a beautiful day just to be in the yard, letting the sun warm the top of my head and arms. He could have said anything and I would have kept smiling and nodding—that is until he mentioned "snake junk injections."

Apparently, I had missed something.

"Yes son, I know it sounds weird but if they can inject alien junk, snake junk, and who knows what else into people, how long before we're not what God created anymore?"

"Well, how do they get the snake stuff into you? I don't want that!" I smiled through a contorted, cartoon face.

"It's complicated, but possible. They can do some sneaky things to people without them knowing, but someday, folks will know what they're doing and they'll still choose to have it put in them. They'll *choose* to do it, but that's a talk for another time."

I looked down at my dandelion and saw it was down to only two seeds. My comprehension of our encounter was summed up right there.

"Look, Dad. It's you and me."

After a long sigh, he took it from my hand and thanked me for the gesture. His sigh could have been because my lack of attention, joy over the gift, or to relieve stress. The "Dad Sigh" was hard to interpret. He left his seat and knelt down, placing his hands on my knees to look me in the eyes.

"Garret, even if this talk was hard to understand, please focus on this: Jesus was fully human, and so are you." He tapped his finger on my chest. "Your *humanness*, Garret, being just a plain human—that's the most precious gift you have. If anyone, ever, for the rest of your life, offers to make you more than that—even if it makes you jump real high, or see real far, or live super long—you *refuse it*." The look on Dad's face scared me and I could tell it pointed to something I couldn't yet comprehend. He stood and stepped away, indicating I was free to go. His last words had that "don't say I didn't warn you" tone.

"The bad guys are going to make it look cool, Garret, and they'll try to make you feel stupid if you don't. You might even be sick, and they'll tell you this will make you better. Remember the crazy story about Esau giving up his inheritance for some stew? Don't give up your human right or authority for some temporary relief. Don't 'love your life unto death.'"

With that Dad rubbed my hair and prodded me to wash up before lunch—and the memory faded away.

"Don't love my life to death?" I said out loud, recalling Dad's awkward idiom. "That doesn't even make sense, does it?"

A light rain began falling outside, tapping its irregular tap against the window. I watched it for a moment before scanning Dad's chicken scratches a final time, and then tossed the book to the floor beside my empty glass. As the pages hit the carpet, the word *son* rattled around in my mind. Brain waves had somehow snagged the word, penned in blue cursive, flying through the air. Diving to my knees from the cushioned bench, I tore at the browning paper, searching for the improbable, heaving breaths, shaking. There it was.

"Son, they are stealing our gravity."

Frantic fingers flipped pages. The book became twisted and turned—its mad handler starved for something more. My father had called out to me from the grave, but when had he written that note? I fumbled backward for the lip of the bench and pulled myself back up into the window bay. The wood creaked under the cushion as I scanned the empty room, mouth agape. My eyes eventually turned outside for any sign of life and found a procession of hurried quail bobbing along our front yard, nervous to find cover before I demanded that they somehow explain all this. Then my bud rumbled an incoming call from Jay, sending the book tumbling back to the floor and my pulse sprinting.

"ACCEPT. Hey, what's up, Jay?" I snapped, trying to calm my jolted heart.

"Nothing man, nothing. This is a prison. What are you doin'?"

"Slackin', of course." A long breath, a pause. "Uh, Mom wouldn't let me come back today, but I'm going to try a new tactic when she gets home. I'll be back tomorrow, for sure."

Should I have blurted out that the aliens were stealing our gravity—that my father had written me a cryptic note from the other side—or that my life had suddenly been thrown into a tailspin? A sensible voice spoke up and warned me to keep it under wraps. When everything's a conspiracy, nothing is. I was angry at my father for telling me so many crazy things that I wondered what I could believe. I took another gulp of air and realized my head was still pounding out blasts of hot pain.

"We on tonight?" Jay asked, his code for "are we training?"

"Ahhhh, I want to, but I'm going to give my cracked head a rest. Last night did me in."

"All right man, see you mañana. OUT."

After Jay signed off, I listened to the drizzle for a moment and waited until my body settled down. Utter isolation soon replaced the person formerly known as Garret. I couldn't shake the feeling that I was being sequestered for some purpose, a future purpose that even the team couldn't help me with. The eerie sense of segregation took a turn for the worse when fear oozed in, a fear of the unknown. My father had instilled a calamitous dread in me, from the threat of snake injections to a hastily-written claim that we'd eventually all float away, doomed without gravity.

Were these myths and conspiratorial nonsense left behind to a fatherless son, or was something he'd warned me about getting in position to strike? Like a colossal set of dominoes thundering into one another, a chain reaction was building a furious momentum, getting louder as it neared.

The first domino to fall was the Meltdown: an event that swept away the old and made way for the new. It was followed by the gravity crisis that was keeping everyone terrified and in need, and now the ETs had arrived.

The word "aliens" should have triggered the tenacious human spirit to shoot first and ask questions later, but not now, not with our planet crippled, its people desperate. Our defenses were down and our hands were out. We were all ears, waiting to be saved.

So what was the next domino to fall?

The thunder rolled closer.

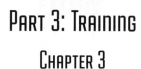

Part 3: Training
Chapter 3

"When it was proven that the world's elite, along with several species of hostile alien entities, plotted and instigated currency crisis and depopulation, the UN and a mish-mash of temporarily formed governing bodies carried out lengthy trials—pitchforks and torches figuratively in hand—to bring the heinous throng to justice. Following a complete ban on firearms, the guilty were executed via guillotine and viewable if one wished to witness the justice take place. Guillotines, at first barbaric and counter to a new enlightenment, were transformed in public perception as a humane and 'tightly controlled method of cleansing.' The UN claimed guillotines could never initiate wars or be wielded to do harm by maniacs in a fit of rage. Only guns posed such violence, and guns would never be used again to take another person's life—if they could help it."

—Piper Corcoran, *Can Things Get Any Stranger? Volume I*

I t watched. From an invisible hiding place, formulating, cunning, it drank in our images without haste. There are no time constraints when you're the unknown, the unseen. It's how a cautious predator preys; enjoying unlimited time to stalk while the target lies defenseless.

How many have been taken, the countless missing? And how many more will vanish? The suffering in secret by the millions of now quieted voices is hard to comprehend. The concept of such a great number stolen is distant until someone you love, with all your heart, is taken to the abyss. At that moment the statistics become so much more, they become cruel and alive. The takers take, and keep taking. They will keep feeding as long as the ignorant and helpless allow it.

But, one in a thousand targets gets the right weapon at just the right time to make the killer into the killed, and that becomes the stuff of legend.

$$\star\,\star\,\star$$

Who knows what the team was bantering about that day, the day I returned to school? I'm certain I would be embarrassed if I heard it played back now. Maybe we were making fun of the Song of Unity booming over the playground, or talking about something petty someone did to someone else. Nothing legendary. And then something shifted close by; in such close proximity it seemed to slosh our souls.

"Hey! What was that? Did you just see that?" I glanced across the faces of my friends and back to the dirt path that ran behind the school. It was a dark and overgrown trail we'd explored many times. Jay, Pak, Beck and I were standing around during break, farther back from the main building along the forest's edge.

After I told Mom I was feeling better but didn't want to go back to school, that I liked the peace and quiet at home—she practically kicked me out.

"Guys, something was right there a second ago. I felt it zoom away and the air brush by us. Dirt and leaves moved along with it, like they were dragged along somehow." Time to regain some composure. I was coming unglued.

"Uhhh, that's called wind, dude. How's that head doing?" Jay was snickering now but the joke would build until he got himself into a hysterical fit.

"Stop for a second," I pressed, "something was there. I thought I felt it *breathing*, or pulsing with energy, so I looked, and that's when it moved away."

"Is this the shadow creature watching you again?" Jay was stirring the pot. "A disturbance in the force perhaps?" And now he'd gotten Beck giggling.

"An 'incongruence in the biorhythms' maybe?" Beck quipped.

"What's that from?" Jay shot back, guarding his prepared string of humor.

"Nowhere, I just made it up, goof. Sounds pretty cool, huh?"

"No, pretty dorky. You've never had a knack for..."

I interrupted and pleaded with them to have a sober discussion.

"Pak? Pak, did you see anything?" He looked down the road and all around, building micro head movements into a perceptible motion, fixing on my face in a full-fledged nod. I wrinkled my brow and demanded more.

"Yeah, I saw it."

"WHAT?" Now I was unglued.

My large friend looked back at the road, along the tree line, and even up to the sky. He was calm. The calm I wished I was. I waited, but not calmly.

"Yeah. I think you're right." Pak conceded.

"You say that like it's no big deal!" I fired back.

"They've been following us a for a few weeks now."

I shot a look at Jay and then at Beck, they were both stunned. Since Pak didn't joke around much he had their full attention.

"*They?*" Beck asked, with a sick expression overtaking her face. Pak snapped out of his distant stare to rejoin us.

"Yeah, they freaked my mom's dog out a week ago. I was out by the street, at the front edge of our lawn, and her dopey little dog ran out to me. When it got close, the dog began to crawl and then it went crazy. It puked and started yapping at something behind me. I turned to look and felt the air pulled away, like what just happened over there."

A long, silent second ticked by before I implored Pak to explain why he didn't tell me this when I was relaying the event at the parking garage. He shrugged and said he thought he might be imagining it. A separate conversation had broken out and I fell quiet in frustration rather than contend with it.

"It's aliens." Jay was talking down to Beck as if the answer was obvious. "I'm tellin' ya. They know we're not onboard with them, their *Way,* their new religion and all that—and they're going to take us out."

"Oh, aliens ate your homework. It's always aliens with you." Beck did not want him to distract from the topic again but he pressed on.

"Laugh all you want, but they're extra-dimensional beings. They could be right here, watching us outside our time and space, and you wouldn't even know it. They're not dumb. We're not going to fall in line. We're a threat to their agenda."

He might not have been too far off. According to Dad, humans had been utilizing captured alien technology since the late 1950s. So these "extra-dimensionals" as Jay called them, must have been slinking around among us since then, likely well before.

My father asserted that official disclosure of a benevolent ET presence would give the world's black projects the cover they needed to unveil their super-tech. After using the reverse-engineered technologies in secret for almost one hundred years, governments would then ascribe it all as recent gifts from the aliens.

Speaking of—Dad drove me crazy every time he would say the word "aliens." Without fail, he would stick two sets of fingers in the air to make those confounded quotation marks around the word. I started doing that with my fingers too, each time he rambled about the subject in hopes he would relent. He said he didn't know if the entities were something pre-Adam, pre-Flood, or what; but they appeared to have the ability to zap in and out of our dimension, looking every bit the part of a deep-space UFO or intergalactic visitor. But it was all a deception to fool us into doubting God as the ultimate creator.

If these beings were not space aliens, quote unquote, and it was all a trick, they would not risk letting anyone hang around who could reveal the truth.

"Maybe they got my Dad and now they're after me?" The thoughts I should have processed internally came out verbally and the team waited for me to expound. I felt their pity fall on me like a heavy blanket.

"Forget I said that. That was stupid. I have no idea what it is." I wanted to cry and let my guard down but knew it was the worst thing I could do. It was time to lead, not wallow.

The conversation came to a standstill and I looked for a way out. I raised my index finger to my lips and gazed back at the others for a moment before speaking. Newt had been suggesting something I thought outlandish at first, but maybe it was our only sure-fire means of protection.

"We should take the 'rides' to school."

Part 3: Training

Chapter 4

"Today, 6-10-36, by boat with several armed men, we delivered food, clothing and blankets to the growing mass of needy filling the end of the long bridge. Multiplying tents and makeshift shanty structures are fast turning the mile long road to nowhere into a floating city, and they've even elected representatives to deal with outsiders.

Their hollow, ghost-like faces staring back both invite and repel me. My braver side yearns to live among them, experiencing their need and humiliation, but my frail side is relieved to hear Evan declare it out of the question."

—Marcee Philmore, *Director, The Philmore Hands Foundation*

The atmosphere hung thick and tense. As we described the day's encounter to Mom, an often-introverted Pak chose the right time to dial up a detailed corroboration of the event. She would have normally dismissed we small three, but with him, she nodded and listened, and then directed us in her usual way.

"The first thing we need to do is pray." No one could argue with that, so we went person to person asking the Lord for guidance and protection. Her request may have felt a formality, but once we began, a palatable clarity filled the room and the tension drew back. When the prayers ended, I broke the silence.

"Mom, we think we need to take our exo-suits to school from now on, in bike mode, of course." She was ready for that, and responded before a half second had elapsed.

"They wouldn't have protected you at break, out by the woods."

"True, but we're just becoming aware today," I shot back with confidence. "We won't be isolating ourselves anymore. We'll stay indoors, or in groups. But when they find they can't catch us alone, they might try to get us coming or going, or do something, not sure. Take us, maybe?" I wasn't fighting fair by exploiting her fears about people disappearing. She let the silence linger and so did we.

Sitting in the "untouchable room" revealed the enormity of the moment. The team's disheveled appearance atop large, white leather couches and ambient lighting made us look like muddy pieces of gravel tossed among a bed of pearls. Mom's morbid, black cat statue continued staring everywhere and nowhere from its glass perch, centered perfectly on an oblong coffee table. Someone's arty idea of having white paint running down its back always flustered me, as if the feline's owner had dribbled hot wax from above to test its reaction. But at that moment, the cat's shocked expression was meant for us, distressed for my stone-faced friends as they sat quiet and intent. Though their hardened look was not a foreign one. The team's strength and resilience shone beyond ours years. Mom was unaware of what we'd become. We were far from average teenagers, but we weren't up against your average mother either.

"No. It's crazy to even consider, Garret. The authorities are not naïve. They're still watching us. How would you feel if this got you-know-who discovered, and arrested?" Mom's voice dropped below a whisper as she mouthed her words. "I don't want to describe too much out loud. Suffice it to say, I think it has the potential to bring much more trouble than it solves."

"You have great points, Mom," I sighed back. "Believe me, we know it's a big decision."

"It IS a big one." Newt's voice cut through the room like a blade and Beck's loud shriek added to the surprise. We set to collecting ourselves as Newton Bigsby turned the corner in dramatic fashion.

"Sorry about that. Didn't mean to frighten you." Newton leaned against the wall and removed his glasses for some vigorous nose massage. He looked beat; more exhausted than I'd ever seen him. He was now as ragged as his lab coat, looking as out of place in that environment as we did. I saw Mom gaze at his old shoes on the spotless carpet but she resisted a reprimand. With all of Newt's concern about us being monitored it was out of character for him to barge up into our house like that.

"I can confirm they are being followed. Whatever it is, it's using some serious cloaking or Electronic Counter Measures, or tech I don't know." We kept staring at him so he continued after a long breath. "Not to upset you all, but one possibility is that Evan is not dead and they want information from him—and taking Garret might be one way of making him talk."

The best of news and worst of news. The thought of Dad being alive was like a forbidden dream. A tsunami of horror was quick to drown away any shred of hope as I pictured him out there suffering. Newt continued.

"Or, it could be something else that just wants to study the team, but why? Unless they are aware of *unusual activity* going on here and want to eavesdrop to find out more. I haven't mentioned this before, but they do have ways of listening to your thoughts."

We sent each other wide-eyed looks, all of us trying to recall everything inappropriate we'd ever thought about. Jay sat with his eyes closed, nodding like he'd been warning us of that for years.

"Is there anyone we can report this to?" Mom asked, knowing the futility. Newt shook his head and reminded her that we had no sound way of explaining our suspicions. Not only did we lack evidence, asking for an investigation contradicted her earlier call for us to remain inconspicuous.

"Newt, aren't you worried about something listening in?" I pointed upward, keeping my volume to a whisper.

"I'm blasting the whole house right now, so they can't see or hear anything, which might send up a red flag of its own."

Mom took a sip of coffee at half-speed as we waited for her reply.

"Newton, please talk some sense into them about taking those things to school." She leaned her head towards our mentor in a coercive manner. He took too long to respond so she added more. "We all know what a stir those bikes are going to create. Can we at least paint them white for heaven's sake?"

"Maybe the attention will help," Newt replied. "Often when someone fears they're being followed, they make as big a fuss as possible, going on the record to say that they might be a target. This can put pressure on an attacker to back off." The response got her shifting in her chair and she didn't dispute his logic.

"To be honest, Mom, we're not that excited about taking them," I whined. "We like to lay low and stay out of the spotlight. The whole thing is going to be downright nerve-wracking. We'll go in as late as possible and slip out as early as we can."

Newt leaned the side of his head against the wall and spoke through an on setting delirium.

"I made them grid-ready, and created titles and registrations as reconstructed or replica vehicles. That won't fly if there's a serious investigation, but if there is we can blame Evan and say he built them before he vanished." He lifted his head away from the wall as though he realized how silly it looked. "I tried to mask their power plants from giving off revealing signatures—not sure if that will be 100 percent effective. It's up to you, Marcee, but I will commit to monitoring the kids all the way there, and I'll guide them home. I'm most curious to see if it stirs a reaction from anything stalking them."

Mom paused and examined the room. "One day. Tomorrow is a Friday. That's it for now. I reserve the right for that to be the last."

I regarded my stoic comrades and they nodded in agreement. Suppressing a smile was easy when I considered the anxious scenario about to unfold.

Newt handed us our pills, his tired body staggering. He declared that the rides would be in the garage by morning. I was sure he wouldn't reveal how he was going to pull that off, so I didn't bother to ask. Newt was a true man of mystery, coming and going from the lab via a method that remained a staunch secret. Where he went when he wasn't down below baffled me. There must have been an entrance into a tunnel system somewhere, but I couldn't find it, and I was warned to stop looking. Dad knew how much I would want to explore a series of mysterious tunnels and sternly eliminated the temptation.

The team started to adjourn, until: "Garret," Mom looked perturbed, ready to make me pay for the whole event now that Newt had gone. After a long pause she asked: "Are you accepting Saul's ill-fitting battle armor instead of trusting in the Lord?"

We settled back into our seats and I scoured my mind for answers.

"That is an interesting thought, for sure. I will consider it—but trust me, Mom, I don't want to blow it here. I know what's at stake." I could see glimmers of truth through the fog but I felt myself reaching out on blind instinct, unsure of my inspiration's source. Years later, my following words still ring prophetic.

"What if—what if these mechanical exo-suits are not the king's armor, but the five smooth stones?"

"Four," Jay said, offering his only conversational contribution of the night.

My mother relaxed and a grin defeated her scowl. She had to turn her head away lest she be taken in by my teenage charm.

The team fixed their eyes on me as she nodded, stood slowly to straighten her skirt, and exited the room without another word. My trio of nervous friends was itching to clap at the clever response.

I hoped the decision I'd just swayed in our favor really deserved their accolades.

PART 3: TRAINING
CHAPTER 5

"Rumors began circulating mid afternoon of an impending confrontation—something vile brewing between Timothy Gorgola and the Philmore boy. This information failed to reach my ears before the day's end, precisely when their showdown occurred. In front of a crowd of twenty or thirty students, behind the stands at the east end of the track, they beat each other senseless. While these things are universally contemptuous, my sympathies fall somewhat to the side of Tim. The Gorgolas fought hard to keep the homeschoolers at home, specifically citing the Philmore family as leaking a poison of backward and divisive beliefs that corrupt the very unity pursued here at Sandpoint High. My observations since the integration is that this has been proven true, 100%."

—Principal Byron Morag, *To School Superintendent Sierra White*

om's transport, my velop, and our four rides took up all the space in our double-sized garage. Dad had used it as his tinkering shop and I remembered several large exo-suits in various stages of build standing out there when I was younger. At one time, it was my place of wonder. I'd venture out to peek in on his progress long after bedtime, testing his mood. Most times it was well received.

"Whatcha doing, Dad?"

"Building robots, son—ROBOTS!" Indulging my fascination.

"I'm gonna be a robot when I grow up." I recall declaring, walking toward him with my finest mechanical-man impression.

"You'll be greater than that, Garret, much greater." He would offer in some variation, his voice filled with love. The mining suits were big enough that I could sit on his lap while he drove them, stomping around the shop. I can still feel the cold steel on my fingertips and smell the greasy smells. I never imagined that someday I would be taking one of his inventions out into the world, especially without him there to guide me along.

My accomplices pulled in the drive within a few seconds of each other, parking their velops on the same side as Mom's transport. As agreed, each brought a late slip to make our tardiness a little less absurd. Telling their parents about our newfangled "velops" was inevitable, something we were dreading. When it came time, we would reveal the truth: my father had created these before he vanished and we thought it would be cool to use them for a while. We would take the fall for my mother and vow her innocence in the whole matter. Unbelievable yes, but we were such good kids that we felt sure we could smooth it over. Mom refused to come outside as if her presence at the event overly endorsed it somehow.

The team marveled at the sight of our top-secret craft about to be paraded in broad daylight. My Control Hat was in my hands when they walked up.

"Newt says we're supposed to wear these on the way there and back, using the Com instead of our buds to talk. He'll be on the line, but won't be saying much. You can still get all your regular calls in them. He rigged it up."

Newt had placed small registration plates on the back of each modular vehicle and positioned them facing out, two by two. It was baffling to me how he had gotten the rides here in the middle of the night without a noise. Never mind that though, I remembered how terrified I was over the whole affair.

We stared in silence as the windshields slid back into their metal chassis, our usual morning chitchat suspended by apprehension. The unfeeling voice from our regular velops was piped into our modified helmets, offering greeting and requesting a location. Despite the difference in our transportation, the destination remained the same: to the asylum, "SANDPOINT HIGH." Our school motto was "Unleash Your Potential," and that's what we were going to do. The procession moved forward, morphing into single file, consumed by the AHS. There would be no finishing breakfast or last-minute homework today.

It felt odd to be shuttled around in our ride armors without using manual controls, but doing so allowed our eyes the freedom to scan for danger. It didn't take long to spot some.

"Uh, control, are you seeing what I'm seeing?"

A menacing-looking black craft appeared out of nowhere in the air above us, sending a chill through the convoy. Nothing about the machine looked familiar but it triggered nature's instinctual warning that it was capable of harm. Darting about as if to get a better look at us, silent and effortless in its movements, we found it impossible to tell if the craft was manned or was some kind of drone. It looked to be using a sophisticated anti-gravity system and hovered around like a weightless metal bat, swooping down behind our group to follow. The team made some nervous comments back and forth before Control cut in.

"That is interesting. I wonder why they're visible. Either they are having a malfunction or they want to be seen. I'm monitoring. Oops, it's gone. Don't worry, I'll keep an eye out. You kids study hard today."

My eyes jumped back to the craft's last location to find a ghostly void. Newt had not wanted to chime in, but had risked it to reassure us. He had the ability to see our vital signs and I'm sure they revealed four very scared kids.

Veering off of Highway 2 onto Syringa Heights Road, and North to Pine, we arrived at the "school" far to quickly for my liking. The parking garage filled up from the first floor up, so since we were running late, we were forced to go all the way up to five. Before entering the stairwell, we took one last look at our conspicuous vehicles, blatant among the many rows of capsule cars. They stuck out like three Jolly Ranchers and a hand grenade in a box of Tic-Tacs.

The halls were my favorite kind of quiet. Overcome by how natural the isolation felt; I wanted to shout something profound. I was on the outside looking in, free to roam and choose my own destiny. My mates were jubilant to have the run of the joint, if just for a few minutes.

Time slid into slow motion as we took a casual stroll through the halls. The smaller ace pilots fanned out in front, three across, with our heavy artillery close behind. Uncrowned kings headed for coronation, about to announce our eminent rulership from that day forward.

Each of us carried on about something, oblivious as to whether anyone else was listening. Jaxon was singing an unfamiliar tune as he extended his arms into wings to glide instead of walk, fighting the imaginary updraft. Hardly a Song of Unity, it must have come from his brother's stash: something about being "free to do what I want any old time." His outstretched fingers clunked against a row of lockers as he coasted by.

Beck was having a serious conversation in hushed tones that only she could hear, complete with hand gestures. The debate must have been going in her favor and she looked delighted with its progress.

And, as if he were seeing them for the first time, Pak grunted to himself about the large "Make Today Ridiculously Amazing" hall posters that he must have laid eyes on a thousand times.

I swore to remember this moment as my finest achievement. A guy couldn't ask for better friends or for a better sense of purpose. I was beaming with an intense pride and joy, right until the plug was yanked from the socket. Principal Morag came into view up ahead. The sight of him drained the color from our faces and replaced it with misery. We had no place to run.

"Ohhh, the homeschoolers," Morag groaned, cocking his head to one side to show his disbelief at our late and simultaneous arrival.

"Good morning Principal Morag! Isn't it lovely out?" Jay extended the words in exuberant sarcasm. My muscles clinched. Why would he poke the hornet's nest on the day we could least afford trouble? I turned towards my cohort, incensed, but found myself all the more astounded. Jay's goatee had become ensnared by a single, bright-green rubber band, pinching the bottom into a ridiculous tuft. I wanted to hide, run away, or die laughing.

My late slip came out in quick-draw fashion to divert attention from his antics. The others fumbled around to produce their own. Morag sneered his hooked nose at the wrinkled notes and ordered us to keep them. Then he dragged his jagged pinky across his greasy bangs and cleared his throat.

"The short bus must have been running a little late today I see. It's hard to keep up with real students isn't it?" He looked jubilant, like a cat that had just cornered four plump mice. "I'm sorry you don't fit in here…a shame, really. There are those who evolve and progress, and those who will have to be cut down to make way for progress. It's called conscious evolution." A few bits of slick hair fell back to their low position.

I went from panic to boiling at light speed. Few words got me as hostile as the word "evolution." I squinted at Morag with hasty determination, fighting off the terror threatening to have its way.

"We don't evolve, sir. We don't believe in evolution, or that were "seeded by aliens" *before* we evolved. So I hope you're not planning on replacing one lie with another here." A mini-gasp slipped from Beck's clenched lips.

Unphased, the principal placed his fingers together as if he were hatching a devious plan. The faint smell of mothballs drifted around us as Morag hissed.

"Whether or not you believe in evolution is not my concern. It believes in you, and it will identify and eliminate what is destructive and not worthy of continuation. You may have already felt this force bite into your own bitter life—*whatever* your name is, son."

Which was to say he knew just what my name was, and who my father was. A furnace stoked hot inside me, cauterizing an open wound. I wanted to reach out and shake his hand for his unintended injection of strength, resolve, and determination to track down Dad's killers. My eyes became squinted as Morag raked his greasy bangs aloft once more, then turned to walk away victorious. Beck looked at me, broken in my place. I let my emotions even out before addressing the team.

"The enemy is real, that's all. I know it and you know it. He's just one of many." I kept looking at the others and repeated myself, trying to infuse the concept into each of them. Not so much wounded as keenly aware of the battle, newfound power surged through me. Slowly, I was becoming more like a predator than prey. The gang disbanded to our respective lockers without further conversation.

Our first class was together, so as expected, the concurrent entrance looked awkward. After a brief discussion on how this might appear, we decided our reputations couldn't fall any lower, so why avoid it.

It was impossible to concentrate on the lesson, and the four of us kept shooting each other looks of disbelief that we'd driven our attack bikes to school. By third period, we'd gone our separate ways and the childish fun had evaporated. I was now stuck with Timmy Gorgola, who was repeating his math class for poor performance. He wasted no time seeping over my way as soon as I took a seat. One of his stooges limped behind like a hyena searching for scraps.

"We missed you so much. *You feeling all better now?*" Timmy finished in baby talk, begging me to box his ears. Nausea took control of my face and eyelids lowered to half-mast.

"I was at school yesterday, genius. You'd better pay attention or you'll be pestering people in here next year, too. See look!" I gestured to the front of the room in amazement at nothing at all. Both Timmy and his friend turned to look, and by the time they turned back, I was shaking my head as if they were the dumbest cadavers in the morgue. On cue, Timmy's young barnacle was chortling. Apparently born without a neck, this goon with poor taste in leaders could only bob up and down like a groundhog pogoing in its hole.

"We're gonna sit here and keep you company—hope that's okay," Timmy's threat became powerless as his retainer lost its position, causing a gurgle and slurp.

"Just don't cheat off my paper, you knucklehead." I turned my homework over, disgusted by his close proximity. He was going to come back at me again, but our math teacher, Mr. Potts, called for the start of class. Mr. Potts referred to pop quizzes as "little opportunities" and loved to hear the sound of his own voice as he announced one. The whole class groaned as he made the pop quiz announcement official, and I was the loudest.

As an engineer's son, you'd think I would have been hard-wired to be good at math. Quite the opposite was true. Further, my circuits felt overloaded from all the wacky happenings over the last few days.

I was thankful that Mom had forced me to study at home. Otherwise, I might have scratched a giant *F* in the margin and saved Mr. Potts the trouble. He passed through the aisle, distributing the quizzes and I could see Timmy glance over at my blank page, testing the angle for eventual copying. Had he no pride?

Most teachers had joined the forties by making tests virtual, using your bud and a touch screen to complete them. But Mr. Potts still favored paper because it had "soul" or something. He put the class on notice.

"Have your homework ready to turn in as well. You'll have fifteen minutes to complete your lit-tle op-por-tun-ity." He paused between the syllables to drain every bit of pleasure from the delivery. "You may begin…now."

I shielded my paper as best I could and dove in. Morag's words about it being hard for homeschoolers to keep up with "real students" fried me and I wrote my first answer through clenched teeth. Moving quickly to the next problem, I vowed this day would not get the best of me, then—my bud erupted.

"Emergency! Emergency! Attention team—They're coming! I'm picking up massive signatures closing on your position. Get out of there—

GET OUT—AS FAST AS YOU CAN!"

Part 3: Training

Chapter 6

"Predictions are hazardous, especially about the future."

—author unknown

The earphone singed my nerve endings like a hot coal. Newt was bawling out an alert far too grave to be a drill over the emergency channel.

My hands vice-gripped the desk as perspiration raced out of every pore. Newt was shouting loud enough that several kids, including Timmy Gorgola, whirled their heads around to locate the disruption. I heard a door crash open in the hallway and Jay calling out for me. I sat frozen as the whole classroom gave up on their quizzes in favor of locating the source of the ruckus. Even Mr. Potts standing to attention could not free my feet from their fixed position. Timmy began a sniveling, wet laugh that caused a chuckling infection to spread desk to desk.

At last, I shot off the chair like a rabbit. My hip carried the desk along for a few feet until it crashed to the floor, papers scattering behind me. I gripped the door handle and used its opening momentum to whip myself down the hall, shoes slipping along the dust-covered floor. Jay was terror-stricken with indecision.

"GO—GO—GO!" I howled as I flew passed him towards the stairs. We shot each other a few incoherent questions before verifying that Beck and Pak were a few floors above us, hopefully in an all out dash toward the rides. A few classroom doors swung open as Jay and I zoomed by, teachers sticking their heads out, incensed at the racket. Once in the concrete stairwell, my feet felt to be floating despite the clomping echo bouncing off the walls. We were on the first floor with four to go.

The rest of the team was indeed already beside our getaway cars, hatches open, when we busted through the large, double doors into the garage. I could see Beck's frenzied pointing as she ordered Pak into his Caliber.

"Garret, ditch your buds—toss them!" Newt pleaded via the Com.

I repeated the order as we flicked away the ear pieces and pressed down our helmets. The hefty camouflaged four-wheeler growled backwards as Pak spun from his spot to make way for us in the lead. Jay's green bike was away first, his headlights illuminating the entire level until I ordered him to kill the lights. Beck and I barreled downhill side by side, our combined width forcing me to crunch an entire whole row of velops in my path. The feeling of brushing through them like flies was as satisfying as I'd always hoped. Newt's urgent voice came on the line.

"They are closing and the signals are difficult to interpret. Do you have visual confirmation yet?"

"No, nothing." I felt collected, my training assuming some control. We'd screeched down two levels before I snuck a quick look in my rear view to see the Caliber obliterating every capsule car I'd missed, scattering their cheap materials into a cloud of bits.

The main, street-level exit was coming up fast, after one remaining turn. A huge threatening shadow stretched into the garage, cast by something moving into position to end our escape. Jay saw it first and announced our grim prospects.

"Holy mackerel! Got visual I think. It's big, whatever it is, and it's waitin' for us. We're blocked in!"

"No, we're not." I gunned the accelerator into the lead, skipping the last turn in favor of straight ahead. Blasting through the double doors into the school's first-floor hallway, I exhaled in relief at the emptiness, its classes still in session. A damage warning for my front wheel assembly blinked from plowing through the divider. Hallway stragglers jumped for cover as four fantastic machines screamed past the doors of now disturbed, and emptying, classrooms.

"Watch for civvies!" I yelled through the Com, referring to our fellow students as the innocent bystanders from Newt's training programs. We barreled towards the first sharp corner and I heard someone plow into the lockers behind me. Jay was grinding against the wall as he tried to steer free. Pak was bringing up the rear, his behemoth contraption filling the hall's width. Newt called to us.

"The place appears to be surrounded. If you are captured, get away from your vehicles ASAP." We knew he meant to blow them up.

"Where to G?" Beck chirped, her voice full of misplaced optimism.

"Not sure yet. The main roads will be choked; maybe eyes in the sky too." I pictured swarms of black bat-craft waiting for us. Then, Beck identified our goal.

"What about the old dirt path?"

"Yes!" I resounded. "Back exit is a few turns up ahead, and it's got the same large doors we need."

Our newfound direction caused a foolish increase in speed. Before I could pull out of the turn, Jay T-boned me into the far wall, Beck spun out and the Caliber went headlong through a glass façade in the corner office. The smell of blackened, burnt rubber and crumbling drywall filled the air.

My bike lurched forward, dragging Jay's front wheel with me, straightening him out. Pak engaged a slow reverse, crunching debris under his monster tires, glass still raining down around him. It was time to gun it, make for the back, and hope they were not expecting us there.

I turned around to see Morag's infuriated face glaring at the improbable traffic jam and his mangled office. The stack of papers he was holding became a crumpled mass. He tossed them away in a fury before staggering our direction.

"Oh, boy. Jay, reverse and get free of me. Go for those back doors—NOW!"

He had the clearance and shot down the next straight away. Beck backed up around the corner and then stomped the accelerator in reverse until she yanked it into another spin to face forward, blasting ahead without losing speed.

Thatta girl, I thought, smiling at her move while ignoring my own lack of action. Morag was alongside me now, only a few feet away, taking photos with his bud screen. I called for the top hatch to retract and removed my helmet. As the windshield disappeared behind me, the cockiest smirk in history painted itself across my face. Our eyes locked.

"The *name* is Garret Philmore. Oh—and nice hair, by the way..."

Morag's jaw twisted sideways, and his teeth threatened to chew off his own lip. I punched the bike's accelerator to blast ahead, barely getting my helmet back on by the next turn. Pak was right behind me as we cleared the corner. Kids were now flooding into the halls so I flashed my front beams to clear them aside. Newt demanded an update.

"Status, please! Garret, what is going on in there?"

"Hang on Control, we're uhhh, busy here, smashing the school."

The red and green bikes were ahead, slowing down for pedestrians. Once through the crowd, all four racers took the final corner, throttling to full speed to blow through the rear doors into the midday sun. Two hundred yards of playground separated us from the dirt path at the edge of the woods.

The moment we hit the grass, the sun eclipsed into dark shadow as several large objects dropped from the sky in front of us. Massive black armored battle suits, fifteen feet high, plunged to the ground with such force that my Brawler bike bounced into the air before regaining its traction.

One of the behemoths darted towards Jay's Brawler bike with surprising speed. Its left arm ended in a giant claw that wasted no time in swiping out for him as he tried to veer around. The robotic devil, the likes I'd never seen, closed the distance on my friend and readied its deadly barb to strike.

Part 3: Training
Chapter 7

"The color scheme of our rides was coming off too juvenile for Jay when he noticed the look taking shape. He asked if we were turning into the 'Mighty Mega Power Poopers;' a bunch of wannabe heroes out to save the world. I assured him we hadn't yet stooped to that level of camp, and attempting my serious leader tone, I reminded them that our squad would likely be facing everything from aliens to disappearing Gs. To that end Jay snorted back that we laughed at disappearing Gs, even zero Gs. 'Heck, we're Team Zero-Gs, baby!' He declared, drawing rave reviews from the rest and missing my point entirely. The name Zero-Gs stuck for our team after that, although we used it mostly in jest."

—Garret Philmore, *Letters on the Lamb: A Collected Journal*

P ak's Caliber rammed into the back legs of the horrifying mechanism, knocking it to the ground and driving over its fallen torso toward our target destination. Appearing as something half creature, half robotic nightmare, I had to fight off the urge just to stare at them like a buck caught in high beams.

Another of the large black mecha closed fast on Beck and me

from the left, so we floored it right; using the one Pak had toppled to cut off its charge. Instead, the huge crab-suit jumped straight over and landed just behind us, sending both our rides scrambling to get back on course.

I called out for a complete view of the scene behind and the horrifying vision appeared on my display. Two battle suits were nearly on top of us, their claws just out of reach. Newt's confident voice came over the Com.

"I see you now. Just drive. I'll send you some help."

A blue glow engulfed the back of Beck's ride in front of me. I exclaimed but Newt cut back in.

"Negative, Garret. Those are emergency boosters. Hang on, I'm increasing your speed."

The added thrust helped Beck and me surge away from pursuing claw monsters to catch up with Jay and Pak at the tree line. I hadn't a second to contemplate how our rides could have "emergency boosters" that I was unaware of. This was not the only covert feature Newt would soon have to reveal.

As the narrow road forced us into single file, the Caliber, second in line, cut our visibility into smog. But dirt alone wasn't enough to turn the sky as black as it became. Something large was hovering above our heads.

"Control, we have company, and we're in a bad formation here. We can't see anything, and I think this trail narrows just ahead. We're going to run out of room real quick." Newt remained calm.

"I'm going to split you up. I'll bring you back here to regroup. Hang on."

The dusty air and forest dissolved into an electronic framework, and I saw the team vanish from my scopes. I felt my wheels bounce off the terrain in that familiar and terrifying thump, and then again and again. More of the clawed suits were dropping to the ground from overhead—and they were close.

As my bike took a sudden, sharp left into the woods, my helmet and shoulder crashed into the cabin wall. I'd lost control and Newt was doing the driving. Brush and limbs pounded against the canopy until B1 broke free and found smooth pavement again. I requested normal visuals, but nothing materialized; only the digital representation of the outside world remained. I wanted to see what was going on with my real eyes, but I feared taking off my helmet and missing any new orders. The Com remained dead despite my many requests for an update. It felt like I was the only one left alive as the radio silence continued. The minutes crawled by until I found myself back into my own garage.

The top hatch slid out of the way to reveal my friends there and unharmed. Four fortunate souls, in awe to have escaped the literal clutches of doom. Newt showed himself and went person to person, making sure we were fully intact.

"Well, I guess your rides were quite a hit today," he said, shaking his head.

"Oh, they were very popular—with all the giant, robotic, grim reapers of death!" Jay burst with awkward comedy; amazed he'd just survived an antagonist of cinematic proportion. Had we actually just seen all that? Did all that? It felt like we'd beamed back into our own dimension after a collective episode of insanity.

Mom's transport whipped into the drive and squealed to a stop. For a moment I wished I was facing another monster-clawed battle armor rather than what was about come out of there. Newt turned to the ragged group to get in one last word before the fireworks started.

"I've been in contact with Mrs. Philmore, and she knows what just happened, complete with images of what was chasing you."

"Fantastic work everybody," Mom bellowed. "I hope playtime is finally over. The authorities might be on their way right now."

Her heels clacked up the concrete in our direction. She wore a sharp, cardinal red business suit, complete with briefcase, looking ready to initiate a hostile takeover. The ensemble's color defied the drab, "blend in with everybody" clothing styles now being pushed on the freed masses. Perhaps this one reacted like a mood ring, altering its hue to reflect Mom's blistering anger. A bit of concern would have been nice, but that wasn't her way. The castigation had just begun when a call hit Mom's bud. She answered.

"Yes, this is. Yes, Chamberlain Maddox, yes, he is home. No, he is far too traumatized to go anywhere right now. What? Yes, of course he would turn it in, but it seems he NO LONGER HAS that stupid bike." She scowled at Newt to confirm that we would be losing them after today. "They abandoned them fleeing from some kind of creatures, and they barely managed to get back alive. Of course I can come to the school. I will be there in less than thirty minutes. I would like to discuss the facility's security, as its obvious you cannot keep the students safe!" Another pause. "I will review the damage and make compensation if Garret is responsible." Her face contorted as her caller levied additional threats.

"I do not have time to entertain such nonsense. I am tending to a disturbed boy who thinks giant things from his school might still be after him. We will discuss the rest of this shortly!"

Mom's vile expression made me almost feel bad for Maddox and his crew, and what they had coming. She huffed at our guilty line-up, a pack of hoodlums caught causing trouble. Her lower jaw extended until she looked like the bulldog mascot from our school. Newt stammered.

"Marcee, this is bad, I know it. The children are at least…" Newt was going to point to us still breathing as a positive, but thought better of it. "Uh, just know I have ways of leaking evidence, or other facts about certain things. If they try to intimidate you, we can make them withdraw." Mom fumed as Newt continued his plea. "We're not dealing with the civil authorities here, but I can make them back off, and I can keep the kids out of sight for a while." Mother's eyes grew as large as a deep-sea fish.

"We are not kidnappers Mr. Bigsby! You three go home! I'll call your parents and explain as best I can. Try not to say anything except that Garret thought it would be fun to show off some of his Dad's old toys today. I don't expect I'll be seeing you for a while, so I would like to apologize for getting you mixed up in all this, and for risking your lives."

The others shuffled out of the garage and Beck turned to give me a last, sympathetic glance. Mom went back on the attack.

"Haven't you had enough now, Newton? I'm sure your full-time skills are needed elsewhere. This project has officially backfired." She moved in close, frothing. "Can't you see that playing with this stuff has taken my husband? And it almost took my only son today. Enough! These things are a lightning rod for death, and maybe you are, too. All you men who like to make war—and killing machines…"

Tears and mascara streaked down her cheeks and she started for the kitchen door before making a sudden directional change for her transport. The tall heels almost got the best of her as she clicked and clocked away. Newt waited until she had pulled out of the drive before risking another comment.

"She doesn't understand, Garret. Our time is up. In more ways than one."

I didn't need his confirmation. I knew it was over.

Part 4: Carpet Burrito
Chapter 1

"If an invention can be turned into a weapon, rest assured they'll figure out a way. I'm more convinced than ever that 'idle hands' are not the devil's playground. It's the hands of men driven to constantly fight against something, real or imagined, and life is too precious to be trusted to them.

They can dress up their toys any way they like, to me it's just more modern war machinery. And it's all fine until someone gets hurt, or more like killed."

—Marcee Philmore, *Director, The Philmore Hands Foundation*

I'd gone upstairs to take a hot shower, and by the time I came down, the rides were already in the lab. Whatever super-powers Newt was using to move them around were quick. As it often did, my journal went below with me in case Newt wasn't ready to get started. He was ready for me this time, and immediately asked that I gear up and change over to Brawler mode for inspection. Happy to oblige as this was likely the last time I'd get to walk around in my robotic disguise. Newt continued to look over our vehicles and was pleased with how little damage they had sustained. There ensued much nodding of the head, intermingled with contented grunting.

The doctor explained away the emergency boosters as something too dangerous to use in the lair. The team would have "bugged him to death" if we knew about the uber-boost. He became unusually irate when I pushed for more info so I dropped it.

As I put on my jumpsuit, I agonized out loud over my inability to fight back against the claw monsters. I'd often rehearsed in my mind the moment when the young shepherd David approached the battlefield to resupply his warrior brothers. I would picture myself in his place, hearing Goliath shout down from the hilltops his curses against God, and wonder how I would react. In his defining moment, David's mortal fear was eclipsed by the power of the Spirit to make the impossible, possible. If the attack at the school was my big test, I'd chosen to turn tail and run instead of facing the giants. Newt shook his head to cut me off.

"Look, it would've been a monumental mistake to try to take them on. You and this bike would be in pieces. You're fortunate their sole aim was capture. They have a particle-beam weapon that vaporizes a target in a single shot. The bloody thing is damn lethal, I can tell you."

"You're right, I know you're right. I was scared silly anyway," I admitted. "What were those things? They're not like any suit designs I've ever seen. It's like they *tried* to make them look evil."

"J8-81 Scimitars. They were in development when I was still on staff. Wasn't sure if they'd ever finish them up. Obviously, they did. It's a unique system where the mecha is integrated with a two-man carrier ship. The second pilot can leave the fighter cockpit directly into the battle-armor, then 'drop-attack' the target zone. They're just the latest playthings of the shadow government to enforce its will."

I asked Newt to print me out a reference of the Scimitar machine and their carrier ships for my journal, then shrugged at the reality of such beastly things.

"But why do they even need stuff like that anymore? We're at peace. All the TV talks about are how wars are over for good."

"From my sources, the black projects have picked up steam," Newt asserted. "The same bad guys I got away from are still in power and cooking up better and better ways to kill."

"What about the new ET overseers though, and the UN, and the CRL? They're not going to let them keep doing that."

"I'm not sure they are two different things, Garret. Listen, sometime before World War II, the world—the surface world if you will—made contact with several kinds of strange beings. From what I've heard, they were subterranean, and they directed humanity towards forbidden science and secret knowledge. One of the races of course, is the infamous Vril, or 'Naga' as some refer to them. Those creeps knew right where we humans could get our hands on gobs of lost technology."

Newt referenced movies and folklore that described Adolf Hitler combing the globe for all manner of strangeness. He verified the scenes as accurate, but that the films didn't reveal just how strange. That madman literally stumbled upon ancient races of creatures living beneath the surface of our Earth. I pictured groups of Nazi officers meeting with what I'd seen of the Vril in photos and video, making deals for who knows what. The breaker in my brain tripped when the image was too unbelievable to be sustained. Newt went on.

"The secret science these entities revealed led to all kinds of corruption. Once humans got their hands on the *magic,* so to speak, we could no longer do without the forbidden fruit. The shadow governments of the world and these creatures forged their Faustian bargain. In other words, we made a deal we couldn't go back on. Legends abound on what people traded these snakes in return for their revelations, and most are too disgusting to repeat."

I finished putting on my jumpsuit and sat on B1's arm-fender, trying to make sense of it all. It was understood that the Tall Grays had many underground nests, but their origin was always asserted as off planet. Newt left me no time to contemplate the subject and continued, talking a mile-a-minute.

"We humans now had access to a high technology that promised to propel us a thousand years ahead. Your father and I both believe it was ancient sciences from the Lost City of Atlantis and the like, as hard as that is to reconcile. The Nazis were the first to get their hands on it, and, eventually, on all the world's powerful governments. Then the race to live forever was on."

"Live forever?"

"I don't want to blow your mind, but one of the ancient technologies these ground-dwelling entities revealed was how to cheat death! Well, in a way. These beings taught us advanced cloning techniques and something called "consciousness transfer," a process where a person can switch from their sleeping, real body over to their cloned body. I've seen it done. It's quite disturbing. People who underwent this consciousness transfer told me how strange it felt, and with every transfer there is some personality degradation that occurs. You somehow become a little less of who you are. It was a flawed method, but I think they were close to perfecting it. So in theory, those with the means could keep jumping from clone to clone, body to body, and never face death. I've been told that large groups of the wealthy and unscrupulous engaged in this kind of clone-hopping behavior."

Newt described how the elite would transfer over to their replicated versions while their real selves slept, to party all night and then return to their rested bodies in the morning—literally no rest for the wicked. Once the ruling class got hooked on that kind of indulgence they were not about to give it up. I was dumbfounded at his outlandish narration. Could life in the shadows have become this fantastic, going light years beyond normalcy? Newt did not give me a chance to wrestle with the idea before going on.

"Rumor had it that those rediscovering these technologies were also working on making 'soulless' clone bodies, and using the large particle colliders to bring in dark entities from other dimensions to inhabit them. Maybe that's what was driving those Scimitar machines today. Your Dad had other wild theories about how the 'beyond black,' projects were trying to bring in demonic hordes from the spirit realm, and was trying to figure that out, too. Evan never met a conspiracy theory he didn't like, and now I must sound every bit as crazy."

I agreed. He did.

Then there was Dad's note about the aliens stealing our gravity. A bubble formed in my throat, filled with air at the ready to divulge my discovery. But Newt was talking too fast, and frankly, I wasn't in the mood to hear my father be laughed at.

Engrossed in his diagnostic review of our Brawler machines, Newt went on about how much of our perceived reality since the end of World War II was a deliberate deception. He cited in a matter-of-fact way how space programs and rocketry became a total sham by the mid-1980s. Electro-gravitic craft, cloaking (or the art of bending light around an object to make it disappear), free energy sources and the like were going on behind the scenes as space shuttles blew up in a tragic facade. Newt called this hidden society a "breakaway civilization," a vast world of guarded secrets, advancing until the day it could be revealed in a manner that did not jeopardize those in control. By his description, it seemed we'd lost the game to these hidden foes.

"So, they won. They got their way, right? Average citizens are starting to see this advanced tech everywhere and giving the credit to our alien saviors,"—just as Dad had predicted. Newt looked up at me for a moment and was surprised I was following along.

"Right, that's where it gets sticky. Just who exactly won here? The power-elite that relished and exploited the forbidden technologies—from politicians, royalty, oil tycoons, and banksters—were all salivating for this hidden world to be brought out in the open. A post-Meltdown world if you will, where they ruled in a new age of enlightenment for the privileged and chosen few. What I'm realizing now is that someone even higher up promised that inheritance and then double-crossed them. Those at the extreme top let the rich and famous take the fall, and are now making it look like all the bad guys have been rounded up. But I think they've just replaced their puppets with someone else, something far more exotic."

Newt's explanation made me feel foolish for not realizing the evil that still lurked in our world. We would never be free of those who wished to do harm to the innocent. I scratched my head and tried to soak up his words.

"Perhaps these beings in control are descended from the original Atlanteans, and they might be calling themselves the 'Nordics' now. Some claim to have run into them in modern times," Newt's face bore a strange grin from humor lost on me. The smile lingered as he went on. "They might have invented this technology in the first place, or were utilizing it in their powerful kingdoms. Could they be the ones secretly pulling the world's strings all along?"

"But I remember Dad saying Atlantis and Lemuria and those legends were from before Noah," I blurt. "There's no way those guys could live that long! And they would have died in the Flood. Are you saying they're still alive somehow, and they were the ones that tried to get us today? Newt, you ARE talking crazy." The doctor continued his Brawler tests, speaking through the preposterous subject.

"Look, these are spiritual, or semi-spiritual beings, at the very top of the pyramid. Your father no doubt explained that Genesis 6 is indeed about 200 Watcher-Class angels abandoning their spiritual plain to have offspring here on Earth. This is a fact that many Christians refuse to except because it's just too scary. The giant monsters born from their unholy unions *weren't no 'Sons of Seth.'* Bah, how that garbage theory ever got taught is beyond me. Pure cowardice, I suppose," Newt wanted to get sidetracked onto that expansive subject but he forced himself to stay on our current one.

"So, if the rulers of the ancient world descended from those original unions, they would have carried a sliver of god-like DNA. They were either immortal, nearly immortal or learned to be so. If these beings are the ones that taught humanity the techniques of cloning and cheating death, maybe that's just what they've been doing to stay alive. Could this group have escaped off world, or underworld before the Flood hit, before their precious civilizations were destroyed? The first angelic patriarchs no doubt passed down the hidden knowledge, and it might have been enough to get their descendants to safety before the wrath of God struck. There is ample evidence to support the notion of ancient flying craft, even trans-planetary kinds."

Newt suddenly caught how ludicrous he sounded and exclaimed with his index finger in the air. "Yes, you're right Garret—I AM talking nonsense!" He shook his head and released a belly laugh before pulling himself back to his work. I was about to mount up, but hesitated to move until Newt had finished telling his tale. He looked up at me again and his attempt to lighten the mood went back out the window.

"Garret, some kind of diabolical force remained in the shadows and reappeared after the Flood to interfere with the notorious Nimrod, making him a kind of super being. His DNA was somehow altered, extending his life span, and maybe giving him extra sensory power. Then you have the giant enemies of Old Testament Israel: the Hittites, Amorites, and Jebusites that 'devoured the land's inhabitants.' Their genetics were modified as well. By whom I wonder?"

Newt mentioned some more colorful names like Quetzalcoatl, a mysterious bearded Caucasian who appeared from nowhere and warped the early Mesoamericans to practice human sacrifice on a grand scale (in one temple alone, archaeologists discovered 136,000 human skulls). And finally the Nazis, who came in contact with unseen forces and then went on to kill millions. He asked if I saw a pattern; I did. Something had been darting in and out of history, teaching humanity secret knowledge that was intended to spell our own doom. I tried to swallow but I was lacking sufficient spit.

The highlighted pages in Dad's book began to bounce around in my brain like a rainbow of lottery balls. *"They will come down again and deceive the world."* It was the dreaded "they" again. Whoever *they* were, it was an enemy that survived outside of time, harboring a deep hate for our race. And apparently, they were going to finish the deal by stealing our gravity.

Newt pulled over a wheeled cart with a portable workstation and began attaching some test lines to B1's power pack. I called for the hatch to open and it started its rearward slide. Staring at the composite-glass retract, a sudden sobriety hit me. At once my thoughts were full of questions already overdue for asking. *Were those crab things just after the machines? Did they get Dad? Did Newt have any idea we were in that kind of danger?* But I hesitated asking as the answers felt uncomfortably obvious.

Then I remembered Mom was at the school scowling over the colossal mess I'd made. I cringed when I pictured seeing her again, owning up to my bad decisions and having to go back to that awful place. My only consolation was that she was in her fierce mode, giving Morag and Maddox their comeuppance.

B1 revved up to full power so I got in and brought us both to our standing Brawler form. I stretched around and jogged in place, punching the air to get into the persona. Any detachment I was feeling was replaced by sudden oneness; oneness with my Brawler machine. The experience was not quite euphoria, but once connected to B1 my emotions ran hot; unleashed to swim and circulate. While outside the suit, my heart felt seized by ice, with every emotion and action nearly frozen by indecision. It felt great to be back inside.

The Brawler system spat forth an infinite list of information, filling every micron of my visual scope. Newt was tapped in and getting a full damage report.

"How's it lookin', Doc?"

"Ahhhh, I am seeing some issues. The front wheel assembly has some damage, which is affecting the shoulders. But all systems held together well."

Our personal calls were still rigged to come through our Hats and a wave of anxiety shook me when I realized it was Beck. It was probably the first of many "punishment updates" that would be coming in from the team.

"Hang on, Beck is callin'. ACCEPT. Beck! What's up? I'm getting…"

"Garret! He's trying to kill me!" Her scream drained the blood from my veins. "It's Kyle—he's drunk and my mom's at the school—GET AWAY!"

The call went dead.

Part 4: Carpet Burrito
Chapter 2

*"It's the unexpected moment, when fear and love alchemize
your actions into an unstoppable force..."*

—Carter West, *O' Mighty Men of Valor*

"Newt—Beck's in trouble! Let me outta here! CALL BECK,
CALL BECK you stupid..."

"Out of your Brawler? What kind of trouble?" Newt stuttered.

"Out of this lab! However you do it, do it fast."

"I'm sorry, Beck is not answering." The phone was proving
useless and so was Newton Bigsby.

"Uhhhh, the last thing we want is you going out there in that suit
right now. Your mother is trying to pick up the pieces, and—"

Smashing his workstation flat, B1's armored hand wrenched the
test cables free of itself, and I placed a large mechanical index finger
hovering an inch from the doctor's chest.

"Newt, I swear, you get me outta here in the next ten seconds
or I'm cramming into that lift and plowing through the house to
get free. Got it? Didn't you hear me? She's in trouble, nothing else

matters. RIGHT NOW!" I ground my teeth and swiped his mangled workstation across the floor.

"Okay," Newt sighed, walking back towards the box, shoulders drooped in defeat. I threatened him over the external speakers.

"Newt, I warn you. You freaking pull the plug on me in there— and you—you can just burn in hell forever..."

"I'm not. You know that wild tech I was telling you about? Well here's some." The empty wall on the far side of the box came alive in a glow of purples and blues, like oil whirling around a watery plain. I let go of the sticks and gasped. A flurry of blinking did nothing to help my mind accept the outrageous sight. The effect was that of an animated cartoon, a portal of light for the characters to zoom in and out of, dashing away to far off places. Newt expounded on the impossible phenomenon like it was old hat.

"A jump-gate. We developed these as far back as the seventies; part of the Montauk Projects. 'Alien Tech' of course. I can let you off a few places, the closest to her is your own garage, unfortunately."

My mouth remained open in disbelief, with a heavy dose of mistrust thrown in. Newt had a warning of his own.

"It's not without risk," he added. "Once you go out there, Garret, there will be no going back. And I'm not talking about the portal."

Those weighty words bore on me, challenging my fortitude. I knew their ultimate truth, but Beck's scream overtook me. I walked towards the gate and leaned over to dip my exo-suit through the vortex of swirling purple light.

Astonishing: in the lab one moment—in my garage the next. I shook my head in amazement and B1 did likewise, but there was no time to enjoy the fascination. Over a ton of mechanized anger took to a full run, ducked under the door frame, and jumped to land alternated in bike mode. I shot away, surging toward her cry for help.

Only 6 p.m. and already pitch black, the wheels of my Brawler tore down the narrow and hilly stretch of Ontario Street, catching air to thud hard on the small bridge spanning the slough. I felt Newt use the boosters to increase my speed as I turned onto Highway 2 and into more traffic. Proximity alarms began to sound in the velops I was shearing past, no doubt spurring someone to call the sight into Central.

"Newt, I do not want to get stopped on the way!" I heaved, hopeful for his support.

"Hang on," he said, somberly. "Okay, you're cloaked now—you are off visual, and electronic counter measures are activated. Drive as though others cannot see you."

"Cloaked? You don't mean invisible, do you?"

"How do you think I got you away from those Scimitars today?"

"Whoa, did not know these things could do that."

"There's a lot you don't know," Newt said with contempt. He was silent for a moment more and then softened his tone.

"I'll grant you, Garret, this is not a good day to call the authorities for help. More like fuel for the fire, but this is rash. Do you have a plan?"

"You know me. I'm making it up as I go. How much farther? CALL BECK," I ordered, but there was still no answer on the line. Newt's directives grew strict as he took charge.

"Garret, you're going fast enough to murder someone with that bike. Please avoid a collision." He made good sense. I was not being cautious.

After a few close calls, I tore left onto 6th Avenue, nearly massacring an unsuspecting family out for a walk. They must have felt the air pull away from their vicinity much like the team had experienced out by the school's old, dirt road. This improbable cloaking technology was allowing an entire hidden world to be played out behind the scenes.

Beck's white-sided colonial finally came into view up ahead, with lights filling every room. I vaulted the last fifty yards and landed on her lawn in Brawler mode, my invisible, alloy feet digging deep and sudden trenches in the dirt.

"CALL BECK…" My due diligence; a last attempt at sanity before the pandemonium.

"I'M SORRY, SHE IS…" Then Newt cut in.

"I am picking up two life forms on the top floor, Garret. But your heart, it's beating at unsafe levels…"

Now under Beck's window, I could see shadows moving inside, sending my pulse racing to the brink. A humongous maple filled the side yard, its expansive branches once the platform for two small kids who dared to climb out on them from the slight roof just below a bedroom dormer. I grabbed at the tree's massive lower limbs to pull my mechanical bulk up into the timbers. Half of its leaves were barely clinging on and they immediately fled for the ground. The feeling of jagged bark under my feet is still vivid, yet, it was not even my feet touching it.

"I admire your tenacity Garret, but this is— Wait, now getting fault warnings; hip, knee. Your gyros are all over the board. Why don't you try knocking on the door?"

Committed, my blue and white robotic arms pulled me higher. Alerts blinked over my scopes with damage assessment and course correction. Limbs cracked and plummeted while I flailed to hook another solid branch. I knew this tree well and realized I stood on the highest limb of any girth. This was the limb that Beck and I had carved our names on in a different lifetime. Unable to see the carving in the dim light, the thought of it made my blood boil.

"Can't I get sound? Can we pick up the noise in there?" I yelled into the Com as a sudden shift stopped my heart. I braced B1's weight against the trunk.

"Yes, you can," Newt confirmed, and a menu appeared, flashed, and then began picking up the uproar of a hostile argument. Beck was shouting.

As if acting on its own, my massive Brawler dove headlong toward the window, smashing through it along with a large portion of the house. Machine-driven appendages thrashed for anchor, sending wood planks and chunks of siding through the air.

B1's mechanical legs found something solid to withstand their weight and I pushed up into Beck's room. She was cornered on her bed, brandishing a shade-less lamp as her weapon of defense. Kyle stood mortified in his gym shorts, curled leather belt falling to the floor. Once so pure, her pastel room was being violated by multiple raging maniacs.

"Garret, there are serious alerts coming across. You've lost cloaking, and you're losing altitude; the structure is about to give way!" I was oblivious to Newt's warning.

Risking one more push, I heaved upward another few feet. Kyle vanished down the hall as Beck dropped the lamp and cried into her hand.

"C'MON!!" I shouted over the external speakers, feeling another shift in the rafters. Those were my final seconds at that elevation. Beck jumped from the bed, barefoot and unsure of where to go. Dressed in only a T-shirt and underwear, the broken plaster and nail-covered floor prevented her escape.

"He's got a gun!" she bawled, doubling over in fear, unable to run or hide. Kyle had charged back into the room, his drunken fingers mishandling an assault weapon. He dropped it along with several clips and ammunition. Shots rang out, strafing the far wall.

A large, circular carpet lay on the floor within reach and I grasped the near edge with both armored hands. Whipping the rug in a wave motion, I covered the lunatic in debris, leaving the carpet empty and Kyle's eyes filled with plaster fragments.

"GET IN!" I demanded, holding both edges of the pink and white rug open wide in her direction. My battle suit crushed downward a few inches through the studs as Beck conceded her fate and leapt in. Wrapping her up burrito-style, my Brawler held the carpet close and hurdled skyward.

Roof, siding, and limbs crackled loose on all sides as we arrived on the ground in a tremendous thud. The gyros held true and kept us upright as I dashed away into the darkness; fully visible and certainly hunted.

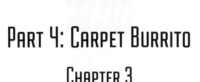

Part 4: Carpet Burrito
Chapter 3

"So persuasive was the mass extermination of those alien, parasitic races, so convincing was their collective and horrible appearance that anything opposing them would seem angelic by contrast. Their annihilation was a blessing now universally celebrated.

But could the devil have offered these beings, sacrificing his own children 'in the fire' the same way he demanded of his followers throughout antiquity? And in doing so played the ace card that secured a total devotion from the hearts and minds of the race he most hated?"

—Piper Corcoran, *Can Things Get Any Stranger? Volume II*

Large composite and alloy feet trudged onward in the dark, while a metal head spun side to side on the lookout for any signs of danger—rushing away from the slightest commotion or light. My eleven-foot tall mechanical mass cradled a pink roll of material, running with it into the night. The scene was not unlike a gorilla that had snuck into camp and made off with a human baby it thought its own.

The Brawler thumped down Alder Street, unseen among its

abandoned stretch of half-completed homes. No doubt the area was being revitalized before construction froze at the Meltdown, and now a large sign pronounced it a future site of government-sponsored housing.

An unlikely robotic jogger passed the last semi-built frame at the lane's end, confronting a well-lit 5th Ave and a slicing pattern of traffic. I darted across amidst honks and a resounding alert caused by an unauthorized object defying the AHS.

"Beck! Hang on. I'm almost at the creek and I'll let you out," I shouted over the externals. "Beck? Answer me!" The audio sensors weren't picking up any sound coming from the roll of carpet, and there was no response from Control as I alternated between shouting for Beck and Newt. Keeping to the less traveled Alder once we'd crossed 5th, we soon reached a familiar spot.

Jumping a short, metal fence, my exo-suit slid on its legs and rear down the steep bank of Sand Creek, nearly drained for the season. A dock stood high in the muck, its end now perched over a shallow stretch of murky water. Cedar Street Bridge towered high in the background, spanning its full 400 feet. The iconic, tamarack log structure looked like a giant millipede stilting its way to the other side of the Byway.

The dank cold of the basin appeared a million years removed from the dry air that warmed this comforting hangout just three months ago. Enjoying Sandpoint's homage to summer, the team had indulged in icy shakes crowded with huckleberries. We watched dragonflies zig from zagging swallows and let our feet dangle over a water plain at least twelve feet higher. But with winter coming it was a damp, frigid and forgotten place.

Light emanated from shops within the bridge's market, and from the steady flow of semi-replacing transports whining down Highway 95, shipping supplies since there was something to ship again. I clicked on a head-mounted beam and carefully set my woven package down on the empty bank, in a layer of lost cottonwood leaves.

The material rolled open to a lifeless body.

"Beck! Oh no no no no no nooooooo! Beck! Rebecca!" Wailing for a response, I let loose of the controls to pound on the cabin's dash. I strained for a moment to be free of the cockpit and run to her, then my hands fumbled back for the sticks. Prickly heat pierced every inch of my body as I fought to deny the consequence before me.

I called out for her again and maneuvered the Brawler's large metal paws to cinch the rug's fringe, rolling Beck around on it, looking for the slightest sign of life. Nothing. Her limp frame flopped over in a contorted pose, the finality of abuse. What the madman Kyle had not taken from her, I had finished off.

I joined with the audience of leafless cottonwoods and stared stupefied by the horror. She lay there almost bare, a cluster of charms around her wrist that would never be given away. I must have crushed her without realizing it.

"Th-tha-that dumb bracelet," I stammered. "That thing should have…" My voice cracked as the knotted frustration over the symbol on her wrist unraveled. A dense haze now made a little clearer; but the truth of it had just been rendered pointless. She was gone. Tears filled the inner rim of my helmet as I threw it off in disgust.

Backing up a few yards, the suit leapt high in the air to land hard in cycle form, a stunt Newt had twisted my ear for more than once. On my knees, encased in the instrument I used to end her life, I prayed through sobs for forgiveness.

"HATCH!" I screamed, smacking the retracting glass with a slippery hand.

As I lifted my head, the most dazzling sight these two eyes had ever seen sat straight up with agitation, reaching for carpet material as a shield against the frosty night. I leapt free of B1, and belted out her name as if howling to the crescent moon. A bear hug pinned the carpet's living occupant inside as my face buried itself in the fabric.

"I thought I'd crushed you Mac! Don't freaking scare me like that!"

Beck groaned and claimed she was all right, while I huffed for breath and tried to seal the rug's seam to preserve some warmth.

The nickname Mac was held in reserve for the most serious of occasions. When Beck had been all but six, she was reading aloud at front of our Homeschool group and the book's character was Megan McDonald, but Beck mispronounced her as Megan Mackadoodle. Henceforth, she was razzed as being that newfound identity but she often beat on us rascals to dissuade the nickname's use. Jay even came up with a Mack-a-Doodle song; a comedic weapon of last resort. But Beck's fierce retaliation made the laugh it got almost not worth it...*almost*.

I held her arms within the rug to avoid any oncoming blows and was relieved to find her sense of humor still intact.

"How can a girl sleep out here with all that racket?" she snapped.

I nuzzled against the carpet, using it to wipe my tears and hoped she wouldn't notice them. Her memory was returning as well.

"Did you just demolish my house?"

"I've gotten a lot done today. Who says I'm not productive?" I heaved, trying to shake off the lingering hysteria. I squeezed tighter. Risking my swollen eyes to her view, my face slid high enough for a runny nose to pop over the carpet's rim.

"Thanks," she said, in total sarcasm.

"Are you hurt?"

"No, I don't think. Not physically, anyway."

Our faces were close. They may have been closer a time or two before, but not with an unseen electrical force crackling in between. I leaned an inch closer and she did not move away. Then a sudden squawking from the Com plundered the moment as Newt's voice drifted out over the cold and empty creek bed.

"Garret! Hello? Come in. GARRET!"

I jumped back towards the bike and held my helmet high, pointing its nose in Beck's direction. I responded into the opening.

"Yeah, Newt. We're here."

"Things are red hot. I've got massive signals closing from everywhere on our position. I've never seen anything like this. They're trying to mask the reading, but I think they're coming up the tunnels to the lab. We are BUGGING OUT!"

Beck was soon at my side, carpet held fast around her.

"Take Rebecca home and get back here on the double," Newt ordered. "Marcee is not answering, so I'm going to have to get her at the school and then swing back for you."

As I listened to Newton's words it felt like a bird was trying to escape my stomach.

It was the dreaded bug-out.

Part 4: Carpet Burrito
Chapter 4

"Gone are the flashy talent and dance competition shows that reigned supreme for decades leading up to the world financial crisis. Now the shows are all about who can give the most material possessions away, to simplify their lives in a new competition over 'plainness.' The messages of these programs are clear: what was once yours is now everyone's. Don't tell, but I miss the old days..."

—Kelley Fenella, *The Death of Hollywood*

"Newt, if we're bugging out, I mean, really out, the team is in, right? I don't want to speak for them, but—" I looked at Beck and she returned a glare, eliminating any thought to the contrary. She shook her head and scoffed.

"Back there? Is he for real?" Beck was picturing Kyle and swarms of CFPO surrounding her fractured house, making the decision obvious.

"Newt, get Jay and Pak through the emergency channel on your way to Mom, tell them we're bugging out, and remind them there's no coming back if they're in." Silence filled the Com. "Newt?"

"Roger, it's your call. These are lives, Garret. Can you afford to make a mistake here?"

I pursed my lips and looked over at the girl I'd almost just killed, trying to decipher brash reaction from leadership. Then Beck leaned toward my helmet to have her say.

"YES, they want that Newt. Just do it." She smiled and gave me a nod. Reassurance; I'd never felt it at such a level. Beck was more than ready to take charge of the team if anything happened to me.

"All right. I'll put the rest of the ride armors in the garage if you all can make it back here. If we can't get them out, they'll be incinerated along with everything else. I'm going to set the lab to blow in one hour. Now, get going!" Newt roared over the Com as I threw on my helmet, realizing only then the magnitude of our predicament.

"Ohhh Newt—what are we going to do? Beck won't fit in there with me. And if I have to carry her in Brawler mode, it'll take too long to get back," I shrugged. "And I can't cloak—and I'm not leaving her. This is bad." A silence lingered before a frazzled Newt erupted in both my helmet and over B1's speakers.

"Good night! Precious seconds are ticking away!"Another pause full of labored breath. "Look—you have a *hover mode* in Brawler. You can, well, *fly* back here." My head whirled towards Beck in amazement as I climbed down into the cockpit.

"If you're serious, you know I don't know how to do that," I said with biting cynicism. "Can't you just remote me back?"

"No. Garret, I am leaving here this second to get your mother. Are you in Brawler mode with your helmet on?" I backed Beck up and made it so, giving Newt a quick affirmative. "Okay, relax for a moment." An *absurd* request. "Downloading now…"

An intense tingling sensation traveled over me from head to toe. Menus appeared in my display showing hover and flight options, and the knowledge of how to utilize them filled my thoughts. The skills to fly *were* where they *weren't* seconds before.

"Whoa, hey, I have hover mode!" I exclaimed, like a young lad who had just been handed an enormous candy apple. Hidden panels sprung open on the Brawler's back and waist, and the drained creek became filled with an imposing brilliance. The force rattled the naked branches nearby and whipped against Beck's carpet and ponytail.

"Are you serious? You're going to carry me? Boy, you're asking a lot!" Beck squinted to shield her eyes from blowing debris and leaves not matted down in the wet. Newt must have picked up her protest, as he was quick to respond over the blaring externals.

"Yes! It's this or walk back! Those pills you've been taking, they run programs and training into your subconscious to be activated on command at a later time. Keeps you from knowing too much too soon. Speaking of time, we're out of it. If I don't see you two again, it's been a pleasure and God bless. As Evan used to quote: 'There are only the pursued, the pursuing, the busy and the tired.' Newton Bigsby, OUT."

I wanted to dwell on the impossibility of Newt's revelation. Had our technical know-how arrived at the point where knowledge and skill could be artificially transmitted into a subject's being? How could I comprehend this advanced flight system without actual study, hours of training? My hand felt the side of my helmet, with its imbedded brain-control interface encircling the interior, and wondered just how *alien* its origin was. I forced myself to stop thinking about the tantalizing possibilities of instant knowledge and moved with urgency. B1's beefy, metallic hand reached for the pink rug, unfolding it on the ground. Beck shot me a last look of disbelief as she climbed in.

"I wish I had a giant toothpick to poke through this carpet!" I joked in a loud, robotic voice, but inside I shuddered at reenacting the situation that nearly killed her.

Blinking like a jackhammer, my mind manipulated the Brawler's arms to pick up the rug-roll and gently cradle it against B1's armored chassis. Then turning to face the embankment, I *wanted* the thrust and gravity displacement to increase, so it did. A blue, blinding light expanded around us. Traction lessened, until we became free of the gunky sand into a low hover. I imagined going up and over the fence at the bank's summit and the flight system obeyed, cracking through a few thin limbs on the way.

Now staring at a downtown still unaware of the flying oddity at its edge, I considered leaving Beck safe and sound in the parking lot that we were magically dangling over. Among the many outrageous decisions I'd been making, the sane option pleaded for proper consideration. But seeing flashing lights of blue and red birthing into swarms, filling the night sky, made me just blast off.

Full atmospheric flight in Brawler mode was only possible in short bursts. This was due to its micro-small zero-point generator, and the inability to pump sufficient energy into the anti-gravity pod for continuous flying. It could try, but that would likely sap away the power needed to run the rest of the suit's functions. So hovering around six feet allowed safe drops when the advanced crystal-cell batteries ran dry. Electro-gravitic power rejuvenated in short order as the generator replenished itself from the quantum vacuum, along with the capacity to take off again. Variable angle, efficient burning hydrogen/oxygen boosters provided the directional thrust.

Six feet above the pavement and accelerating, it felt like I'd done it a thousand times, albeit without a petrified girl swaddled in a pink carpet, zigzagging down a crowded street at night. Not sure one can ever train for that. But the ability to execute missions of flight, which had been latent the unconscious realm, were now free to control my actions.

Cedar Street was suddenly full of the CFPO, blocking our more direct route west. We'd have to blast down First Ave—going the wrong way on a one-way street—to reach Pine, and eventually Highway 2.

We glided toward First, past the building-side mural of a sprinting, blue caribou that was painted well before I was born. It had always looked terrified to me, running for its life, and now I knew exactly how it felt.

The whole town had turned angry while we had our little moment at the creek. Whirling lights in every direction signaled we'd just won a jackpot of trouble. They danced off the underside of the town's low-hanging clouds while sirens wailed—and people screamed, pointed or ran. But the first obstacle to come in front of my face was my own smile. It was a blast to fly, period, but blowing away this quaint pedestrian setting suited me well. I was a spoiler, a disrupter, enjoying every second. The only thing uncomfortable about it was how comfortable it felt. Thirty-two miles per hour is what the indicator read as we blasted ahead, flying against the tide of vehicles cruising their way around the one-way loop.

"Hold on. We're weaving through traffic!" I warned Beck over the speakers.

Stupefied looks, proximity alarms, and gaping mouths remained in our wake as B1's rear thrusters basked the area in electric light. The Brawler's alloy feet scraped over velops packed in three-deep along the curb, bursting windshields as I veered too far left and right.

The scene was ridiculous, like an improbable event that takes place right before everything goes haywire in a fiery, red explosion. I wanted to marvel at the view but Beck could not afford a distracted driver.

A group of sign-carrying protesters crossing First scattered as we neared Church Street. A panicked picketer tossed a sign high in the air that said something about "My Jesus Ain't No Alien" as he dove for cover. Its cheap wood and paper disintegrated against the Brawler's hull as we burst through.

Blinding spots zapped on from above, placing us inside blazing, brilliant circles. Just *wanting* to know what was projecting the beams created an identification display on my visual scope. It was a few of those metal bat craft, and their vital statistics began to scroll across my menu. They looked to be drones after all, but I could spare no more of my focus. My full attention was needed to navigate a thousand dangers, except one alert was now exchanged for another. A flashing indicator showed orange steps vanishing inside an outline of my Brawler's back-mounted generator. Within seconds the ability to fly evaporated. I was now reduced to a tedious run, eliciting a scream from my reluctant passenger.

"Hey! I preferred the flying thing! You're killing me in here!"

Beck sounded in good health but I knew she would tough it out beyond her brink. Recalling the sight of her limp body splayed out on the ground sent a fresh arrow through my brain. I tried to *think* B1's arms through a gentler grip as a charging CFPO cruiser bumped our alloy leg from behind. We nearly toppled to the asphalt before the Brawler's gyros sprung us plumb and kept us in a jog.

Up ahead, a pair of civil defense exo-suits plodded around the corner at Pine Street, thwarting our escape. Standing obtusely just outside Sandpoint's enduring Panhandler Pie-Shop, these symbols of the old and new could not have been more dichotomous. The mecha were heavy and slow, but came armed with powerful stun batons that neutralized electronics on contact. Their elongated shoulder armor looked like dopey elephant ears and they walked with the same level of grace. Newt had laced his simulations with them so I was not unfamiliar.

"Uh-oh, two big power armors up ahead," I updated Beck. "Is this where King Kong has to put down Jane and fight the Tyrannosaurs?" Not a second elapsed before I heard a muffled and angry roar.

"Heck no! Jane will call for help and get you busted!"

"Never mind," I stated, as the power indicator again read full. B1 shot upward in a fiery arc, propelling us well beyond 200 feet. We cut diagonally toward Pine Street, high above several building tops.

Something like a "whoooa-ho-hooo" escaped me as Beck and I swooned to the starry night. Things sure looked different from that angle and we quickly lost our bearings, juice and altitude. The flight system automatically brought us back to ground level as its power spent itself away. Fearful hands shook against the sticks as I finessed our landing close to where the main road turned southwest. Once again grounded, B1's awkward run was leaving crunched chunks of pavement and sounding alarms trailing behind us.

Anti-gravitic capability would soon regenerate but I noticed our thruster fuel was already running low. I wanted to tell Dad the Brawler's flight range was seriously lacking, a capability he kept from me, and wondered what else I might discover as Beck and I took off again, ripping down Highway 2 toward home.

The distance from our pursuers gave me a moment to consider my actions. Whether brash, or as a daring leader, I'd made my move— and was now enduring their counter move.

The outcome was anything but certain, with death but a hair's breadth away...

Part 4: Carpet Burrito
Chapter 5

"They reckoned that below 278 degrees kelvin all matter should remain perfectly still, without heat or motion. This temperature is the 'absolute zero point.' However, instead of a tranquil state, there was a boundless, surging force of energy. It's been said that a coffee-cup sized sampling of space has enough power to instantaneously boil off all the world's oceans. Long ago, searching deep within the quantum lengths, great and tenacious minds took hold of that energy. Unfortunately we cannot claim the bragging rights. It's now been handed to us from the most humbling of sources, our creators."

—Dr. T.R. Hornbrook, *Mercury Magnetic Vortex Propulsion*

"CALL NEWT."

"I'M SORRY, HE IS NOT—" "Yeah, yeah. Newt, you'd better pick up soon!"

Ontario was its customary reserve of hush until a flying exo-suit whooshed over the narrow stretch. A small blue sign reading "Entering Dover" flapped madly as we rocketed beyond the slough.

Beck had once claimed to be the inspiration behind the motto "A Hidden Jewel Discovered in Dover, ID," then I reminded her that she was born and raised in Sandpoint.

The image of Beck and I ice skating just below the bridge flared to mind, and I wondered if we'd ever get the chance again. The helmet's sensitive interface allowed me to somehow feel her within the roll of carpet against our chest. *Our chest;* the line distinguishing where B1 stopped and I started was blurring the more time I spent inside the incredible suit.

Expecting to surge over our development's tall, iron fencing, I noticed both gates already open wide. Several velops and transports were making their way out of Hemlock Hill and the Flagstones were among them. Why sensible people were leaving was not a mystery. A thousand strobocops looked to be dancing among the wooded lots like some kind of pagan ritual of fire. Overhead beams again drenched us in light, advertising our homecoming as we vaulted over the exiting vehicles, heading straight "where there be dragons."

If downtown had been lit up like a Christmas tree, this was Rockefeller Center. SWAT trucks, hover cars and jet-packed Darths of the night sky all twinkled with brilliance, portraying the dramatic end of our road. A bevy of flying men were taking off and landing in what looked like practice, their bulbous heads and hoses still sucking the life from their own bloated chests. My stomach twisted as I waited for them to finish their hunt, and for the first shots to be fired. Yet nothing made a move to prevent us from passing.

The great mass of CFPO stood gawking at our soaring robot as I flew over and around them in a mad race home. Chamberlain Maddox was holding a bullhorn, standing with a large group of officers at the east end of our drive. His jaw swung loose as if on a busted hinge as we floated past, setting down outside the trio of garage doors. Commanding one to open, it revealed a welcome sight. I called out to my friends over B1's sound system.

Pak and Jay were inside, jump-suited in their mecha underwear, frazzled and frightened. The quick activation of the door and my thunderous salutation sent their already fragile nerves into low orbit. Like a giant shutting eye, the closing door extinguished the clarion of jabbing light outside. Instead of multiple squads pouring up the drive demanding our lives, the sea of authority remained in place. They had us surrounded, yet were holding back.

I lay the carpet down and Beck sprang out like a jack-in-the-box, furious over her choppy ride. Despite the tense situation, the guys dug into their repertoire to comment on her state of undress. She was in no mood.

"Don't even—" Her fist raised and clenched hard in their direction. Beck swiped her jumpsuit off the front cowling of her red cycle, gave a growl, and withdrew as much as possible to throw it on.

Checking my position, I returned B1 to bike mode to face outward along with the others and dismounted. Someone needed to take charge of the situation and be our calm, collected leader, but an incredible sight threw me off course.

"Holy, sweet mother of..." I whisper-shouted, removing my helmet to reveal a sweat-laden mop of hair. Mounted atop Pak's Caliber car was an immense gun: a hydraulically driven, seven-barrel Gatling-type auto cannon. I reached out to verify its reality and the imposing barrels rotated with a smooth oiliness under my touch.

"Where-did-you-get-this-thinggg?" The stunned words escaped me in a rhythmic cadence as I noticed that the rest of team's vehicles were equipped with obvious weaponry and indistinguishable devices. Pak was fuming.

"Our rides were like this when we got here. I was going to turn around and leave but that's when the company arrived. I did NOT sign on for this man. This is crazy. We destroyed the school. What— we're not going to get in trouble for that? We're going to start shooting people?" He looked at the team with fierce eyes and I groped for a way to intervene. Big Pak continued and made his position clear.

"The Bible says not to kill. There are dads out there—with families! I'm not a killer, no way. No way man…"

He was right. The decision that lay before us was crucial. I was about to agree with him and concur for the group when Beck, now clothed in black, cut me off.

"You know that thing my Mom is married to? They're just like him." She pointed to the garage door, insinuating the great force beyond. "The red list, green list or whatever, that Mr. Philmore talked to us about—conservative Christians and homeschoolers are right on that list under veterans. Who do you think is going to go door to door some day to get those people—to get US? It's them. They already killed thousands during martial law and when they took all the guns! We're next."

She screamed it out, expecting our collective agreement. Pak took a deep breath and readied himself for reassertion despite the tears peaking at us from Beck's eyes. She staggered and I steadied her. It was time to calm everyone down before the barking got out of hand.

"Look, we're not killing lunch-bucket dads today, or anybody else." I put a hand on Pak's granite shoulder and tried to connect the three of us. "Newt just told me about a whole bunch of stuff. The things that came after us at school might not be all human, and they're a lot different than those cops out there who are just following orders."

"Yup, aliens." Jay muttered to no one's surprise.

"We're not going to hurt them, and I don't think we'll have to." I looked at each member of the team, establishing eye contact.

"As crazy as this sounds, these suits can fly and turn invisible, cloaking or something, but Newt's got to download the feature to us.

We can't activate it on our own. We've gotta get him on the horn and make a peaceful getaway—okay?"

I backed up towards my ride to try to raise Newt again. The group decompressed while Beck distracted them with tales of our flying adventure.

"CALL NEWT. You'd better be there my friend!" Nothing. Not a peep from Control. I wanted to slam my helmet down but thought better of it.

I took a look out the slender, front window and hoped for an encouraging sign. The ocean of fury remained the same formidable sight, maybe worse. A giant spotlight careened over the window and I jumped to the side, turning back to my friends more frayed than before. Jay was staring at a heap of equipment on the floor so I asked if he knew its purpose.

"They're for your ride. Newt told us to try to load them if and when you got here. But they're too heavy and this lug won't give me a hand."

"That's' right, not going to..." Pak said with complete determination. Nervous and irate, Jay leapt to his feet and started shouting in his direction.

"You know, I just don't get you. Didn't you hear Garret? Humans do not pilot those crab suits! If they had gotten a hold of one of us this morning, what would you have done, pray for it, Bible-Man?" Pak's large hand moved so fast it could not be seen by the naked eye, grabbing a fistful of Jay's jumpsuit, dragging his face into range.

"I flattened one of those things as it reached out for you, you little punk, while you were running away. So I don't want to hear—"

"Hang on there my massive friend..." I tried to pry the two apart while Beck stood by, hands on her hips in mild approval. "It's the middle of the flippin' night, we're strung out and exhausted beyond belief. We've got to pull together—wait, I'll pray. C'mon, let me pray for us right now..."

Pak's muscles deflated like a puffer fish collapsing its quills, showing I'd chosen the right arrow to shoot into his brutish heart. My comrades attempted to wander in opposite directions until I reached out and pulled us into a facing circle. "Help me pray, you guys. Mom says that people only pray as a last resort, instead of when they should."

"I don't know what day you've been living in, but this *is* the last resort." Jay decided to start his own prayer to help me out. "Dear God, we're about to be horribly murdered here and I would just like to…" I jabbed him and reached for everyone's hand.

"Lord, please help us right now. We don't want to hurt anybody, and we're not sure of what to do. Please give us guidance. In Jesus' name, Amen."

We opened our eyes and looked at each other as a strange sense of relief swept over our group. Jay, Beck and Pak stood perplexed at the feeling of euphoria, a strong relaxation in the tension, but I knew better.

"They're blasting the Gs!" I shouted, and reached out for an old paint can on a nearby shelf. Tossing it end over end in the air, its descent was slow and exaggerated. The team readied a test jump before I stopped them. "Beck, Pak—mount up. Jay, let's see if we can get these things onto my ride now."

Jay looked thrilled by the notion. As we began grappling with the Brawler add-ons Newt had left for B1, I could see through the side window silhouetted movement in our garden next to the house, sending my hands into their full shake. I envisioned shots raining through the glass any second, or something crashing through the door as we ran out of time. The sight of a slender, female form disappearing into her red cycle distracted me into asking for a last affirmation.

"Beck? Are you alright?" She turned her helmet my way and gave me a strong thumbs-up before sinking into her ride. Jay tugged on my jumpsuit.

"Newt said they were plug-and-play easy as long as you were powered up." He motioned me over to hit the power and we set about arming B1. I had always wanted weapons, but now the thought of them was wholly disconcerting. The two, top-mounted sensors were removed and exchanged for large pods, their outer doors concealing the contents. Jay was quick to direct the gun mount, displaying a knack for assembling the parts, and observing that Beck had something similar we could replicate on mine.

It was then that I managed to grab ten seconds to look over what Newt had attached to our "attack vehicles." In addition to Pak's top-mounted cannon, each forearm held double tubes of something unknown. Beck's red ride had twin gun mounts and what looked like top-mounted missile pods, eight tubes per pod. Jay's green bike had the most bizarre-looking addition: twin conduits running from his back-mounted generator to each forearm, where they met up with strange containers.

By the time we mounted my second pod, it weighed almost nothing, and our feet were struggling for traction along the floor. I was astounded at the fortune the lower Gs had just provided us, should those weapons prove necessary that dreadful night. Taking another paint can from the shelf, I tossed it up into an environment almost devoid of gravity. Jay grabbed for his bike at the leg, using his hands to crawl along it and climb into the cabin. I did the same. The fresh oxygen inside my Brawler was a relief from the thin, departing air in the garage. A flashback of terror slapped against me as I relived being pulled aloft from my backyard. I shook it off and called out to the team.

"Guys, hang tight, let me scope it out first." I changed over to Brawler mode, hunching to clear the ceiling, and used my wrist camera to spy out the small, front window. "Hey heyyyy! Wait a second here!"

I called for the door to open. As it rose, an incredible sight lay before us. The blockade was breaking up and making its way out of the area, even the airborne units. I ducked B1 under the door frame and the team changed into robot mode as well, following me out onto the driveway. Four colorful exo-suits jumped for joy, and even tried to high five, missing. We bantered around theories about why they were leaving but we were just too darned tired to care. For whatever reason, the hounds had been called off and our source of terror was fading from view.

Wind-borne leaves remained aloft as the air collected an increasing amount of weightless debris. I used my Brawler to pick up a large brick from Mom's landscaping and toss it toward the road. It continued a hundred feet or more before bouncing lightly along the street and into a cluster of bushes. I felt concern for my neighbors, for their safety (and for being seen in that get-up), but the more I looked around, the more the area appeared abandoned: Not a person, cat, squirrel or sign of life was visible.

"Whoa, this is amazing," Pak murmured. "We're in almost no Gs." He sounded the most relieved of all of us as he hopped his hulking Caliber suit down the drive. My relief evaporated as I remembered everything set in motion.

"Guys, we've got no time to celebrate. Newt set the lab to blow. It's going to go up in about twenty minutes. He's supposed to be getting my mom right now and coming back for us, but we can't wait around for him."

"TING—TING—TING—TING!"

Blaring alarms filled my display as threat and proximity alerts danced everywhere. By the chatter across the Com, I could tell that it was the same alert in every unit. Jay couldn't make sense of it.

"I'm getting readings all over. From up above, behind us, I mean—I dunno, all around. We're surrounded. We're surrounded…"

Part 5: Firefight
Chapter 1

"Only the brave Garret, only the brave..."

—Evan Philmore

We scanned the midnight sky but all that could be seen were a few, slow-moving clouds, their edges brilliant from an intense moon. But then a hum started low, building quickly into a bone-rattling vibration that permeated every inch of me. The ground trembled as the wind whipped and arcs of electricity flashed about the firmament. The illusion of three massive clouds gave way to gigantic ships, which decelerated and glided to a stop over our heads. The team said nothing. Like masked robbers, fear and awe had relieved us of our vocabulary.

Moonlight glinted off a host of smaller craft, disembarking and scattering into formation. Several squads raced over us low, filling the air with a vortex of swirling rubbish, branches and dead leaves. Another row of fighters lined up a few hundred yards ahead, dropping their cargo of blackened and clawed death machines into Hemlock Hill. One of the sinister mecha crushed through the Voegle's sun porch, blasting its rear jets as it did so. Their roof flickered with lingering flame as the beast stepped free of the rubble in our direction.

The scopes on my Brawler's display rollicked with activity. Electronic finders blinked and flashed at over the fifty adversaries now eager to end our short-lived game of cat and mouse. Each Scimitar battle suit bore twin ruby eyes, glowing one on top of the other; a sight we were spared in the daylight chase. I cleared my throat for an absurd and final declaration.

"This is where we hold them. This is where we fight. This is where they die..."

Few stood against many in firm resolve. The moment hung with profundity. Darn if Jay couldn't just let it hang there.

"Uh, *they die?* Is something wrong with your sensors? If you listen real hard, that bell is tolling for us, my friend. I know you always wanted your David and Goliath moment, but I was hoping we weren't going to be around for that."

Ready to bite back at Jay and demand his unwavering loyalty, the bottom fell out of my heart. Overwhelming odds had crumbled bravery's fragile edifice. We would all be killed; slaughtered. Abandoned for reasons unknown, my Heavenly Father had turned away. There would be no climactic defiance. We would not overcome. Evil would win the day and there was nothing I could do about it. I was blanked, with no idea of what to say next. In my place, a host of unfamiliar voices flooded the Com.

"We have link up. All coded communications now being broadcast on high-frequency, variable channels..."

"Analysis shows all weapons systems online; cloaking not responsive from unit B1. All others are activated with flight systems unlocked, diverting power now..."

We listened, stunned, as the confident voices piped through our helmets.

"Downloading Operation FIREFIGHT and all prior training capsules. Weapons now synchronized. Targeting will exclude all unit members…"

Then the download came, a head-to-toe shiver of instantaneous enlightenment. Within seconds we were fully trained, military combatants. Pak was the only one who didn't enjoy the magically transmitted talent, protesting the upgrade. Jay wanted to carry on some nonsense about how invincible he felt, but Pak ordered him to shut up. The Com kept flowing with emotionless pronouncements.

"Estimated twenty seconds of combat time before enemy forces abandon capture attempts and switch to destroy. All units stand ready…"

"Commence operation in ten seconds, mark…"

More enemy fighters discarded their shimmering, black battle armors. They filled the streets and positioned themselves into an ever-tightening noose. There was no time to think or debate. I had been through this drill fifty times, whether in a dream or reality—it made no difference. They had made their counter move and now it was my turn.

"I'm not a killer," Pak said, making his final statement before a change in orders came across for me.

"B1, remain in position with hands raised as a diversion. This might buy us a few seconds of confusion."

I had not counted on that, but it made sense. A lot made sense now. Then the command came as the last of the sand drained from our hourglass.

"Commence attack sequence: FIREFIGHT!"

The team took a three-step run before changing into their rides and disappearing, cloaked from view. I raised my suit's arms as instructed, eliciting very little reaction from the opponent. A few of the giant Scimitars ran forward, but were at a loss, trying to pull the missing team back up on their scopes. A brief moment passed and that's all that was needed. Jay's green Brawler appeared deep behind enemy lines, as I knew it would. Scores of enemy battle suits picked up his signature and turned his direction, but it was too late.

White-hot lightning fell from the sky onto his antenna array. The devices on his forearms glowed for a split second before bolts of death shot away in three hundred different directions. The dark-colored ships and suits grew much darker, their red and white signal lights snuffing out as dozens crashed to the ground. The neighborhood went black, and so did I. The force from the impact sent my Brawler hurdling into the yard face first. I had to let go of the electrified Control Sticks as the whole cabin became cooked. B1's display flashed warnings and damage reports as it pulled itself upright.

Pak's Caliber materialized close to Jay and sent its forearm projectiles straight up over the battlefield to set off an explosion of orange, like lava spewed from a volcano. A smoky veil blanketed the area as tens of millions of sparkling smart-filaments filled the air. Our targeting would be unaffected, but enemy systems would now find it hard to lock on to anything, especially us.

The contents of my pods were indeed missiles. I followed mission protocols and let them fly at the half-mile-long motherships. Only four were available for three different targets, but these highly advanced, surface-to-air missiles would accomplish a great deal. As they streaked towards the gigantic ships, I crossed my fingers that the filaments would make their countermeasures ineffective. I changed B1 over to bike mode and moved to the end of our driveway. Pak was supposed to be covering me but his cannon remained silent. The Com took note of his deviation.

"C1 has not opened fire; should we do a system override?"

"Negative."

That was Newt's voice! I didn't waste a second.

"Newt, you mad genius, you planned this all along," I chided to provoke a response but he offered none. I heard Beck's panicked shouting as her Brawler came into view with the others.

"He's not going to make it—they're coming in." She meant me.

My threat warnings were active, but I was too busy playing, and now it might cost me everything. I punched the accelerator in a mad dash to join the team, becoming part of their defensive line, but I remained isolated, a sitting duck. Unable to get target lock, the contingent of enemy fighters was holding their fire until close range.

Beck's red Brawler switched to bike mode and broke from the rest in my direction. She let loose a salvo of stinger missiles from her top pods at my would-be killers. B3 changed back to Brawler mode, skidding my way to let fly a half dozen more. Her missiles found their target, vaporizing the squad of enemy fighters above our position. The explosions hurled my bike into her battle suit, and sent both of us grinding across the pavement in a heap. I changed over to Brawler but my suit tumbled and lay helpless on the ground.

"My gyros are screwed up. The system is trying to recalibrate. I hope it's not dead!"

I could feel Beck pulling me and B1 up to our knees, the painted heart on her suit's shoulder filled my optics. Then she let out a horrible screech and was no longer there.

Part 5: Firefight
Chapter 2

"Instability in the home is renown for causing deep-seeded issues with the children living under its roof. So it was with the people of Earth when they realized their future was uncertain; that their mother, after much abuse, might not have the strength to care for them any longer..."

—Warner Roxwell, *Our Backs Against the Wall*

An enemy battle suit had taken to full flight and reached out its giant claw to pull Beck's red Brawler overhead, no doubt on its way back to a mothership. The Scimitar's pair of powerful, back-mounted rockets left a blinding stream of fire across the sky. Unable to remain a neutral observer any longer, Pak snapped to his senses and let loose.

"Someone's going to answer for this!" he screamed, whirling his loud Gatling-cannon into action to find Beck's captor. Tracer rounds tracked the flying crab across the sky and pulverized it into hunks of falling metal. Her Brawler suit plunged towards the ground with the Scimitar's black arm still digging into B3's armored waist. The Caliber's targeting system showed its extreme precision, turning even the remaining claw to dust without harming her. My heart stopped until she hit her counter-gravitic controls, righting herself to jet back our way.

Her rate of descent revealed that the bad guys had shut off their gravity blaster, no doubt disappointed it hadn't been effective in terrifying us. Another female voice bearing a slight southern accent came across the Com, more nervous than the rest.

"Alert. The enemy is now resorting to deadly force!"

Pak was off the chain now, yelling into the Com and wreaking carnage everywhere. Enemy ships and suits burst open across the dark horizon. The crackle and pop of explosions pummeled my kidneys and invited panic. There was smoke and fire everywhere, chunks of craft, houses and trees catching fire; all of it a violent, swirling chaos. I concentrated on steady breathing as B1's diagnostics blinked green and my gyros reset. Once on our feet, I scanned the clouds for motherships to find two damaged, belching out sparks and fire. The other was no longer visible.

"Control, what about the other mother craft?" I asked, as a young-sounding male voice reprimanded the question. His tone reduced me to the amateur I was.

"It blinked out, B1. Stay focused on available targets. Wolf team, launch. Try to give us some room to set down."

A dismal feeling was descending about the battle's progress. The remaining mothers were spewing out fighter after fighter, despite their wounds. I felt like I needed to get my friends away from there before things got any worse.

"There are too many. Beck, activate your shield. If they don't back off soon, you guys are going to have to cloak out and make a break for it. I'll go in another direction and try to buy you some time."

I remember Newt telling us that the small circle on top of Beck's red bike was an extra sensor. Now, with the downloaded combat scenario, I knew the truth. The funny thing about instant awareness is it's hard to remember back to when you didn't know something. It's as if you always did, even when you didn't.

The circle telescoped upward, high over Beck's smoldering missile pods. From its perimeter, a pinkish, luminous dome fell over our group. Projectiles and beam-type weapons could pass out of the dome, but would prove ineffective incoming against the shield, at least until its limited power ran dry. It deployed just in time as bolts of plasma impacted over our heads, absorbed by the barrier.

B1 was tracking clusters of enemy carrier ships and I could see a squadron circling around for another run. Their triangle shapes silhouetted as black demons against the night sky. The fighters had already dropped their Scimitar battle suits but their payload of bombs could obliterate our position—not to mention the enormous mother ships might open fire any second. I called out to the team.

"Guys, get ready to change modes and split…"

Without warning, three regular army J-22 power suits in full flight, propelled themselves into the enemy squadron's path. They loosed a host of attacks against the oncoming triangle ships. Explosions snapped open and permeated the atmosphere. Parts hailed down around us. Then someone from the army unit called out over the Com.

"It's now or never; Cavalry 1, get those kids outta here!"

What was not part of the mission download was a large ship materializing in the cul-de-sac a few hundred feet behind us, its bay door open and waiting. The vessel appeared and disappeared as though its ability to vanish was breaking down, but our course of action was obvious. The four ride armors of team Zero-Gs fell back into vehicle mode and collectively sped for the safety of its holding bay.

Once inside, I retracted the windshield and removed my helmet, blinking at the miraculous view. All my friends alive and blinking back at me. The ship was taking off and the tremendous roaring wind from the open rear door drew our attention. The team threw our helmets back on, not knowing what might be greeting us on this unexpected lifeboat. That action may have saved our lives because just then, the great ship heaved. The night itself exploded into a bulb of furious white. Blinding light from a hundred suns invaded the hangar area, along with a dense murk of smoke and fumes. As if the escape had not been spectacular enough, we'd made it off the ground and away from Hemlock Hill just as it imploded.

Gasping for air inside B1, the sticks shook violently from its trembling pilot. My scrambled mind raced through an index file of everything that had just been vaporized, including Dad's final note.

Amidst the clearing smoke, a lone, olive drab J-22 army exo-suit rocketed onto the ramp and up into the flight bay. The ship's large rear door groaned and sealed behind it. Hell's miasma dissipated from its shell as it thunked our direction.

The team remained motionless inside our rides as the lumbering attack suit approached, faceless and cold. Multiple blast points littered its hull, and an olive paint job more chipped off than on. Smoky wisps meandered from barrel tips as it stood there, the unknown pilot swaying for breath within.

"Bloodthirsty" was the title over a hand-painted wolf sinking its teeth into an unidentifiable strip of flesh. The graffiti decorating its battered, metal plating, completed the picture that we'd left Kansas and were headed straight for Mars.

A row of four holding ports sat on the far side of the bay, with one port occupied with a similar armor, only less battle worn. The J-22 clunked its way over to the docking area and backed into an empty slot. Lights turned out on the armor's exterior as high-pressure steam spat forth as escaping exhaust.

Several clamps bore down to secure the battle suit in place and the J-22's front entry popped loose. A vein-laced, hairy arm pushed open the hatch to reveal a driver matching our expectations. Bald and snarling, he flung himself out and onto the cold flooring in a way that defied physics. The mountain of walking muscle gave us a menacing snarl and whipped open a forward doorway.

With a violent slam, he was gone.

Part 5: Firefight
Chapter 3

"Each member of the team seemed to take their turn at both pacifism and warmongering, and never at the same time as each other. While this difference in philosophies would have disrupted most units, it actually served to balance this unlikely group."

—Birdie Vilmos, *And Then There Were Four*

"W here…are…we?" Jay sang the words up and down to the vaguely familiar *Twilight Zone* theme song.

"I don't know, but at least we're all alive," I whispered. "Whoever is flying this ship must be friendly, or we wouldn't be. Someone yelled to 'get the kids out' over the Com, so it looks like these guys swooped in for the rescue."

Pak was the first one to dismount. Looking drained and half alive, he staggered toward the metal fore-door. If it had been much farther away he would have fallen before reaching it. His black body suit was drenched, making him look like an exhausted swimmer exiting the pool after a marathon swim.

The rest of us cut short our gawking at the hold's contents and caught up with him. I wasn't aware of the extreme fatigue until my feet reached the deck. Legs wobbled with weakness, eyes argued for sleep with every blink. If only there had been a bed within my next ten steps.

Pak pounded the door for a brief second before it hissed open. There stood Newt, face full of joy the first second, pulled through the door by his coat the next. Pak flung him two-handed up against the far wall, keeping double fists full of Newt's semi-white jacket. Out of character, Pak hurled his words unrestrained.

"You used us, you creep! We were just your little lab mice. You were making murderers for fun, just because you could." The team piled up behind the assault, but hesitated to grab those big arms, rationalizing reasons to wait this one out.

"If you could just give me a moment, I can try to explain," Newt stammered. "I understand why you're upset. I had hoped it would not come to what you just endured. Please, let me…"

Pak gave a last shove and snort, choosing the hatchway to the unknown rather than stay and hear Newt out. Bottling up my nagging questions, I chased after, leaving the others to hear what the befuddled doctor had to say.

Pak was ten feet ahead, unresponsive to my calls. In this exhausted, irrational state, he was seeking another coat to grab, demanding answers from the next available body. I followed him down a long corridor, ignoring closed hatches on each side, into an open area of the ship's fore-section. I was thankful to find a warm and disarming scene waiting for us.

Three rows of six seats faced toward the front of the craft. They sat empty except for two mothers—Beck's and mine. Mom and I embraced as she gave me a guarded look, avoiding any spoken detail about our current whereabouts. It was one of those "hope we didn't just go from the frying pan into the fire" looks. Ms. Sprankle,

Eleanor, had a stunned but pleasant glow. She was a little glassy-eyed, like she might cry, laugh, or do both at any second. I wanted to say something like, "Sorry for smashing your house," but I didn't feel sorry in the least. She would never set eyes on the damage anyway.

In front of the passenger area stretched a dividing wall with open aisles on either side, and beyond that was a circular control center. As I peered around the divider, I could see Pak talking with a few technicians who were all seated around the center module. Four had their headsets down around their necks, showing they weren't taxed with any current duties. Several others sat on the far side, absorbed in their screens and buttons.

With Pak's fury culled, I debated my next course of action when sobs erupted in the seats behind me. Beck and her mother had reunited. Their pleasant embrace stood in stark contrast to the fuming bald madman that stormed in from the bow of the vessel. Newt had no sooner stepped into the area than the furious man in fatigues began berating him. The soldier knew how to shout.

"THIS? My men died for *this?*" The raging man pointed our way as if we were inanimate objects on a ledge. I felt bad for poor old Newt. The stars that had once filled my eyes for him tumbled from the sky, one by one, as he drew the fury of so many in such a short time. He looked like an inept child, who didn't know how to stay out of trouble. Newt embraced the role of absent-minded professor and fumbled for words.

"Team, this is Major Brody Freeman. He is a highly—"

"SAVE IT!" The loud rebuke made everyone jump. Major Freeman looked at Newt like he wanted him to say one more thing, giving the excuse he needed to shred him like paper. Fuming Freeman walked toward me with purpose, knowing I was the ringleader, the real burr under his saddle. He bellowed into my personal space, his sweaty nose pressing against my forehead.

"This whole thing was a complete disaster. THERE'S NO WAY you'll ever make up for two of my men—two of my friends!"

If true, and I reckoned it was, the rant was called for. His friends deserved someone to be that angry. The major's lambasting demanded the weight of their deaths be contemplated, and at the right time, I planned to find out everything I could about them. Why had these soldiers thought us worthy of the ultimate price?

"Back off, Wolfman." Someone pushed between us; someone whose small stature belied her fearlessness, and someone who smelled much better than the Wolfman. "Name's Minerva." She reached out for a shake with one hand, sending her black eye shields up into her flight helmet with the other. "I fly this rig."

"Well, why aren't you flying it then?" Brody grimaced, trying to send her the same saltiness he'd been giving us, but his failure was perceptible. It came off more like a brother teasing a sister, revealing that some day we might be able to upgrade our status with him to just mild abuse.

"We're on auto and cloaked. What do you want me to do, play solitaire up there? Millers' got the helm, reeelaaax..." The mood in the cabin had taken a colossal shift. Suddenly Bloodthirsty didn't seem so bloodthirsty. Of course Jay had to test it.

"So what army are you a major in, anyway?" Freeman paused for half a second, appreciating that somebody had volunteered to send him back into his tantrum. He made two quick steps towards Jay to move within spitting distance. The audience braced for impact.

"The Green Elite, punk! I know you've never heard of it because you're a momma's boy, and shouldn't even be here!" His shouts were less scary now, and he was morphing into a parody of himself. I looked at Minerva for reassurance; her smile gave it to me. The major pressed on.

"The only thing you can relate to is being green, punk! There's nothing elite about what I'm looking at here…" Major Freeman's face wriggled in far too close to Jay's, his normal procedure. Maybe Jaxon was just too darn tired to be scared because a grin claimed the area under his nose.

"My last name is Green. Really, it is." A few of us stifled our awkward smiles. If the major turned away from Jay for a moment he might turn back to a goatee laced with rubber bands. Freeman seethed, scanning us all in disgust.

"Well, doesn't that just figure? Minerva, you got your wish, the super kids are coming over to our side. Congratulations, they're all yours…" With that, Major Freeman vacated toward the back of the ship. Waves of weariness overtook me until I collapsed into the nearest seat.

Four of the techs had gathered around to watch the action, three females and one male. They appeared to be in their early twenties. Despite the violent scene, their faces remained cheerful and intrigued, as if they were looking over the litter for which puppy to take home. Pak's big body slumped into the seat beside me. His head smacked against the rest with a thud.

"I can't believe it. Those J-22 suits that took on the Scimitars, did two of them just die for us? That ain't right man. That ain't right. They're dead? Somebody's gotta pay for that. We're…responsible… for…" His voice faded and his faced drooped to signal a departure from the waking world. I looked on his slumber and savored the idea. My eyes drug themselves upward toward Minerva for a few final seconds of consciousness.

"How long is the flight? Oh, thank you by the way."

"That's okay. Don't mind ol' Bloodthirsty. He's a good man, and the best there is." She nodded with respect and got lost in thought about the men not coming back. "You've got three hours Garret, enjoy it." She patted my head lightly and turned to walk away, to where I cannot recall.

Part 6: The Collins Elite
Chapter 1

"Our martial arts instructor, Master Barrão, teaches us an exhausting mix of techniques, with much of it focused on smooth movements and a cadence almost like dancing. We're to remain in constant motion, making us a frustrating target for any forward-advancing opponent. He shouts at us to keep our 'ginga flowing' and to 'bake in those good habits!' I can hardly lift my legs from today's session so I guess I'm pretty baked."

—Garret Philmore, *Letters on the Lamb: A Collected Journal*

An eager rap on the door sprung me upright in my cot. I spent a few seconds in the moment—that moment where you fight the fog and try to remember what got you to your current location. The rapping came again and pulled me out of my stare. Even in that groggy state it was instantly apparent I was no longer on a flying ship. As I looked around bleary-eyed, nothing crystallized. I opened the door about a foot, unsure of what could be standing on the other side.

"Morning, do you remember me? You were pretty out of it back in the hangar."

An eager face, a few inches shorter than mine, was chipper and ready to start his day. I recalled him as one of the techs from the big ship. He may have helped me get to that room, but those details were sketchy. The "container" where I found myself was as much a metal box as anything else, and it felt cold and stark as his voice echoed behind me.

"Glynn Azuka, I was your board op, or 'fight tech,' from the big battle last night. You know, you did much better than I anticipated. It was my first real combat action. I think you—"

My stance became unsettled, shifting side to side to show I wasn't ready for this conversation. Glynn caught himself with a quick apology and informed me that there was a change of clothes beside my bunk.

"Let me know if those don't fit. I took a guess at your size. I'll wait for you right out here. I'm supposed to escort you to lunch and show you the ropes, so to speak. That's the last time you ever get to sleep in. This place can be—"

I shuffled in place again, closing the door enough to signal I would try on the outfit in question. It's never wise to be rude to one's host, but I wasn't sure how else to achieve progress.

Every inch of my body ached as I pried out of the black jumpsuit. My head pounded from dehydration. Desperate for water, my pace quickened as I donned the well-fitting, camouflage pants and dark green T-shirt. The tan boots were a bit big, but workable.

"Hey, those look right on," Glynn said. "Guess I guessed well then. I'll bet you've never had fatigues on before. There's going to be a lot—"

"Can I get some water? I'm dying of thirst…"

"Yeah, sure. We're going over to the mess hall."

I followed behind him down a narrow, metal-lined hallway,

turning sideways when necessary to let others go by. Every surface appeared washed in a dirty, brown film, with dried and fresh leaks of ooze seeping from the paneling's seams. The smell was that of a machine shop, and the stink of old oil pushed hard into my olfaction.

Glynn continued to babble, much of it lost in the clattering foot traffic and commotion coming from passing rooms. My unfamiliar face conjured a few looks from the hall's flow of army-looking types, but their considerable busyness left most without the time to notice. Glynn was excited about his assignment.

"Mess hall is just ahead, Garret."

"Yeah, good—I just need some water."

"Right, we do have that. So you're in luck."

Yet, there were more pressing concerns than whether this place, wherever it was, had water. Burning questions hung on the tip of my parched tongue, but I dreaded the thought of asking Glynn. His long-winded answers might delay that drink for hours.

He called out a greeting to someone down the hall and we turned to enter a large room. Jay was there, being led by his board op, a young girl I also recognized from the escape craft. Her hair was pulled back into a bun so tight it strained her dark skin, which was the same color as Jay's. A patch on her lapel read "CORAZON." She ushered me into the hall with a "good morning" and a gentle motion from her hand. Jay and I acknowledged each other with jutting chins. He commented on my "nice pants" that were identical to his.

I was relieved to see Beck already seated inside. She glanced up at me, but lacked any perceptible enthusiasm, turning back to her conversation already in progress. It looked like she had managed to land a tech friend with whom she had instant rapport. An alarm blared inside my gut as I dashed for the water fountain.

Lapping the briny, warm water allowed me a moment to think about our predicament. The excitement of our new surroundings was displaced by trepidation. I worried over the thing I held most dear: the tight friendship between Beck and me, a friendship that kept the world at arm's length. This new environment left me with none of the control I was used to.

"C'mon Garret, before the rush hits!" Glynn was beckoning me on, far too cheery for my state of mind. I forced myself to make the best of it.

"The food's not bad most of the time," Glynn grinned. The gruel the mess hall staff was handing out looked to betray that opinion, but I was hungrier than I thought and the aroma of comfort food had overtaken the oily stench.

The four of us filled our trays with chicken gravy and biscuits, and joined Beck and her companion. They tried to stifle their giggles as we filled in the seats around them. The patch on Beck's new friends' fatigues read "KAVITA" and she avoided eye contact with me by glaring at her food. Looking somewhat East Indian, her thick mass of long, black hair was clipped back, leaving the remainder to dangle free.

I kept waiting for formal introductions but none came, only small talk and a reminder our debriefing was at 1300 hours. A nearby clock read 12:10, so I figured 1300 must be fifty minutes away. Just below the clock sat a hastily, spray painted sign: "MESSENGERS" in red, with a cliché red circle and slash running through its center. While not very creative, it was wholly informative. We were breaking bread with the resistance.

"I wonder where big Pak is? He's probably hibernating and we won't see him for a month." Jay had just finished speaking when Pak made his way into the lengthening chow line. His female guide, two feet shorter than him, was pointing out items of interest with enthusiasm, despite his conspicuous yawn and arm stretch. The fatigues suited Pak and I wondered if his dad would have mustered some pride over him. I tried to imagine just what other conversations might be happening back home. Pak and Jay's parents, The CFPO, the school—did they think us criminals? Dead? I decided not to dwell on it any more and took another heaping spoonful of chicken and biscuits.

Mom and Eleanor arrived with an escort; their progress slowed by a queue that stretched out the door. Seeing my mother in a military uniform gave me an epiphany! Business suits be darned. Those army fatigues were just what she needed all along to bring our house under tighter control. Their conversation was drowned out by the hall's increasing noise but I was able to get Mom's attention with some mild waving. She sent me back a half-hearted wave of her own and resumed her discourse without missing a beat. Knowing Mom, she would be running some type of meeting by day's end. Her tour group didn't even attempt to sit near us despite open seats in our vicinity. I would get my space here as I always had. Pak's duo joined our growing clique.

"Hey guys, this is Ivy." He nodded toward a girl who sat down opposite me, so I continued my patch reading: "BAYLOR." Ivy Baylor had a nice ring.

"Ivy's from Georgia," Pak said. "She grew up on a farm." He didn't offer much eye contact with me either. His complete focus was fixed on shoveling down his grub as fast as his fork would allow.

"Yeah, but I pretty much hated it." Ivy's timid voice was laced with a cute Southern drawl. She chirped out a nervous laugh and did her best to stop any attention building her way. Her straight, brown hair hung only a few inches below her standard-issue cap. Soft mumbling kept making its way out of her mouth—something about "going back to the farm and enjoying next time,"—but her words trailed off.

The CORAZON patch broke our uncomfortable silence. "Why do they call you 'Pak'?" Assuming my large friend was about to offer the canned answer I'd heard a thousand times, I was stunned to hear him begin an unfamiliar anecdote.

"My family's Greek, and in Greek, when you add -*aki mou* after a name, it means 'my little.' So 'Phillip-*aki mou*' means "my little Phillip.' Well, my older sister couldn't pronounce that, so she started calling me Philli-*Paki-mou*, which basically morphed into 'Paki-moo.' When I got older, I hated the name, so my parents cut it back to 'Pak,' I can live with that, I guess."

A simultaneous roar spewed from Beck, Jay and me. "WHAT? You never told us that!" We exchanged shocked looks and enjoyed the breakthrough event.

"I knew I'd never hear the end of it, so I kept that to myself," Pak alleged, keeping his eyes firmly on his lunch. "You guys are brutal. Don't tell these three anything. I'm tellin' ya—they're brutal..."

The attention shifted back to the team as we scrambled to argue against the charges. Somebody pointed out the irony in "my little" anything having to do with the massive Pak Pateras and a collective howl broke out louder than it should. The KAVITA patch covered her face with both hands, terrified by the social ruckus. I tucked "Paki-moo" away to have it ready for the right occasion. Yeah, he had been right to keep that from us. It felt good to laugh again. It felt good to be alive.

At ten minutes to the hour, we started to clean up and head for the debriefing. I hoped "debriefing" meant I would get answers to all my questions. As I scraped the remaining food scraps from my tray into a large trash can, a quote Dad had written down in one of his study books rushed back to me: "It's only after you've lost everything that you're free to do anything."

A chain of events, built link by link, had brought me to a unique location, to that place in time. Was this a grand escape from the world I had never felt a part of? Had last night been my victorious David and Goliath moment, or had I roused the wrath of the Philistines and would soon regret it?

"Velops"

enVelop Single Seater XI

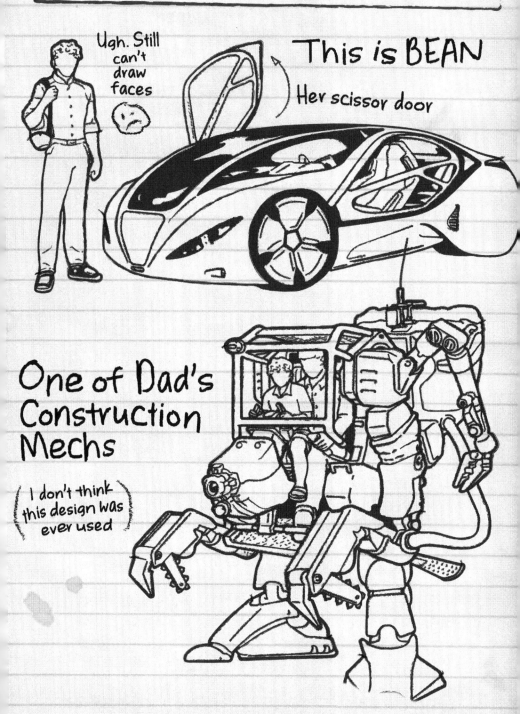

Ugh. Still can't draw faces

This is BEAN

Her scissor door

One of Dad's Construction Mechs

I don't think this design was ever used

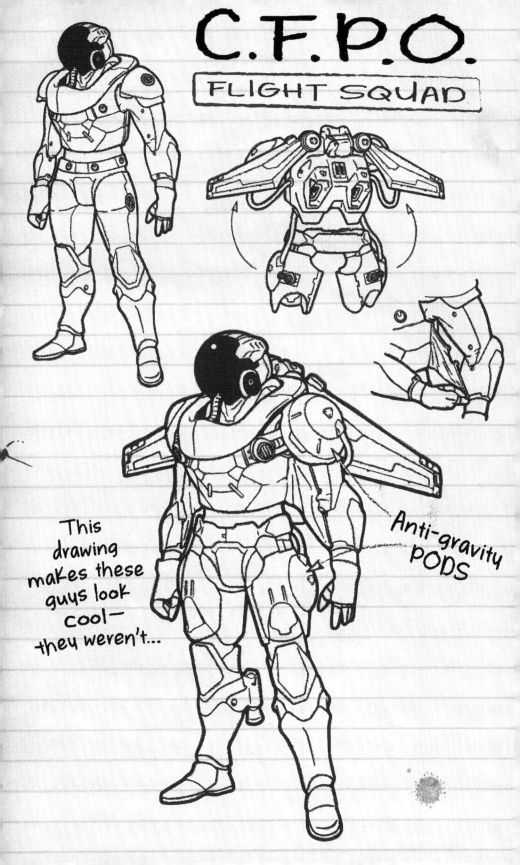

C.F.P.O.
FLIGHT SQUAD

This drawing makes these guys look cool— they weren't...

Anti-gravity PODS

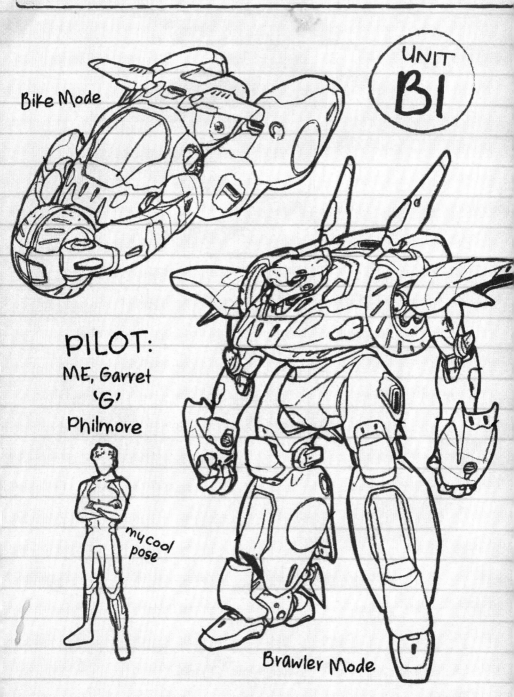

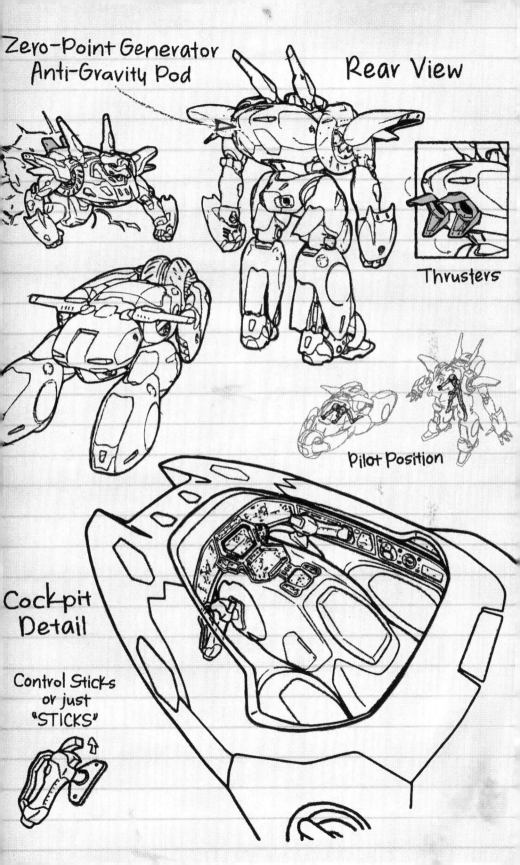

Zero-Point Generator
Anti-Gravity Pod

Rear View

Thrusters

Pilot Position

Cockpit
Detail

Control Sticks
or just
"STICKS"

BRAWLER
VARIABLE MODE

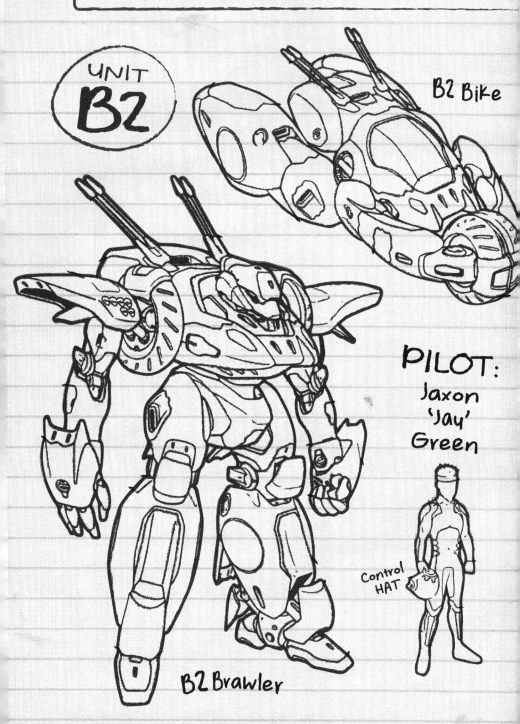

UNIT **B2**

B2 Bike

PILOT:
Jaxon
'Jay'
Green

Control
HAT

B2 Brawler

TYPES

POWER ARMORS

Beck's Bike

UNIT
B3

Queen
O'
HEARTS

PILOT:
Rebecca
'Beck'
Sprankle

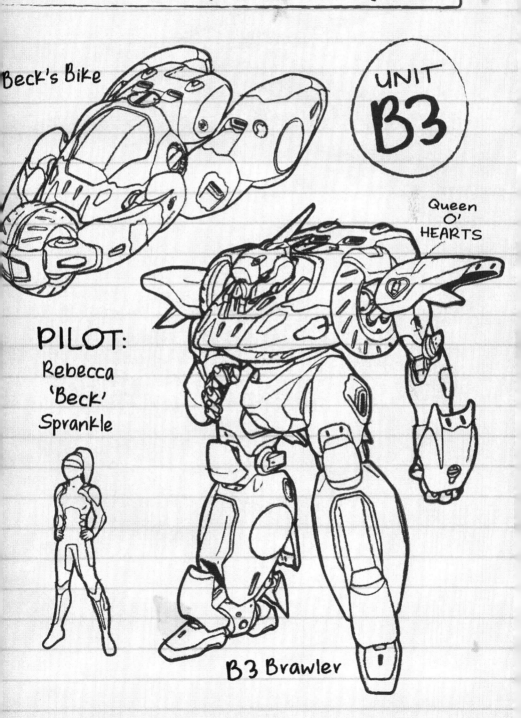

B3 Brawler

CALIBER-TYPE

VARIABLE MODE POWER ARMOR

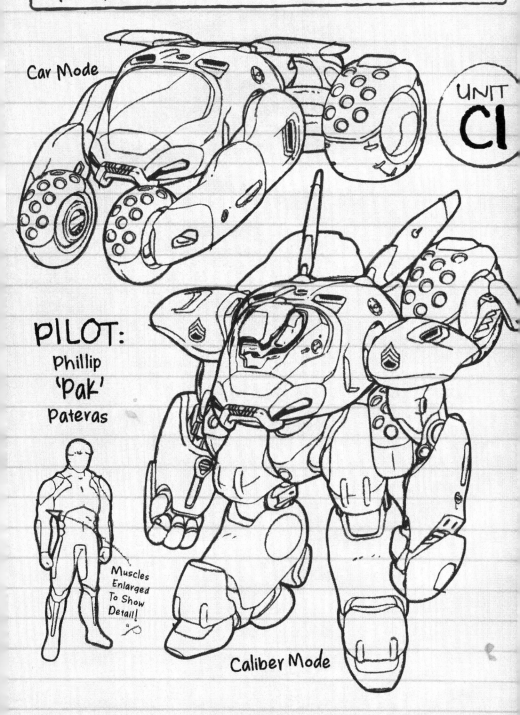

Car Mode

UNIT
C1

PILOT:
Phillip
'Pak'
Pateras

Muscles
Enlarged
To Show
Detail!

Caliber Mode

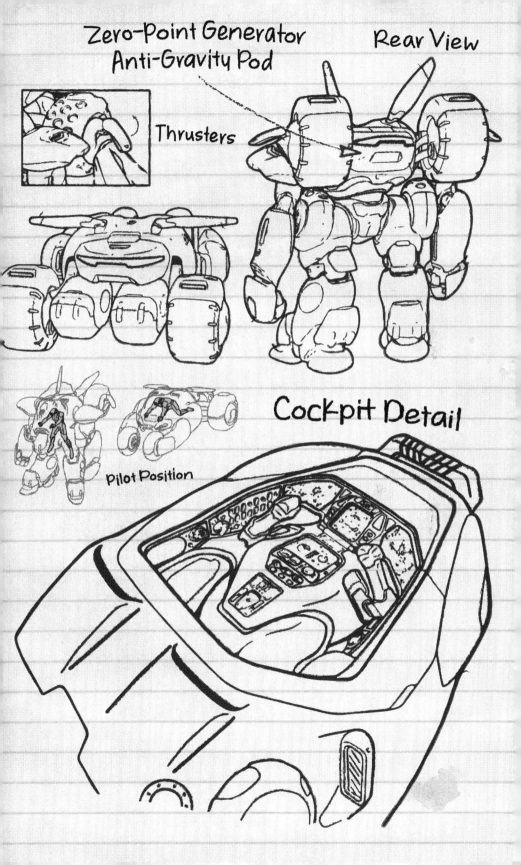

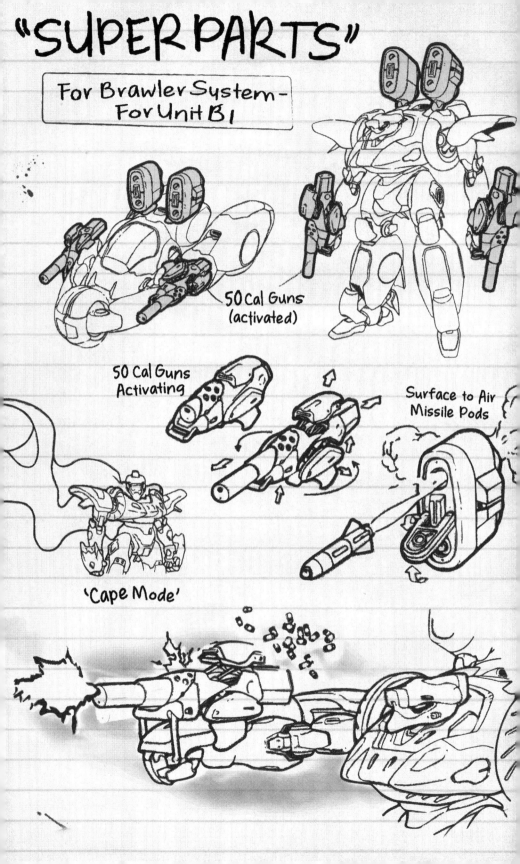

POWER PARTS

For Jaxon's Brawler B2

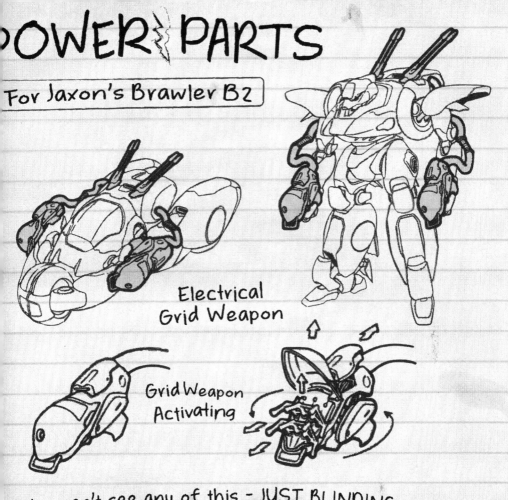

Electrical
Grid Weapon

Grid Weapon
Activating

You can't see any of this – JUST BLINDING LIGHT

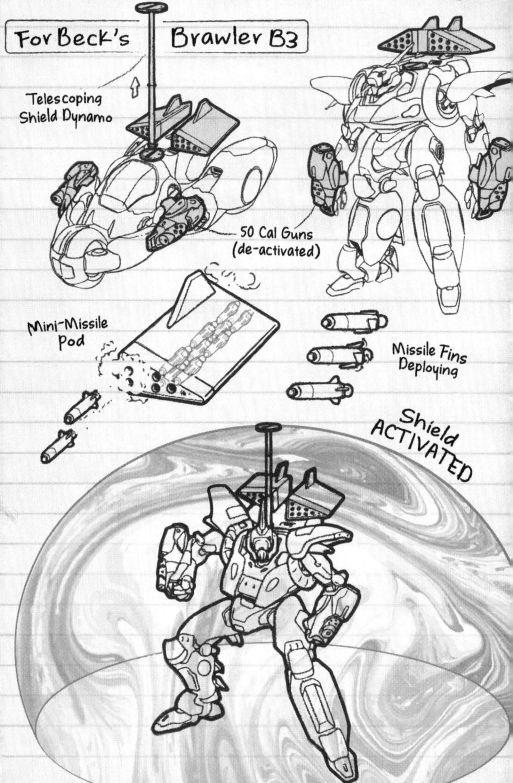

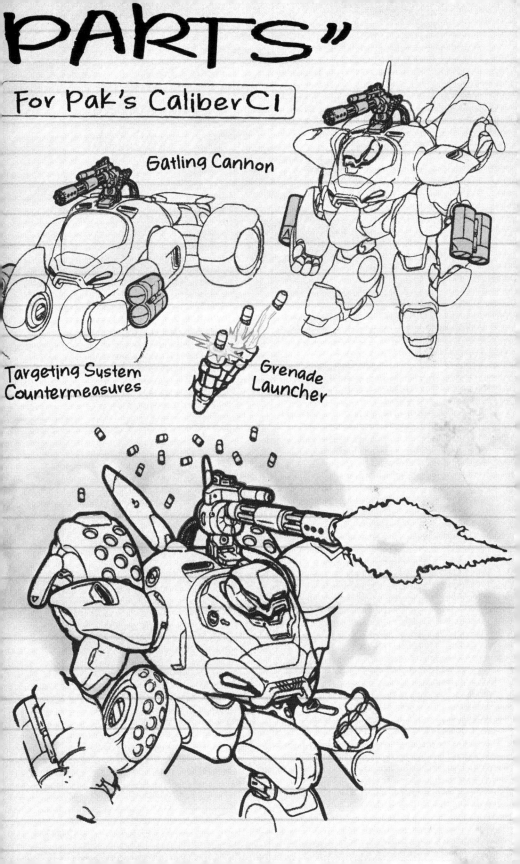

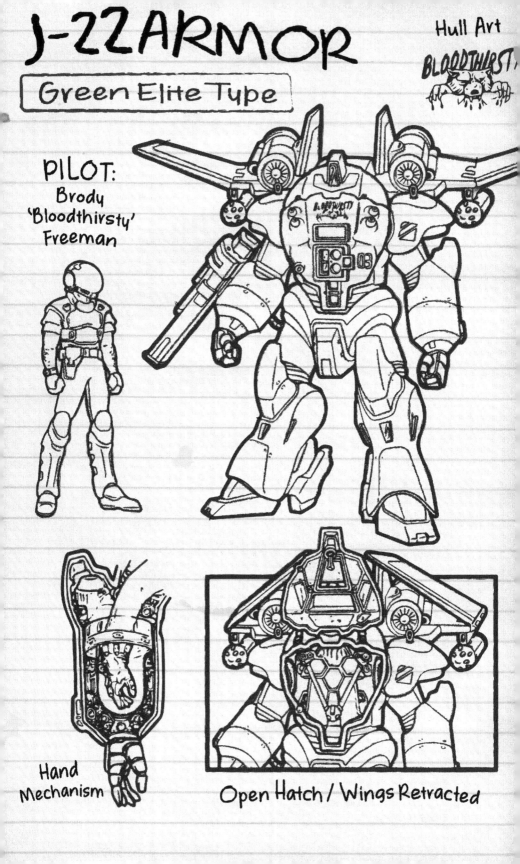

CAVALRY 1&2

GREEN ELITE DROP SHIPS

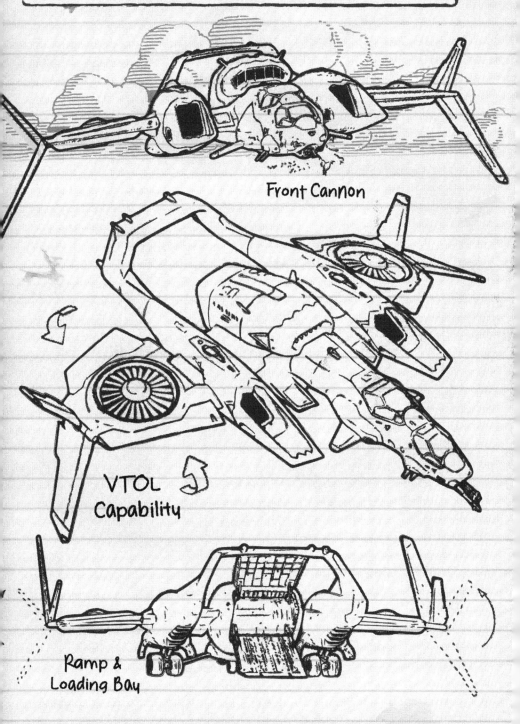

Front Cannon

VTOL
Capability

Ramp &
Loading Bay

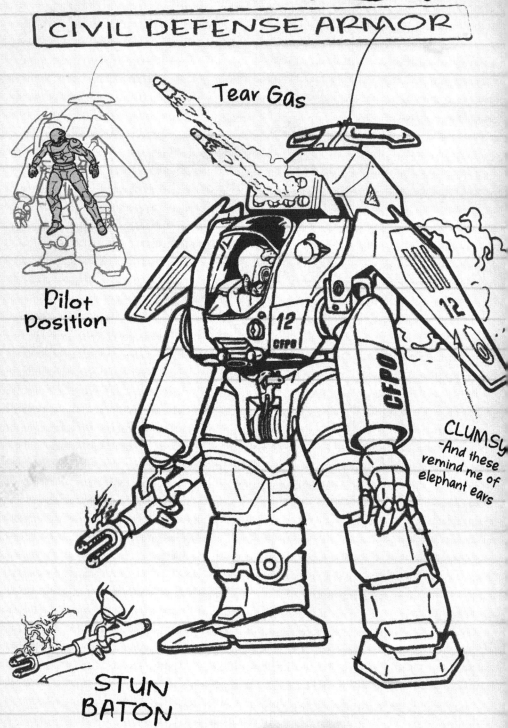

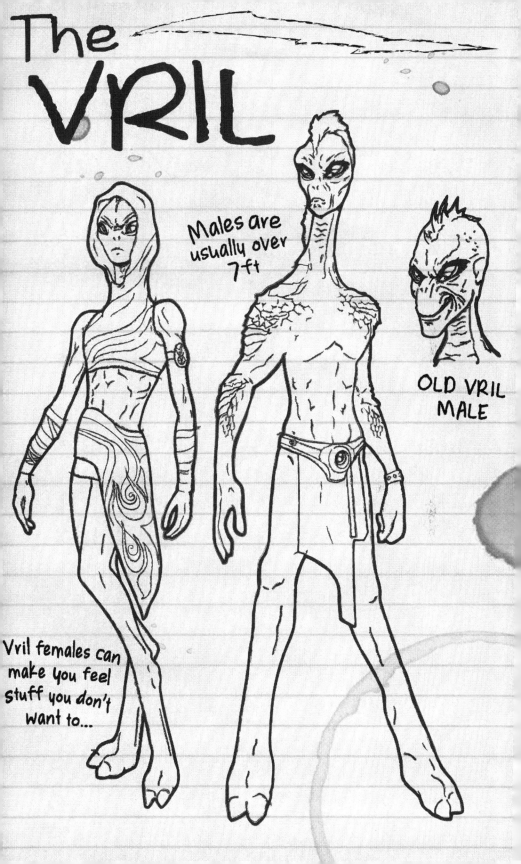

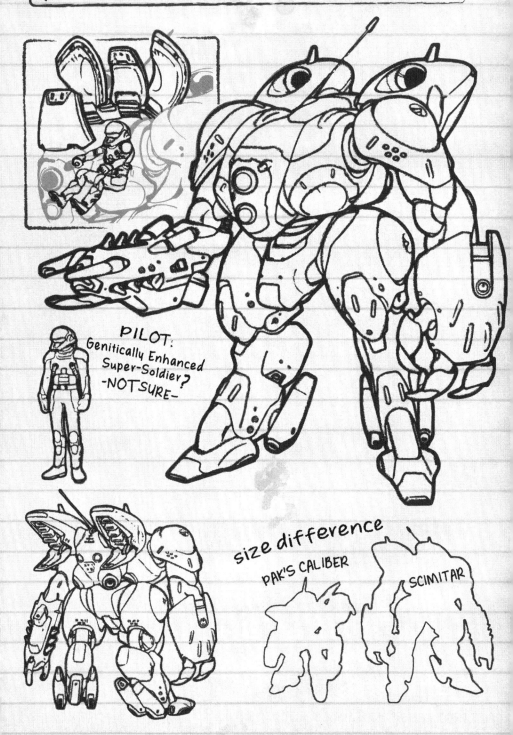

SCIMITAR

CARRIER FIGHTER

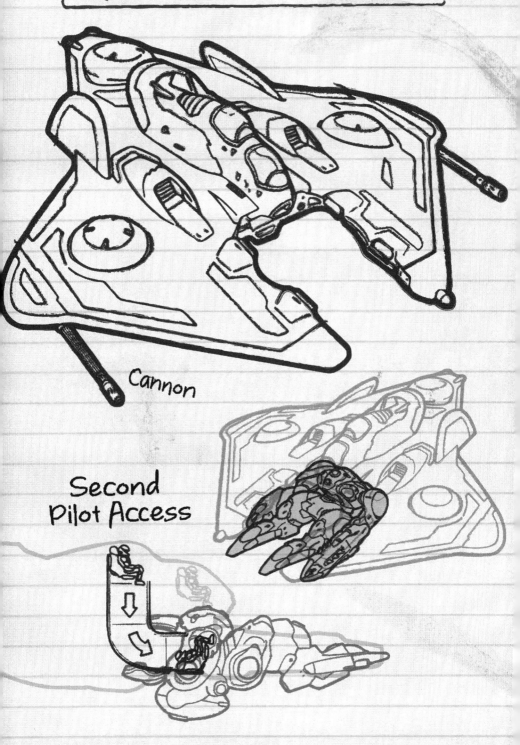

Cannon

Second
Pilot Access

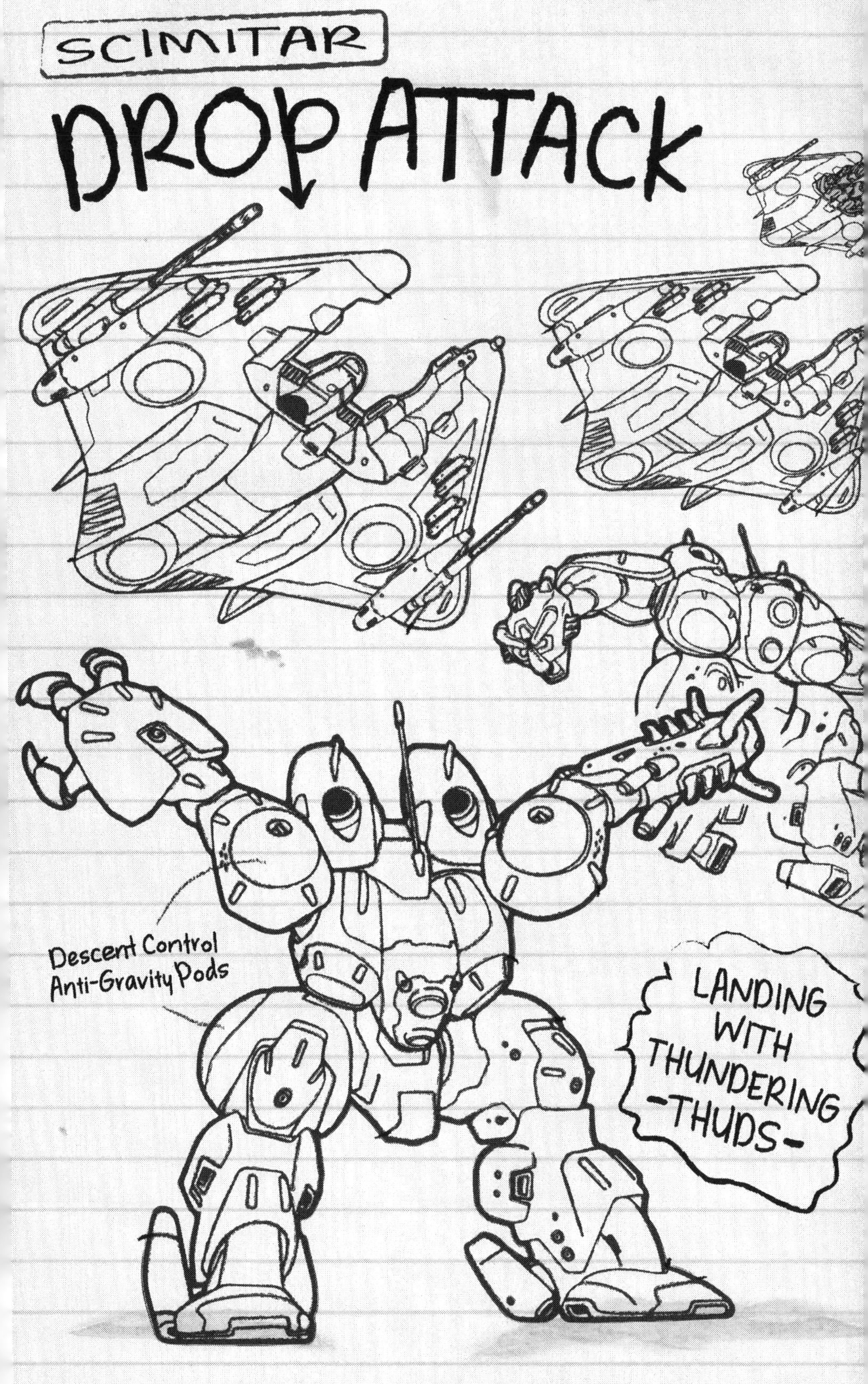
SCIMITAR
DROP ATTACK
Descent Control
Anti-Gravity Pods
LANDING WITH THUNDERING -THUDS-

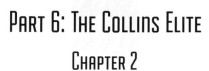

Part 6: The Collins Elite
Chapter 2

"Looking back, it's hard to imagine the citizens of the world not becoming aware, and then vengeful, over the nearly 3,000 Deep Underground Military Bases (D.U.M.B.S.) built all over the planet to the tune of twenty billion each. Before the internet went down, many strong voices sounded the alarm but governments everywhere just kept saying there was nothing to see, move along. Disinformation artists denied it, distracting everyone with effective deception. As Joseph Goebbels said, 'If you tell a big enough lie and tell it frequently enough, it will be believed.'"

—Piper Corcoran, *Can Things Get Any Stranger? Volume II*

The meeting was held in a large room, with over thirty people in attendance. A variety of military uniforms dotted the crowd; a few lab coats, several uni-colored jumpsuits covered with insignias—all engaged in their own murmured conversations. It smelled more like a gym's locker room than old oil and I was already wishing the air would catch some movement. Our lunch group remained together, with our fight techs taking every other seat. Someone wearing a lab coat broke from the crowd toward the front and called the meeting to order.

"Hello, everyone. My name is Dr. Uri Kalko. I am the head of special projects here at Outpost 6. We find ourselves in a unique time, challenged as never before—but I believe in a bright future, a future made possible by our great past."

Dr. Kalko was a small man, looking frail from a life's work that had taken everything. Balding and pale with a strong German accent, he held a half-length pencil and waved it as he spoke. His strong spirit contrasted the quivering hand that wielded it.

"I apologize to those of you who have heard our origins recited before, but I believe it wise to remember one's roots and the cause for which so many have already fought and died. As I look out at these youthful faces here today, I am filled with renewed hope."

Dr. Kalko opened his lecture by reminding us of a time when humans thought themselves alone in the universe, and of the first UFO sightings 100 years ago. Dismissed, the sightings gained little credibility and graduated into the lore of science fiction. Dr. Kalko went on, beaming with pride as his story built.

"The Collins Elite—secretly formed in the early 1950s—was comprised of personnel from within the U.S. government, military, intelligence, and science communities. This group concluded that not only was the UFO issue real but that the craft had nothing to do with literal extraterrestrials. Remaining in the shadows, even from fellow agencies, the Collins Elite were privy to information few could acquire or grasp, even if they had access to it: That UFOs, or "aliens," were an occult phenomenon, and notorious figures such as Aleister Crowley and Jack Parsons had opened the door of our world to them through their performance of ancient, satanic rituals. The remnants of the Collins Elite carry on today, in this room, and in hidden places throughout the globe."

Dr. Kalko even managed to make those awful quote marks with his fingers when he said the word "aliens." Dad would have loved that.

The doctor continued, directing much of his talk our way with a kind delivery.

"With NHEs or nonhuman entities, and their craft now pouring in from other places or dimensions, the evidence mounted. Debris from several downed vehicles was collected in the late 1940s, with much more soon to take place. The public thought the rumors were a hoax, while those who found the craft viewed them as extraterrestrials, beings visiting from far-away worlds. The Collins Elite ascribed to neither view. They believed these were orchestrated events to give the illusion that deep-space alien life existed, and at the same time lure us with outlandish new technologies. And the *Vril...*"

Doctor Kalko trailed off. His hands met together at his mouth, and even his eyes shut in a moment of mock prayer. I looked about the room and read many nervous faces. Some eyes got bigger in anticipation, others looked as a loss. The doctor took a slow breath and rejoined us.

"The Vril...hardly "alien." Instead, the very seed of the serpent himself. Gone *perhaps,* but still bruising our heels. They are a talk for another time..."

The frail doctor shook himself back into his original speech and went ahead. He spoke about a rash of extra-dimensional craft crashing, or being shot down by various governments around the world, in a tone that suggested this information was commonplace. Humanity's brightest began a race to reverse engineer the technologies found within these craft such as "dynamic-counterbary." This repulsive force made flying machines act contra-gravitationally, allowing them to "float away" without jets or rockets. Sounded familiar (my own backyard jumping to mind) and terrifying.

New energy sources were also discovered within these captured UFOs, giving not only our aircraft designs unlimited power but also civilization itself. By the early 1950s, science and technology sectors touted that we were on the verge of an electro-gravitic breakthrough, with public designs on the books for Mach 3 anti-gravity craft. Then, the subject went taboo, with anyone discussing such matters roundly mocked. Somewhere, someone or something had decided these advancements, as well as the truth about countless alien ships flooding our airspace, would remain classified. The doctor remained amicable despite the subject matter, adjusting his round lenses higher on his nose every few sentences.

"But with all the public sightings it soon became impossible to deny the existence of these ships, so, in 1956, UFO investigation groups endorsed the extraterrestrial hypothesis. The Collins Elite suspected this as being an act of disinformation, designed to draw attention away from the mounting demonic and paranormal evidence it was gathering to the contrary.

"Momentum built towards this deception and soon complex alliances formed to promote the idea of extraterrestrials. They found allies in the New Age movement, transhumanism, Freemasonry, luciferian Illuminists, and anyone who wanted to end Christianity in favor of the next Golden Age—an age when superior beings from the heavens would again show true enlightenment to mankind.

"A priesthood of sorts was disseminated to bring about a climactic series of events that we believe we are in the midst of even now. I, for one, am enthused to have Dr. Bigsby with us and to see if anything can yet be done to turn the tide in favor of good—before it's too late. Allow me to now introduce our revered base commander, Colonel Milo Reed."

If Dr. Kalko was the picture of gentleness, Colonel Reed resided at the opposite pole. The colonel strode to the front of the room, his biceps bulging from short-sleeved fatigues. He barked out at us like a cornered, junkyard dog.

"The Shadow Government—the black helicopters of legend—they were not dismantled by the new government, I assure you." Reed used a long pause to look over the room.

"The top tier remains, ready to do the bidding of its high priests, who have now removed everyone else from the equation. They're more heavily funded than ever before, upgrading their black copters in favor of trans-planetary warships of all sizes, mobile power armors so advanced it makes our stuff look like it belongs on the trash heap."

The colonel stood an imposing six feet, six inches, with tan skin and silver hair showing under his rank-adorned cap. He used a rolled up manila folder as his only prop, smacking his hand with it for emphasis or using it to point toward random individuals to verify their focus. The room was alert.

"My grandfather was one of the original Collins Elite, and he worked to find out the identity of these mystery military units, the ones in favor of human abductions. These sniveling cowards made dirty deals with the so-called Vril. In exchange for technology, they traded human slaves with those long-necked freaks, and this *treaty* may have involved one of our own presidents..."

Reed bit the side of his own cheek and crushed the end of the folder. He was a man long bent over his secret war, rage still bubbling like a cauldron.

"They let their puppets cut the world's population down before betraying and blaming them for all our woes in the World Court. Their minions—the rich and powerful, political rulers, nonhuman entities—some legit, some manufactured—got caught with their pants down when the music stopped. They popularized the term 'Illuminati' right under their noses and then handed 'em over to the lynch mob. Now the world thinks we're set for a future of peace and prosperity. It looks like our alien saviors are here for our own good, but that's just the set-up they wanted. People; the great deception, the great falling away, is now set to begin." The colonel looked me square in the eye to see if I'd turn away. I didn't and he went on.

"There's no one left to fight them. Only a scant few, like us. You are among last resisters, and we are dwindling. Lost two more yesterday. If we could please have a moment of silence for Corporal Maximuk and Private Boscoe, who perished bringing Dr. Bigsby and Dr. Philmore's family safely here."

My heart sank as the reality of these men's lives, given up for me, became stark. I wondered if they had any family on base, or what they'd been like to hang around with only two days ago. Sacrifice was no longer an abstract concept. It was the only reason I was still alive. The colonel's voice cleared its gravel and he continued.

"There are several new faces here today, including the ones from Dr. Bigsby's group. You're probably wondering where the heck you are. Well, don't! That's just the way we like it. Our enemy can scan thoughts. Let that sink in. Don't even think about your location. Just know you're about a half mile underground, in what might be the last outpost of the resistance. If you are unhappy with our fight, our way, or what we're trying to accomplish, I'll gladly air-drop your sorry butts back home the next chance I get."

Then, after Reed spoke the word "screen," a large, floating monitor materialized, featuring an aerial photograph of a scorched landscape. Colonel Reed pointed his folder at an image of a blackened smear.

"This crater *here* was the Philmores' home…"

From a few rows behind me, Mom let out a muffled gasp.

PART 6: THE COLLINS ELITE
CHAPTER 3

"Like Dr. Karla Turner, the legend of Phil Schneider existed beyond the outer fringes of conspiracy theory. We now realize that he not only sounded the alarm, but also had come face to face with the Vril and risked everything to tell the world. After a dozen attempts on his life, the 'Establishment Hierarchy', with their vast secrets to protect, murdered him. Phil's talking videos warned us from the grave for years before we lost the net. Now that the Dulce Wars and other early battles with the 'Tall Grays' have been well documented, the bravery and heroism of Mr. Schneider must be fully acknowledged."

—Piper Corcoran, *Can Things Get Any Stranger? Volume II*

My eyes bulged as I thought about my mother's immaculate décor being incinerated in one big puff of smoke. But my mind raced to Dad's things—especially his books, and all of the highlighted pages now gone.

So much for the development, I thought. *It went from Hemlock Hill to Hemlock Hole. And Sorry Popo and Gigio, I trust the end was quick and painless.* As the colonel revealed the extent of the damage I prayed our neighbors had good insurance.

"They've had the whole area on lockdown," he said, "with no one allowed to come within a few clicks of it while they clean up all the evidence. The neighborhood had been evacuated by the locals, so there were few civilian casualties." By few, I hoped he meant none.

Colonel Reed continued to point out various downed craft and wreckage. He explained that Newt had sent a secret communiqué earlier that day, detailing the school attack and how the team had barely escaped with our lives. The colonel then dispatched Cavalry 1, our eventual rescue ship, to gather intel and remain in the area on high alert. Reed nodded toward Newt who was sitting on the far side of the room, signaling his turn up front. Newt said a quiet "Thank you" as the colonel stepped back to give him way. Newt looked like he hadn't slept in a week.

"Thank you, Colonel. Thank you, friends and colleagues. I'm pleased to be here—long-term at last—and to have brought some of the prototypes with me that Dr. Philmore and I developed at our secret lab in Northern Idaho.

"As some know, I was troubled after escaping the black projects, and when I reunited with Dr. Philmore, he wanted nothing to do with the military. I owed much to the man, so I agreed to work at his facility and help birth his idea for a radical new, variable mode, power armor system."

Newt's skin was blood-flushed and sweaty. His decrepit appearance made the presentation look more like an interrogation than a briefing.

"I never shared with Dr. Philmore, Evan, where this base or any other outpost was located. I kept this from him for security purposes and to alleviate the pressure that might cause on our working relationship. He wasn't keen at all on the idea of a rebel force getting a hold of our work, even a God-fearing group like this one, but, as we saw the potential in the new C-Type Caliber system take shape, he warmed to the idea."

Newt described how Dad claimed to be on the cusp of discovering the source of Earth's waning gravity. He took special care to address several people in the crowd who had strong objections that such a phenomena could be artificially induced. Newt didn't say what he personally believed but gave a vote of confidence that Dad's findings appeared sound. Discovery of my father's note: *Son, they are stealing our gravity* was locked tight within me. The little voice, not sounding so little anymore, screamed it would be foolish to bring it up. I wasn't even tempted to do so. Newt had to stop and collect himself at the memory of his old friend.

"Evan thought he was getting close to a breakthrough in his investigation and suspected he was being followed. Shortly after, he and I talked of jumping out to this installation with his family and all his research, but then he vanished, poor chap. I urged Mrs. Philmore to come anyway, but, as you might expect, she wanted to grieve and, if possible, give her son a normal life. I frustrated many of you here by withholding our research. But with Evan's concerns, I wanted to honor him, and Marcee, and wait until the proper time..."

Newt talked about the Brawler and Caliber designs and called for their schematics to appear on the screen. The sight of our transforming suits caused an increased mumbling among the attendees. When Newt mentioned our team's impressive skills after training for such a short time, I had to suppress a smile. But my blood pressure surged when he went into what he called "virtual, capsule-induced, combat training." The idea of pill-programs running simulations during sleep, with actual awareness to be triggered later, still astounded me. I imagined what else I might "know" without the actual realization of it yet. I felt kind of sick as I pondered Newt fiddling around in our brains. He claimed it was only an emergency precaution, that the process did not bend the will. It only provided the skills necessary should the subject chose to take action on their own. Newt looked at Pak and tried to stay strong, but he faltered and took that moment to ask for a stool. Someone rushed one up to him. He sat down, stroking his swollen face for a moment before resuming.

"I never intended to force them to do anything, and deeply regret it if they feel violated."

Pak's demeanor remained cold and unmoving.

"Evan's disappearance still grieves me so," Newt lamented, veering from the uncomfortable subject by looking at the ceiling, as if Dad were somewhere up there, being held hostage in the ventilation system.

"Perhaps he HAD discovered something about the gravity problem. I can't be sure, since Evan withheld his findings for security reasons. Then when forces attempted to capture Evan's son and his friends, there were reasons to suspect they might also have discovered our secret laboratory. With that possibility, it was no longer safe to use the jump-gate to evacuate the area. They could have sent interference into the flux field, causing us to simply go nowhere. We could not have risked that option."

Newt looked like he was about to dismount his stool when he added something I'd hoped he wouldn't neglect.

"Oh, and to Jaxon and Phillip, I wanted you to know that I urged your parents to come with me last night. However, I barged into their meeting like a madman, and it's no wonder they decided to remain. They will be questioned, but knowing nothing, they will be left alone. They are safe. Perhaps at some later date we can get them out. Don't lose hope."

What our former mentor failed to consider is that Pak's father already had "the cancer" and there might not be a later date. Newt then identified and addressed Mom, and said something about how the two of them had agreed that adding Dad's research to the Collins efforts was appropriate so long as certain protocols were maintained. I turned around to see Mom give everyone a solemn nod. Colonel Reed showed some humanity by helping Newt to his feet and thanking him for his contribution. As Newt found his original seat, the colonel called after him.

"So, please doctor, prepare a demonstration of these variable exo-suit systems later this evening, 1700 hours. Nothing fancy, just an overview of their capabilities. We'll clear a space on the flight deck. Let our people know if you need anything." I wondered what that might entail as performance anxiety vice-gripped on my already rattled nerves.

When Major Freeman joined the colonel at the front, I vowed to step up my workouts. The two men bulged with lumps of camouflage and muscle, reducing my faint manliness to a flicker. Colonel Reed asked the major to detail the fight and discuss any tactics or patterns exhibited by the enemy. I was surprised when Major Freeman called on our group for perspective, allowing us to comment. It hinted of respect, making me feel a part of his task force, even if it was only the lowest rung.

Fervor kicked up in the room when the talk turned to the weapons tested and their results. Jay's green Brawler and its lightning blaster were the most anticipated and celebrated. The wicked contraption far exceeded expectations. A superconductive electrical weapon, it drained away power from the aerial grid, with the ability to direct it to as many as fifty targets simultaneously. Jay's lightning fried twenty-nine ships and suits, and caused a four-state blackout that was still in effect. A large portion of lab coats and military types in the audience agreed the device might not ever be viable again, as forces of the shadow government would be scrambling to erect safeguards against its destructive power.

When I recounted the Gs being zapped, both in my back yard and in the garage just prior to the assault, the topic of a possible enemy gravity weapon sent the meeting off kilter. Several groups voiced their disbelief and began arguing amongst themselves. If Dad's note felt off limits before, it was vault-locked now. Colonel Reed let the bickering go on for a few moments until the volume built into a rabid shouting match.

"Look, people, we're just telling it. You can debate it in due time and include your opinions in your regular reports. I think that's all for now. Pastor, wrap us up here."

Prayer at that moment was another bizarre event at the end of a long list. A kind looking gentleman stood in the middle of the room, wearing a cream turtleneck, an out-of-date gray sport coat, blue jeans, and dark-rimmed glasses. He was glossy bald on top, but had a coal-black beard that climbed up over his ears and wrapped itself around the back of his head.

"Hello, welcome to the new faces," the man said. "I'm Pastor Babineaux. I look forward to meeting and talking with each of you. We do have services on Sunday in the mess at 0900 hours after breakfast. Attendance has been a little light of late. So I hope you will all join me there tomorrow morning. I don't ask for any money, so that can't be scaring you away." He chuckled at his own joke, turning about the room to display a gentle smile.

The pastor offered a short prayer and the colonel shouted out a last reminder about the night's pending demonstration. I was feeling even more nervous about it and I looked for Beck to test her reaction. Scanning the dissolving crowd, I could see her and her KAVITA friend gabbing with each. It looked as if they'd muzzled in all their words throughout the meeting and now they were bursting forth all at once. The two were almost to the exit door when I considered calling out for her. I changed my mind. Something about her was already gone.

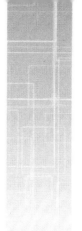

Part 6: The Collins Elite
Chapter 4

"One of our groups in the Air Force raided an underground base near Montauk in Sag Harbor, Long Island, in 1996. The information they uncovered about mind control, depopulation plans and the coming alien saviors was more than mind-blowing.

Finding out about my grandfather's secret life, and discoveries like these, forever cemented my loyalty to the cause."

—Colonel Milo Reed, *Life Inside the Collins Elite*

The tripe stew, or "Cau Cau," as the mess staff called it, was looking more like modern art than a breakfast. An aluminum tray was its substitute canvas. It was far too early to be eating food like that. I missed the smell of Mom's cinnamon toast and the comfort of an ordered life.

Arriving with only ten minutes left for breakfast, the line was nonexistent and so were most of the patrons. A flurry of activity had begun about the base and I was still trying to clear the cobwebs. I'd ignored Glynn's knocking until he had given up and went away. So I missed Jay, Beck, and the gang. Doubtful they even noticed my absence, though my mood was not one suited to be around anyone anyway.

The previous night's demonstration of my piloting prowess had gone about as badly as it could have. My Brawler got a brutal beat-down from Brody's superior combat suit. I should have expected actual contact once he powered up his armor and clanked into test area. He thinks the Brawlers are toys, gimmicks, and a waste of resources. It was proven when he knocked me flat and stood on my chest to drive home the point.

Pak, reluctant to participate because the R&D staff in attendance was salivating to see his Caliber, asked Newt to remove the weapons systems before he would mount up. Newt hemmed and hawed until I thought Pak might punch him if he didn't comply. But after Brody made a fool of me, Pak did what he's always done: take on our bullies. When their armors started roving in circles like two sumo wrestlers ready to collide, Newt asked the colonel to order a stand down.

Initially, I was more incensed with the dent Major Freeman had made in B1 than I was by the blow to my ego. Though considering there's not a spot on his combat armor without a dent, I realized how skewed my priorities were. Power armors were not objects to shine up for a weekend date. They were war machines plain and simple, a means to an end. I'd wanted to be free of the social trappings of my town and school, and there I was. Nothing mattered at Outpost 6 except "God, cause, unit, family." Major Freeman exemplified this and his easy victory made it impossible to avoid my shortcomings. Now I was dealing with a hangover called "I'm not the hot-shot I thought I was."

I'd always imagined "Garret" as the G in Zero-Gs, but maybe the name was merely declaring itself better off without me.

But what would Beck have done in my place? She might have flattened the major. As much as I would have liked to see that, my pride was grateful that she wasn't the one who ended up saving the little boy who couldn't. Though Beck didn't seem the least bit concerned with my failure. Whenever I risked a glance to find her in the crowd, she didn't even appear to be listening to her KAVITA shadow, her mind off in the deep blue. Cheating death had not brought us closer together. It had succeeded in killing something; killing our friendship, killing the team.

"Hey there, sport." Minerva plunked down across from me, bursting with energy. She leaned over to look up at my sulking face. I noticed her surname patch for the first time: "DOON." A sight better than that stew, her long hair flowed free of her flight helmet. The mane of curly-brown locks bounced around like she'd just stepped out of a salon. A strange streak of blue ran down along one side.

"You're not torturing yourself about last night are you?" she demanded. "C'mon! You just got here. Get right back up in the saddle, kid." She patted my arm to transfer some of her positive energy but it was time to accept my ineptitude.

"Eh, well, I wish I would have known it was anything goes. But I'm not sure I could have done anything about it anyway."

"It's not you. It's that pretend suit you're driving," Minerva said, itching the side of her nose with a perfectly painted pinky nail. "You need to take a spin in one of our *real* combat armors. They're kinda old, but they're *bad*. I'll take you down to the hangar some time and let you power one up. Ol' Bloodthirsty won't know what hit him."

I nodded not at the truth of what she said, but at the fact that her talented pep talk had left me no other choice. My forehead bunched and I attempted a serious tone.

"How did you get mixed up in this?" I motioned to the room around us. Minerva's eyes darted about and she hopped up from the bench. Her mouth opened to say something but she never got the chance.

"Well—Good morning, everyone! I'm glad to see more of you here this week than last."

I was facing the far wall, heedless to the comings and goings behind me until Pastor Babineaux's voice turned me around. Twenty or so folks were seated in the mess hall now, their metal trays exchanged for Bibles. I turned back to ask Minerva what I should expect, and whether I should run, but she was at the exit.

"Hey!" I shouted a whisper after her. "Aren't you staying?"

"No, it's not my thing," her face scrunching to reinforce the point. "I'll catch you later." With that, she took the corner.

"Can I open us in prayer?"

Pastor Babineaux's clothing was the same as before, only the cream turtleneck was now exchanged for a black. His face bragged an irresistible smile, and his silken voice could make even a prison camp tolerable. Maybe that was his true purpose there. I was relieved the gang had forgotten about the service or was avoiding it, leaving me as an anonymous observer.

We sang some traditional hymns, a few people shared what God had been doing in their lives, and then the pastor spoke for such a short time that I wished he'd gone on longer. Any misgivings about the man were evaporated before they had a chance to form. Remaining seated after his dismissal, my insides wanted something they were certain this bearded saint had the power to give.

"Hello, Garret." Pastor Babineaux wandered over and sat at a parallel table making himself comfortable. The mess hall was now empty and quiet except for the occasional distant clang of breakfast cleanup.

"What's on your mind?"

The words tumbled out of me: "Did you ever have the feeling that you were supposed to be somewhere? Or that a message was made for you?"

"Many times," the pastor answered. "Is the Lord trying to tell you something? Maybe He's called you to a purpose soon to be revealed."

The conversation felt like it could have been our fiftieth talk and I didn't even know how he knew my name.

"Not sure," I eventually replied. "I did get a vision once at our house church that I was sharpening my sword for some future battle. I guess I'm in it now."

"And how do you feel about that?"

"Conflicted," I said. "Doesn't the Bible say to 'turn the other cheek' and not to kill? But aren't we at war? Is it different in war? I mean, did Jesus end war and killing for His followers?"

The pastor readjusted his position on the bench and let out a long sigh, slowing the rapid pace of our conversation.

"You said you felt like you were sharpening your sword. Well, Christ did say quite a lot about those: 'They that take the sword shall perish by the sword'... 'If you don't have a sword, sell your cloak and buy one.' There are more scriptures I could recite, and on the surface their meanings may seem to conflict one another. But in the end, I think our own swords matter little. It's only *His* that makes a difference. Jesus said, 'I came not to bring peace, but to bring a sword;' a double-edged sword of indefensible, spoken truth. This kind of sword can be quite problematic to our ways of thinking."

"If I take up a sword, I will die in battle, then?" I pictured dying in the great Battle of Hemlock Hill and contemplated if that sat well. It did. Going out in a hail of plasma fire against the bad guys seemed a fitting end for the hero I imagined myself. But sudden and cold sweat broke free on my skin when I remembered my moment of doubt at the Firefight: believing God had abandoned me to a horde of deadly Scimitars. Shame over a blatant lack of faith, I had not risen tall in the face of terror, trusting in the unseen God. I'd lost all heart. I'd blown it. It was difficult to shake off the rattling memory and focus on the Pastor's ongoing dissertation.

"Yes, of course it's possible you'll die," he answered, adding, "but not taking up the sword can end in death as well. Jesus set the example of non-conflict, giving up His life and asking the Father to forgive His assailants in the midst of crucifixion. To forgive those who persecute you. It's hard to get around that."

"So what we did the other night was wrong?" I asked. "We shot down a lot of those ships. There were pilots in those, but Newt says they're not human."

"We have to be careful not to rationalize our actions."

"What are you doing here with this group? Are you trying to talk them out of fighting?" The pastor pursed his lips for a moment, weighing his response.

"Dr. Bigsby has some valid points, and I've seen the evidence," he said. "Those enemy soldiers are more manufactured than they are born, but I'm still not sure. What I am certain of though, is that there is a force coming against humanity that is purely evil, and not of this world."

I almost put my fingers in the air to make the quote-marked "aliens" signal before the pastor had a chance. He of course went there, and expounded on all that I'd heard from Mom and Dad a million times. The visitor's sudden appearance saved our world, but people's faith in God had plummeted. *Blah, blah, blah* I thought. I sighed and realized I wanted to talk about Garret—my life—my problems. The pastor failed to read my impatient expression and continued.

"They're not just targeting Christianity. They want to place themselves in the position of authority, in the position of creatorship. The Church was and is weak, and will fall like a house of cards when presented with this new false gospel. The pre-Meltdown Christian body was overtaken by comfort, undone by entertainment, and unhinged from God. And we still haven't regrouped. The gates of hell will not prevail against us—but it's sure going to get dicey for a while."

"Are you saying we *can* fight them, then?"

"Jesus says to love your brother and your neighbor. These things are neither. You will have to listen to the Holy Spirit for guidance and be obedient. These Messengers may be some type of *unsanctioned creation* that God is set against, as He was in the past. It's possible we are passing into a time when God will use some of His people to execute His wrath on the *reprobates,* so to speak, but the price will be high to be one of those slayers." Pastor Babineaux left me no time to respond before going on.

"Chronicles tells us that someone named Benaiah slew two lion-men of Moab, whatever they were. Another of David's mighty men killed three hundred enemy warriors with a spear, and was honored for it. Is that what you want—to be God's judgment against the wicked? Blood spattered all over your face, your muscles aching from the slaughter? You look like a fair-haired, innocent boy to me. Or are your looks deceiving?"

The pastor's smile and sympathetic look reinforced what he really thought.

"Do you mind if I call you Pastor B?" I asked.

He closed his eyes and exhaled a soft laugh through his nose.

"No, of course not. I'd be honored." There was a pause before he shifted gears. "It's not right for a boy to lose his father. I heard he was a good man. I'm sorry for your loss."

"No, it's not right," I said. "I would like to find out who did it and wring—" I heard the hate slip out as if it were someone else.

"'Vengeance is mine, says the Lord.' I'm sure you know that one. I'm done preaching for today, but I will say that revenge can eat the soul. It violates the attitude God commanded us to have towards our enemies. As strange as it may sound, you're better off praying for whoever it was, and petitioning heaven about their unjust deeds. Perhaps God will lay them at your feet. You may end up amazed and thankful for His intervention, with your conscience clean."

Looking away from Pastor B's gaze, I realized I *did* want the blood of those who killed my father to be dripping off my face and onto the floor. Like striking Timmy Gorgola and watching him gasp for air, I wanted to enjoy watching Dad's murderers pay.

How did Jesus pray for those crucifying Him? He even asked the Father not to hold their sin against them. I felt incapable of anything like that. Maybe I *was* destined to die by the sword. Pastor B managed to speak even more kind and soft than before.

"He who overcomes in one trial merits a sharper trial still, I've heard it said..."

I tried to hold back the tears begging to come out but they were beyond resisting.

"Look around here, Garret. Spirits are low. These people are looking for a leader, an inspiration. They don't need another gun. They need a man of faith who shuts himself in with God, who prepares his heart before Him and who learns to hear His voice." He paused for a moment to let me cry it out and rubbed my hair with his pudgy fingers.

"Wouldn't you rather march around the enemy city and SHOUT the walls down than to lunge at it with a pick and shovel—or sword?"

I didn't have the patience to walk around a city, nor the faith. Pastor B was imploring me to take the high road and I felt it calling. But instant justice, carried out by my own hands, felt a lot more gratifying. It wouldn't bring Dad back though. Just then, a resounding announcement boomed through the mess hall, stealing away the quiet.

"Attention. Attention. A through D Groups please report to the Operations Center right away. REPEAT: A through D Groups please report..."

"That's us—" Pastor B put his hand on my shoulder as I wiped at my face.

"Me even?"

"Yeah, you're with me. C'mon."

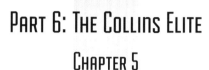

Part 6: The Collins Elite
Chapter 5

*"The good Lord has placed me here to do more than just be
a comfort during difficult circumstances. I must steer His
sheep back to Him despite the horrors of war. But can one be
guarded and peace loving, yet strong and supportive of their
cause—simultaneously? I mean, it can't just be praise the
Lord and pass the ammunition."*

—Jasper Babineaux, *The Atheists have Left the Foxhole*

The casual feel of the debriefing room had been replaced by
nervousness, made more so by a packed house with many standing
along the back wall. I was wondering just how many people were
there at the facility when I saw a sign I hadn't noticed before.

A piece of board several feet wide had been bolted into the metal
paneling, creating two distinct ooze marks from the incisions. In
permanent marker, carefully written, were the words "To make war
we must and will harden our hearts—General Tecumseh Sherman,
1864." Pastor B and I slinked through the crowd and settled into an
open spot, with my shoulder touching against the board's sharp edge.
Colonel Reed strode to the front of the room and called for a screen.
He looked to be bearing a great burden.

"The CRL had their regular spill-the-beans session today. However, I can assure you it was not more of their usual fluffery. Hear for yourselves." The colonel backed away from the screen as a recording came to life.

The massive hall where the Council of Resplendent Light met looked chaotic, yet somehow more festive. The lyceum appeared darker this time, with white lighting running along its endless aisles. The monitor zoomed in on the stage as a man with a dark complexion and snow-white smile, stood. His golden nameplate read: *Rakesh Kadam, Teacher.* He dabbed his forehead with a cloth and returned it to his pocket before presenting.

"We are pleased to announce there is indeed something big waiting for us up ahead." The speaker took his time, looking far to his left and then right, allowing the excitement to build. "The age of nations has passed and we find ourselves in the pregnancy of a new and gifted era: a global, interdependent and universal age. We must now adjust our individual and group interests and attune ourselves to the collective and supreme synthesis about to take place."

I wasn't sure if anything of substance had been said yet, but by the tense look of everyone in the room, it was forthcoming. Would we all soon be talking like that?

"A sentient energy is leading us to life ever-evolving," Kadam continued. "It is this fountain-source from which all truth flows that we will receive our race-awakening. The time of its dawn is at hand. At this transitional moment, questions are more vital than responses, communication is more important than doctrine. If we can put aside our differences and seize the moment, a divine guidance will raise our collective consciousness. Our fears will fade away."

The gentleman sat down, and a young Norwegian girl, not more than sixteen, stood up amidst a barrage of flashing cameras. Her name tag read: *Almina Berglund, Student.* In a voice strong with a native accent, she spoke.

"As we approach this transition from animal-beings to co-creative beings—a swath may be incapable or unwilling to evolve with us. Their temperaments are not viable and may threaten to sink us back into the same morass, the same sea of greed and corruption from which we almost met our end. We survived the 'Second Crisis,' but we may not survive another unless we eliminate the poison which remains."

Almina looked calm and confident as she addressed the millions watching her broadcast. One could almost see a slight smile as she continued.

"These persons are recalcitrant, keeping humanity from its rightful and glorious destiny. We must engage in a selection of the self-centered, with coercion if necessary, but we will soon move past the enforced stage to a free stage where a natural desire will exceed any needed imposition so that humanity can go forward along our lighted path."

It was brilliant to have had the most innocent and young among the CRL espouse their most violent of decrees. The teen spoke of weeding out the unwilling from the willing with as much force as necessary.

"We will witness a grand phenomenon that represents a final division of mankind—based no longer on class, riches, or fame, but on fulfilling one's unique capacities in this revised spiritual hierarchy. A new stratum will materialize, but then disappear as the reactionaries are replaced by those who engage with whole hearts in this quantum shift."

The girl sat down in favor of another member, gray-haired and bearded: *Edward Wright, Carpenter.* He had the look of a retired cashier at the local hardware store, but spoke with the passion of a man who had just found his freedom. Edward alluded to the next Golden Age, a millennium of peace there for the taking, along with a profusion of upbeat clichés. I was about to tune out the endless blather when Edward's countenance grew into an impatient tone of rebuke.

He asserted that humanity could not afford to wait until change was comfortable, his fist pounding a single strike on the podium in a very un-CRL like gesture. Edward glared at the expansive crowd and warned that there were other "interested parties" ready to clench upon our weakened state if we did not re-engineer our civilization based on the alien saviors instructions. The uproar in the auditorium mirrored that of the tense Collins troops packed into the briefing room. His proclamations turned even more shocking as he revealed that our space friends were about to escalate their supervision.

"At the beginning of the New Year, the Messengers will bestow to the people of Earth the first twelve of thirty-six 'Trusims.' These are the essence of salvation, the knowledge that spared their race so many ages ago from being swept away and forgotten in a tide of evil and selfishness. It is a magnificent honor to receive them, and I speak for all the Council when I say this will be the greatest event in human history."

An unsettled shuffling sound spread across the Operations room as many became uncomfortable in their seats. Countless hushed debates kicked up only to be stifled by the Council member's ongoing oration.

"The Messengers realize we burn to know their name, or their race, so that we may eliminate all doubt and give ourselves to the cause," Edward stated. "However they stress that this great transition is not about them, but about us, and for our benefit they will remain hidden for now. Yet, they know our frailty and have agreed to reveal an aspect of themselves so that mankind may see the ally working on their behalf."

Mr. Wright took a deep breath and gathered himself before dropping his next bomb.

"On January 1, 2046, our gracious benefactors will declare a new era by flying their fleet of interstellar craft over major population centers in a display of love and solidarity. Not only a show of strength, but of encouragement and celebration so we may be bolstered by those who have come alongside us for this great journey!"

The giant auditorium erupted in flashing lights and tempestuous emotion. Loud conversations broke out all over as I remained fixated on the monitor. Questions from hundreds of reporters barraged the stage.

"Can you identify these other *interested parties*?"

"Their craft, are they transports or warships?"

"Are they the same objects that were recently seen over Northwestern Region 1?

"These Truisms, are they laws? Will the Messengers use their ships against us if we don't follow them?"

I looked up at the pastor as he looked down at me. His smile was subdued but persevered.

"Were you expecting this, PB?" I had to shout my words over the climbing noise. He winced, tilting his head as if to decide whether or not he had.

"Yeah, I think so," he sighed, then smiled a little. "PB?"

"You give me an inch and I'll take a mile," I smirked back, but he was already somewhere else.

PB looked back towards the front monitor, though more through it to something beyond. He squinted and I knew he was praying for me; praying for us all.

Part 6: The Collins Elite
Chapter 6

"'Other interested parties' is how the Councilmen phrased it; a soft touch upon heavy, heavy words. Just who or what is watching us at this very moment, biding their time for attack? If we do not come together as bees in a hive, uniting for the good of the whole, then we have no chance against the wasp and bear that prowl for humanity's honey. The Vril, eradicated from our sector with help from the Messengers, may have left us broken gravity as a parting gift. Perhaps they triggered a ticking bomb during their last gasp, as classic villains so often do—and now we're paying the dear price. We must wise up, collectively, and prepare for a coming war in the stars, before we're all of us, doomed."

—Warner Roxwell, *Our Backs Against the Wall*

It had been just over a week since we arrived at Outpost 6. Our old selves had been replaced by angry and edgy look-alikes, with the strained relationship between Pak and Newt making matters all the worse.

Dr. Kalko's team wanted to study the Caliber system and they needed Pak's experience to run stress tests and put it through its paces. The stress tests were aptly named, as every time Pak returned from their lab he was stressed and testy.

The tension ended up working to our advantage as Pak traded time with Kalko's team to get us some restricted R&R. Despite the base being on semi-lockdown the colonel granted us a day out as long as we kept it quiet and made our exit before the morning rush. The original agreement was for just us four, but it was obvious Pak had grown fond of Ivy and negotiated our "fight techs" be included. He didn't have to twist base command's arm since Jay's tech, Nia Corazon, was a local and it made sense for her to act as our guide. She had a destination in mind but warned us it required a two-hour walk there and back, and that we should cash it in early the night before. By the way everyone was rubbing their eyes I wasn't sure they'd listened.

The group gathered in the darkened flight deck before Nia lead us down a long concrete tunnel, up a short elevator ride, and through several hatchways. A checkpoint stopped our progress and we fanned out to change into the clothing she'd picked out for us. Our drab fatigues were exchanged for bright fiesta wear. An uncontrollable giggle hopped from person to person as we spent some time pointing out how crazy we all looked. Jay was sporting a poncho and a ridiculous knit hat that he would have normally groused at, but one got the feeling Nia could talk him into anything. It was rare to ever see Beck in a dress and she looked great. The long black and red material was adorned with red fringe sewn in waves along the bottom and on the sleeves. Her leggings were teal, and her shoulders were wrapped in a shawl of every color. It was pure fun to see everyone in disguise, off for adventure into the unknown.

Two lethargic grunts scanned us and took some notes before letting us go ahead. They confirmed the Gs were normal in the area and that we should have no problems. My interest grew intense to see what was waiting for us on the surface.

After passing one more yawning guard, we emerged under a million flickering stars that spilled out forever in every direction. Space looked close enough to touch, with swirling galaxies stretching from horizon to horizon. A long swipe of purple and indigo at the far edge hinted at a coming dawn. The unfamiliar sounds of distant night animals clacking away added to the strangeness. The air had its nip, but it was sure warmer than Sandpoint on a November morning. I sucked in a breath so deep I nearly passed out. Fresh air, I'd missed it. Boy, had I missed it. Steady inhalation flowed in and out and I closed my eyes over the sensation.

Nia stilled our curiosity about the locale by saying it was a "mountainous, subtropical region in the southern part of the world," and that's all we needed to know. The key she said was to "not want to know" where you were or let yourself think about a location at all. It would be easy to find out if we tried, but it could endanger everyone at base operations. It felt impossible at first to avoid thinking about something but it was far more thrilling to leave it a mystery.

We each carried our share of necessities; food rations, water, and emergency medical supplies. Pak was loaded down the most and reveled in the challenge.

But Glynn was far too talkative. His endless commenting barged into every thought I tried to formulate about my new environment. We were walking single file so I fell to the back of the pack, increasing my distance from him. Suri Kavita, Beck's tech, had started to loosen up and no longer acted petrified around the team, although she still huddled close to Beck most of the time. Pak and Ivy's humble personalities meshed well and they remained in a perpetual, hushed conversation, just beyond everyone's ability to listen in.

Our destination was the nearest town and the local market there. Anywhere would have been fine, just something to contradict the notion that all life had ended the moment we arrived at the outpost.

A winding path took us downhill most of the way so heading back was going to be much more work. Nia talked of altitude sickness but everyone fared well during the rocky trek, despite the thin, dusty air. A rising sun added twenty degrees but it never took the temperature beyond a mild summers' day. The mountains reminded me of Montana and the drives we made to Yellowstone before the Meltdown, only this was much greener. My homesickness plummeted and I found myself eager to get acclimated there, wherever "there" was.

After a little more than an hour we could see the misty shape of a far off burg, nestled at the valley's base. A herd of sheep made their way from pasture to pasture amidst the sound of roosters and church bells. I felt bad for missing Pastor B's service but Nia insisted that Sunday Market Day was not to be missed.

Our anticipation built the closer we drew to the growing commotion, until the tumult spilled out of the town to drag us in. A man in an even wilder poncho than Jay's greeted us with a blast from his conch shell, waving us onward. They were drinking the gritty, local coffee, but the festive atmosphere made me wonder if they weren't adding something more. Nia was anxious to start the tour.

"I know from the outside it looks shabby, but I grew up on this. Mother always called Market Day a 'kaleidoscope' of color, sounds and aromas. Many of the stands have been operated by the same families for generations, using products from ancient times."

The carnival atmosphere so contrasted the dreary base it exploded our senses. Children played along quaint, cobblestone streets while wood-burning ovens wafted the scent of fresh baked bread above our heads. We walked along aisle after aisle of vendors haggling over prices, hawking hand-woven hats, rope and anything you could imagine. Groups of ladies Nia called "mamitas" were cloistered everywhere, gossiping and laughing, their backs full of swaddled children. Vendors husked corn for tamales as buckets of crab advertised their freshness by kicking or attempting their escape.

"This village didn't suffer much in the collapse. They supported each other and lived off the land as they always had. And there's no fancy equipment to help them deal with a Gravity Alert; it's called 'siesta and wait it out with friends.'"

Nia smiled but nothing made me want to scowl more than the thought of a G-Alert spoiling the day. Her commentary flowed free, covering every detail.

"We have an entire area dedicated to a thousand types of potatoes—and there's an aisle just for entrails, you'd like that." She tugged at Jay to emphasize the joke but I doubted he knew what entrails were. "C'mon, I will take you to my favorite place for fresh juice. They make it from star fruit, cherimoya and pepinos."

Nia's hair was pulled back in a bun, though not as tight as she wore back at base. The small, black ball was encircled with a colorful ribbon that matched the dress she managed to twirl every few seconds. Nia was proud of her culture, showing it off to an eager audience. After a few hours of exploration Pak was ready to eat.

"Hey, that smells awesome. Let's have some of that." He was drooling over the barbecue as the man turned some kind of skewered animal that sizzled in its new position. Nia beamed at his decision.

"Oh yes, good choice. I'm so glad you picked this, it's one of my favorites; it's called 'cuy' or guinea pig. It's a local delicacy."

"Guinea pig? Isn't that like a rat or something? It smells great. Let's do this, I don't care." Pak sat down at a bench along the front of the makeshift restaurant and pounded both fists on the well-worn table. *Eat a rat?* I thought. I would sooner starve.

Nia knew everyone there and relayed something about our tour group in Spanish before making a few jokes and paying for the meal. Those that protested the cuy were treated to a delicious ceviche with spicy seafood risotto. Jay sensed Nia's disappointment though and went all in for the guinea pig. Watching him contend with the charred carcass provided the lunchtime entertainment. Its whole body was there, legs spread out and claws still attached. Its face still bore a kind of shocked expression. Pak had almost finished two of them by the time Jay had stopped poking at it and got underway. When Pak reached out and tried to steal his too, Jay grabbed it back and shouted, "Gimme Pig!" The choice of words left us howling.

"My twin brother Voncho and I used to raise them for meat when we were younger and sell them to market restaurants." Nia went on to say that her father was a jungle lumberjack that had run with a rather rough crew, and her mother was the camp cook. She and her brother were a tough two-some themselves so joining the military was a natural course.

"Voncho ended up being a courier in the Army and found himself in the wrong place at the wrong time. He misheard the receptionist telling him to wait and instead entered a meeting room where he saw some of the large skull people, living ones." I exclaimed over Nia's wild report.

"Wow, whoa! You mean like the elongated skulls found in South America?" Dad said they had tested the DNA of those skulls and they didn't appear to be human. He said a notable whistle-blower named Karen Hudes had once confirmed they were still a living race, 'Homo capensis' she called them. The former World Bank employee had also claimed that these beings remain out of sight and in some position of authority; authority over whom was a good question. These long-skull entities were not among the long list of scary bad guys we rid from the Earth, so I guess we'd missed a few. Our tour guide's story added one more oddity to a life turning out so much stranger than fiction.

"Yes. Many of those skulls were found along the coast not far from here. They've all been confiscated now. After the incident, my brother started researching them and his commanders must have been monitoring. Voncho complained of being followed and treated poorly. After a few weeks he seemed not himself, distant and absent.

He warned me to get out of the Army and hide. And that's when someone from Collins contacted me and brought me in. I haven't seen my brother or family for two years."

Our jubilance evaporated as Nia grieved, but within a few seconds three of the young girls she'd been bantering with approached our table arm-in-arm, lightening the mood. The one in the middle held out a ripe tomato towards her, signifying some kind of inside joke that sent them all to laughing. A second girl held out a knife as Nia explained.

"Tradition goes, if you can peel a whole tomato without breaking the skin and create a rose, you are ready for marriage."

At that, all heads whirled to look at Jay. A colossal guffaw burst forth turning his dark cheeks a ruby red. Jay pulled his knit hat down over his eyes as Nia peeled the tomato with skill, creating a flower from it before our eyes. She broke a piece off as she neared its completion and feigned a lack of readiness for marriage after all. Jay was relieved to end the game.

We left the table stuffed with local fare and set about buying a few trinkets to remember the day. As we passed by a row of old women seated on the ground, one of them called out to us in Spanish. Their collective dresses merged into one mass of blinding fabric, hiding every set of legs in a way that suggested the group might be buried in the ground up to their waists. I'd never seen skin so dark and wrinkled, with deep grooves running over every inch of them. They were parched and weather-beaten roads. Still, they were beautiful—but not attractive, if that makes any sense. As Nia knelt down and began to listen, the old woman in the center kept nodding and pointing her crooked finger at me.

"These are medicine women who sit in the market selling medicinal herbs and diagnosing symptoms for the local people. She says you are the one, *the vital one*."

Part 6: The Collins Elite
Chapter 7

"We are but seeds in a vast, cosmic garden. Somehow, the energy essential to our evolution became cut off. When? Who can know? But the gardeners have returned to care for what they'd begun so long ago—and now we will grow up to reach the stars."

—Susan Thompson, *We Are All Children of Noble Light*

"**U**h oh, what did I do now?" I pointed at my own chest, shaking my head to say it couldn't be.

The old woman looked at me with sparkling eyes—almost like a child's. She set about gathering materials in front of her and babbling with the rest of the elderly ladies who joined in with their own babbling. She laid a piece of paper on the ground and began to toss in flowers, corn and confetti. Pak came over behind me and started to pull at my shoulders. His expression said—"don't mess with witch doctors, man." I tended to agree.

"She is preparing a *despacho* for you, a prayer ceremony," Nia said, as the woman interrupted her with a louder exclamation. Still more pointing ensued. "She says you will 'step on the dragon's tail.'"

I turned to look at Beck but her shoulders were already shrugged in my direction. "Someday, you will step on the dragon's tail and she wants to offer a prayer of thanks on your behalf."

"Is that so? Tell me more. Do I make the dragon mad? What will he do to me?" Pak halted my approach toward the medicine women and started dragging me down the street. He'd always been buttoned up pretty tight about avoiding spooky stuff and I was having too much fun with it to walk away. Nia stayed behind to talk for a moment and then ran to catch up.

"She gave you this bracelet," Nia huffed and puffed, "saying you'll need it for protection to safeguard you on your coming journey." It was a simple beaded bracelet, with a traditional pattern much like the town's colorful ponchos and hats.

"Awww man, don't touch that stuff." Pak reared up to smack the bracelet to the ground but Beck reached out and took it.

"I'll keep it for him and pray over it so it's safe." Beck rolled her eyes and started sizing it up on her wrist, just behind her charm bracelet. There the charms dangled before me, glittering in the sun. They mocked me from their safe place.

"We can head up the hill and look at some ancient ruins, but after that we should start back." Nia had proved an excellent guide and I hoped this trip was the first of many.

The thirty-minute haul to the ruins sapped my remaining energy but seeing the spectacular stone citadel waiting for us at the top gave it all back. The gargantuan fortress, which overlooked the lush valley below, was well worth the trip. Nia described the stones as weighing as much as 300 tons each, yet built in such a way that a single piece of paper would not fit between them.

Built by what hands for what purpose? I thought, feeling like a gnat next to the colossal structure: a gnat in the endless string of history, and a tired gnat at that. A G-Alert induced siesta had started to sound good after all.

No one wanted the day to end so it flew by. When we reached the base we were quiet and altogether dragging ourselves to the finish. Finding our way into the secret entrance under the cover of darkness, we changed clothes in the tunnel and staggered our reentry so the group was not pouring in all at once. It was late and most of the hubbub about the outpost had died down. I'd just closed the door to my metal box and fell down on my bunk when a rapid knocking jolted me upright. The door swung open to reveal Minerva waiting in the hall, impatient, but looking salon fresh and smelling better than ever.

"Hey kid, I've been looking for you all over!" Her enthusiasm surprised me.

"I was on kind of a special assignment. I'm pooped though, bet you can tell." My eyes struggled to stay open despite how good she appeared to them.

"Well, I said I was going to show you one of our armors and let you try it out. C'mon."

"What—now?" I whined. "Oh, I dunno, captain. Can't we do it tomorrow?"

"No, the hanger is quiet and maintenance just reloaded Cavalry 1 with the J-22s. I think you're made for each other. Wait, why are you moping around and arguing with me? I'm a superior officer for God's sake! Let's go."

With that she reached in and pulled me into the hallway. Her assertiveness had given me a boost of energy, along with the prospect of trying out an actual combat mecha. I reckoned to have enough left in the tank to see it through.

The hanger was dim and still, with the two large drop ships centered in the enormous space. Cavalry 1, and a non-functioning Cavalry 2, looked heroic, like twin, stalwart watchdogs guarding Outpost 6. Unlike any aircraft I'd ever seen, their inverted wings and dynamic profiles were powerful and inspiring, contradicting the run-down appearance of most of the other equipment around the base. A series of Cavalry sketches would certainly find their way into my journal. I stopped to gawk at them so Minerva ran through their highlights.

The drop ships were able to take off and fly undetected by utilizing an advanced electrochemical, high frequency helix cloaking device. The bases' hanger doors were camouflaged and hidden atop a rocky hill, opening and closing like something out of a James Bond movie. The lab coats had figured out a way to project the illusion of a continuous rocky hilltop there to avoid the doors being spotted by drones or satellites, and the surrounding property was privately owned and fenced off to avoid eyewitnesses. I caught myself breathing hard into icy hands and wished I'd grabbed a jacket.

"How did a rag-tag group like Collins get their mitts on these bad boys?" I asked, resuming my hand puffing.

"Dr. Kalko's team defected in them. I was part of that exodus. I used to fly missions for the black ops, for super soldier and power armor training. They're pulse-proof. Everything could have been."

"So you left the regular military to come out to the middle of nowhere? Are you down with their *cause* an all?" I wasn't sure what the cause was, and maybe she wasn't either, as she neglected to answer and walked on at a faster rate.

The rear ramp was open to Cavalry 1 and her quick pace took us up and into the bay. The interior gave me a comforting feeling despite its eerie green cabin light. Four teenage kids had managed to survive a fight of epic proportion and find solace there. I shook my head at the graphic memory, feeling nearly as tired as I was then. Major Freeman's battered suit stood motionless in its familiar place, with two other similar armors flanking it. Minerva went up next to one and pushed open the hatch.

"Do I need a body suit?" I asked.

"No kid, these are old fashioned. You don't need anything like that. The arms on this hulk work like the legs on your Brawler, exaggerating your movements, but with a lot more torque. This here is more like a flying tank. Get in, you'll see." Minerva had a New York swagger and a rough voice to match. She was downright persuasive if not pushy.

The railing in front of the suits acted as a ladder and I used it to climb inside. Getting situated within the J-22 took quite a gymnastic feat to extend both arms into their mechanical sleeves at the same time your lower body slid into place. The fascia of the open hatch contained the start up controls so Minerva backed her bushy hairdo into the cockpit while she reached up to flick them on. When she turned around she hovered close while I stood pinned inside.

"Seems a shame to put this helmet on just yet," she said, as my eyes grew big and mind drew blank. Minerva dangled the helmet I wished I had on.

"Well, isn't this nice," Major Freeman barked, his grimacing face cracking the silence. "What the heck are you two doing in here?" I would have jumped out of my skin if not incased inside that war machine. He smacked a greasy crescent wrench into his open hand and stomped our way. "You can't just climb into one of these things whenever you want. You're busted, kid."

"Yeah, yeah. Whatever lame brain. Are you holding that tool to try to look smart down here? Garrets is with me." Minerva wasn't rattled by Major Freeman's bluster. She started chewing a piece of gum I didn't know she had and walked his way a few steps to cut off his approach. It was official. Going to the hangar was a bad idea. I longed for a jump gate that would transport me back to my room.

"Cavalry 2 is almost up and running. You'll see. Then I won't need you or this bird to get me around anymore," Brody said with a snarl.

"I'll believe it when I see it. That thing is beyond your skill." Their standoff grew more intense and looked less like kidding around with each passing second.

"Speaking of something beyond their skill—what is this joker doing in a J-22?" Major Freeman walked up close to the battle armor, taking advantage of my immobility. "Look punk, why don't you go back to your little transformer toy and leave the fighting to real men? We've got, what—two months until an alien armada threatens to end all free will on planet Earth? And you're supposed to be our great white hope? Don't make me laugh, kid! Pathetic." Though half afraid, he still got me riled.

"By the look of things around here you could use all the help you can get."

The major's head was yanked back my direction as if pulled by a chain, then I found out what riled really was.

"Help? HELP! This isn't kitchen duty! I'm on a suicide squad and my number is punched. The odds aren't just overwhelming—they're catastrophic!" The major was back to spitting almost every word and grabbed the armor's hull to jerk it around in frustration. "I formed the Green Elite with over fifty men. Good men—fifty. There are eight of us left. EIGHT! You have no concept. Your reality is about to hit a friggin' freight train my friend. Help—*help?* Being in the Green Elite is like hiding out all day in a pile of manure catching flies, waiting for your time to come, for the almighty hammer to drop and turn out the lights." He leered at me then slammed the wrench hard against the suit's metal skin. The loud clang made Minerva recoil and step back. I winced but kept my eyes on Freeman's.

"I'll know soon enough whether you've got any guts, kid. We don't have much time left." He spit a wad onto the deck and turned to walk away. "Carry on, love birds…"

"Thanks for the speech, Brody, I'm sure he's all tingly inside and ready to die in a blaze of glory." Major Freeman did not respond. His heavy footsteps grew faint as he moved down the airship's rear ramp.

As much as Bloodthirsty Freeman acted like my enemy, he felt like my strongest ally. I was sleepwalking through a minefield—and something was trying to wake me up. If I didn't start asserting myself others were eager to take control. The pleasant day had made me soft, Beck's smile and flowing red dress had made me weak. And now I watched as the tiger and snake argued over who got to eat me for lunch. Downtime was an illusion in the jungle; something's always on the hunt.

"Put the helmet on," I ordered. Minerva responded and grabbed a headset so we could communicate. "Okay, run me through the basics."

Some of the fun had gone out of it for her but she turned out to be quite a good teacher, with no more signs of funny business. My mind drifted towards Brody's words. An alien fleet was going to show themselves to a waiting planet in a few short weeks, a desperate world ready to do their bidding. Who was I to stand against something of that magnitude?

Part 6: The Collins Elite
Chapter 8

"How can blindly vowing allegiance to these beings from space accomplish anything but to taint the fullness and purity of our faith? Much worse than any erroneous push towards modernism, this is the very pinnacle of heresy."

—Father Dangelo Ettore, *Society of Saint Pius X*

"To offer any resistance to this most necessary shift in our Church's structure would be to fight against the very heavenly signs sent to lead us to this conclusion. The culmination of Fatima, Pope Pius XII's vision over the Vatican Gardens, and even of Constantine himself—are upon us! Who am I to contest divine intervention?"

—Cardinal Eliseo Giotto, *Vatican City*

"Only a little more…" Whispered Major Freeman over the Com. The left hand of his J-22 combat armor had been modified into a powerful cutting torch and I watched its glowing tip sever a cluster of thick elevator cables. The process was taking an enormous amount of time, time we didn't have. My nerves were making me short of breath when at last the hissing sounds gave way to a tremendous, thundering roar. The elevator plunged several stories and pounded itself into the basement level.

"That did it. I'll mount the detonator up here," he whispered again.

The major had selected me for a "vital mission" as he called it. We would break into a UN World Currency Center somewhere in Brazil and raid their data banks before blowing it sky high. Outlandish, but that's what my world had become. He assured me the facility was still under construction and abandoned, so confrontation was unlikely. The major was also confident that if we executed the mission December 31st, the eve of the new year and the much anticipated massing by the alien fleet, we would catch their security forces off guard.

Major Freeman initially opposed my presence anywhere in his vicinity, but after a dramatic about-face he'd spent the last month and a half training me on the J-22 attack suit. Minerva was just as surprised by his improved attitude and kept a watchful eye on our progress. Then, only a week ago, his motivation revealed itself when he picked me for a secret operation. Major Freeman said he would have preferred Boscoe and Maximuk, the two men lost during our rescue, but fate had narrowed his options (meaning we had). No one on the team knew I was involved in this Collins mission except for Jay, who was circling around at that moment co-piloting Cavalry 2 until the major and I were cleared for extraction. Jay's interest in piloting had coincided with my J-22 training. He'd proved himself a natural, though neither of us could take full credit as the virtual, capsule-training cut our learning curve by 75%.

Aside from the pilot Captain Miller and Corporal Robek, the large vessel cloaked high above was empty. The Cavalry ships were large enough to demand more hands but Major Freeman was paranoid about a possible mole and kept it to a skeleton crew.

Upon our initial briefing, Jay and I argued the mission didn't seem a worthy enough cause for crusaders like the Collins Elite.

That's when Major Freeman revealed the details that secured our loyalty. He claimed he had information that the UN and International Monetary Fund were hatching the mark of the beast at these facilities and we might be able to throw a wrench into their plans. If that was not enough to convince us, the major claimed to have a "man on the inside" who agreed with his assessment. This person was in charge of installing the security system there and had seen information first hand that corroborated the major's story. Fully down with the Collins cause, our inside man would ensure that all the alarms were disabled and timed with our assault.

"No man can buy or sell without joining their new system. It's the Mark, its gotta be." The major laid it on thick and Jay agreed right away, danger be damned. I requested a night to think it over, a sleepless night, then signed on. If the mission didn't go well maybe I would get to see Dad sooner than I thought, unashamed for not having cowered before the beast. Besides, who better to go out fighting than the devil himself?

The plan appeared straightforward: at 2300 hours, Corporal Robek hit the building with a sophisticated pulse weapon to knock out the two night watchmen on guard. The number of guards was down from the eight they'd identified during earlier reconnaissance, confirming a lighter holiday staff. The corporal then moved on to disable the electrical grid receptor for a few square blocks around the facility while Cavalry 2 jammed any outgoing transmissions. Major Freeman and I dropped our combat armors close enough to break into the loading dock area without being seen. A stolen schematic showed we could cut the cables on the freight elevator to clear enough room to fly our suits down to the basement level, which also happened to be Information Systems. Piloting the two J-22s, we would then have the firepower to blast through anything in our way, grab some incriminating files, set the charges and get out.

Once inside, I could see the interior was lush with marble floors and columns, glossy walls abounding in metallic trim and fine art of every kind. The construction looked complete. Maybe the UN was waiting to roll out their new monetary system until after the alien fly over terrorized everyone into compliance.

Major Freeman said he didn't want to chance a remote detonation due to possible interference with the structure, so he jumped from his J-22 to mount the firing control on the main level. A traditional blast cord would deploy from his battle-armor as we flew down the shaft. We would trigger a two-minute countdown from ground level once we had both safely reached the surface.

I had to go first since the major would be letting out the bomb cord. My metal suit clunked its armored feet toward the lip of the black pit and jumped off. Plummeting several stories in the dark sent my stomach lurching through my throat. The shaft's tight fit caused the rotund exo-suit to scrape against the walls several times on the way down. I missed my familiar blue Brawler with its light and streamlined design. But the J-22's retro rockets fired in a controlled manner just like our practice sessions, slowing my descent for a soft touchdown. The walking tank was awkward, but its brute force and armored skin were double that of B1. The arm control system acted as an extension of my own arms and hands, and was easy to get used to. Using its powerful metal claws, I pried open the doors with ease and walked free of the shaft, activating my night vision to get a look at the lower floor. Major Freeman got the all clear and joined me at the bottom. I tried not to sound scared, but I did.

"I hope this is Information Systems. I don't recognize anything from your drawings."

"Cut the chatter. Keep your wings retracted and don't run them into me or the walls. You lose a wing and you might not be going home. Let's move..."

The major used his rear thrusters to scoot down the hall like some kind of armor-plated hockey player. The blast of light from his jets blinded my night vision and I lost my eyesight for a few seconds. He was long gone by the time my eyes adjusted and I struggled to finesse his same scoot maneuver, instead of lifting off headlong into the ceiling. Since I was carrying half the explosives any impact could prove fatal. The cord was still unraveling behind the major so I had the breadcrumbs I needed to catch up to his position. He was already at work cutting into a sealed hatch, the target database.

"After I get us through these doors, I'll take the explosives and plant them while you raid the drives. Be quick about it, I'm outta here once I've got them all set." Major Freeman's angry orders caused my fears about him to resurface. Our friendship hadn't grown much over the last month and I wondered what made me trusting enough to be around him with explosives. My voice cracked as I scanned the endless walls of darkened computer equipment.

"What if we can't get localized power to the database? We won't be able to get anything from it, right?"

"Just hook that pack up where I told you and it'll boot up, guarantee it." The major finished his cut, backed away from the hatch and used his massive mechanized foot to kick the panel down with a thud. He continued his impatient demands.

"The opening is too small for your suit, so get out and do it by hand. You only have a few minutes. I'm going to set the charges. Good luck..."

I popped the hatch and began my struggle to get free as he removed the explosive packs fastened to my unit. Unlike the major, it was still quite an effort for me to get in and out of these iron eggs on legs. The helmet's night vision worked just as well a second time as Brody's departing blast blinded my eyes again and sent out waves of blistering heat.

Frantic among aisles made of solid computers, I found the main terminal under a sign that read: "Security: Our First Priority," and opened a small suitcase device that was supposed to do all the work. The cables attached as advertised and I flicked on the power.

Major Freeman was not rife with detail but according to him electronic "squiddies" were going to run the lines and break through any security walls standing guard. The power pack would provide just enough juice to wake up the database without booting up the whole system. The display inside the case indicated the search was on but it hadn't locked onto anything yet. Captain Miller in Calvary 2 interrupted the radio silence to heap some more stress on the already precarious situation.

"Bad news, guys. Signals headed your way. Looks like civil forces but we're scanning the area for any other activity."

Bad news for sure.

Part 6: The Collins Elite
Chapter 9

"If Dr. Philmore has in fact perfected an effective cloaking device in such a compact, attack unit, we need to convince him our cause is worthy of it.

Or better yet, the Lord's cause is."

—Dr. Yuri Kalko, *Recovered Technical Notes and Journals*

Major Freeman was quick to jump on the line.

"Roger that. We've been ratted out. I'm almost done with the explosives. You get anything yet, kid?" *Kid* was Bloodthirsty's informal call sign for me. Just then the squiddies found their target.

"Yeah, getting something," I responded. "I'm gonna need a minute!"

"You have five. After that I'm blowing this Popsicle stand." He meant it.

Ignoring the sophisticated timer in the helmet's display, I chose to look at my watch—Dad's old watch—and decided to pull the plug at two minutes. The data-retrieval indicator was not like the movies where a convenient progress bar would tell me when the download was complete. I'd be pulling out with no idea if we'd been successful.

Major Freeman had been fair in describing the data-grab as hit or miss, but I was hoping we'd hit it big. Cavalry 2 came back on the line.

"Wolf team, you're going to have company in five! That's cutting it too close. We're beginning our approach."

This'll leave me only three minutes to get out, I thought, as sweat gushed from everywhere. The oversized watch got checked again.

"Charges are set, kid. I'm going up and back to the dock. When you get to the top activate the detonator. You'll have two minutes from that point. Freeman, OUT."

Ten seconds, c'mon... I watched the thin hand smooth forward as long as I could stand it, yanked the cables, and then dashed for my waiting armor. In my haste I failed to fish both arms into their control sleeves as my legs sank into place. This almost dislocated an elbow and kept my left arm inside the main compartment. Try as I might I could not lean the opposite way enough to feed my arm into its sleeve, at least not within the next five seconds. It was the wrist that bore Dad's watch so I rechecked it. Time was disappearing as the orange seconds hand whirred on. Unable to reposition myself quickly, I settled for one arm inside the cockpit with me. I closed the hatch and scooted back towards the elevator shaft. Freeman came back on the line.

"C'mon kid, I'm back by the dock. Let's go! Set that timer."

Brody sounded genuinely concerned for me. If I made it out alive I just might enjoy an elevated status in his brigade. The weighty J-22 hovered into the chute before its jets blasted me upward. I struggled to keep a centered approach vector and scraped along an inner wall most of the way up. Just as I reached the main level something got hung up and hammered my robotic shell to the deck. From the waist down the exo-suit still dangled in the open shaft, and its immense weight began dragging it backward. It would have been an ideal time for them to hit the area with their G-Zapper and lighten the load. I dug my one working elbow hard into the marble and felt it shred the floor before taking hold.

"Something's got me. I'm snagged. I can't get free!" My exclamation brought another unwanted update.

"Wolf team be advised that there are about fifty vehicles, air and armor support. They are taking up position at the front of the complex and making their way back along the sides. You are OUT of time." Then the major made a desperate offer.

"Kid, do you need me to come back? It's going to get bloody if we gotta shoot our way outta here. Status? –OVER…"

A vivid picture swirled in my head of Major Freeman killing twenty or so men in the rescue attempt, as we both got blasted to bits. A pair of mavericks caught breaking and entering; killed like dogs.

"No, I'm all right. My knee plate is caught on something and it's almost loose. Take off sir!" I half-hoped he'd refuse and come back for me.

"Okay C2, I'm coming up. Don't forget to set that charge, kid!" Then there was that: blowing the place up. It was not how I imagined my first Collins mission unfolding.

I was going to have to let go and fall back down the shaft. Then use my one, functioning arm to swipe away the cable, and hit the jets before I smashed to bits below. As I was about to execute the reckless plan, something hit the slow motion button, conforming my brain into mush. My escape window was seconds from closing, yet a calm, apathetic feeling washed over me. I heard a voice say: *"It's your time."*

My muscles relaxed and my eyelids grew heavy. Questions filled my head. *What had even brought me here? How would I be remembered? What had been left undone?* I'd thought about writing a note in case something disastrous happened, but in the end I couldn't find the words and vowed to return. *What would happen to the team, to Beck?*

A steady gnaw I'd ignored over Christmas—in that sardine can of a base—bit down hard, paralyzing me into inaction. The pain of alienating my friends had become a deadly parasite I denied giving a ride. And that parasite was now friends with one already onboard and sucking me dry: the ache of losing my father.

It was obvious that Beck and Pak had struggled with depression over the holidays. Yet, I remained aloof, avoiding them, absorbed in my training. I shielded myself from my best friends, shielded myself from their rejection. I'd let an emotional chasm stretch wide on all sides of me. Then the voice came again; *"Garret, its time to sleep..."*

The elbow that held me aloft lost its hold. Horrid sounds of scraping steel screeched as several tons of body armor careened over the edge. The cable tangled around my armored knee lost its grip and fell away. Rockets fired to slow my descent before retaking the momentum to propel me skyward. The J-22 suit collided into the door frame on the way out, the angle proving just true enough to plow me out onto the main level. Alarms beeped and flashed inside the suit as it groaned to right itself. I took off my helmet and wiped my face with a hand I shouldn't have had access to. Woozy, I could hear somebody talking to me but could not discern the source. Tiny words were coming at me from somewhere—from inside the helmet. I blinked hard and put it back on as the fog lifted.

"C'mon, G!" Jay cried out to me from Cavalry 2. I shook my head to counteract the numbing force. "Wolf 2, come in! It's getting hot out here, over..."

"I'm here, Jay. What's the situation?" I asked, as Captain Miller took over the Com, his voice laced with panic.

"The buildings' flooded. They're coming in. You'll never make it to the back; you're closer to the main entrance. Set the charges and run the gauntlet out the front. If we see you we'll uncloak and attempt a pick up. If you miss we'll have to blip out. You've got one shot."

Sounds of thumping footsteps echoed in the distance. I moved to the end of the hallway as sensors outlined a pair of civil defense armors and a few squads of men taking up position. Beyond them was the front entrance, the way out.

Limping my suit back over to the detonator control, I reached a metal finger toward the flashing button. My own promise not to kill "lunch bucket dads" came back to me, as did Pastor B's exhortation for non-violence. *I can't kill these people. What a mistake this was. Sorry Dad, I made a mess.*

I stared at the red button for a few more seconds before turning to make a break for it. The J-22's right leg had taken too much damage and was not responding. The skating scoot-maneuver was my only option. Skidding around the corner, I punched it full thrusters right at the ominous force assembled against me.

Small arms fire impacted every square inch of the suit as I braced for the harder stuff. Damage alerts sounded out while visibility dropped to nothing. A power armor reached out to grab my limp arm as I blasted past at over 100 mph. It ripped it clean off sending a rushing wind into the cockpit from the open cavity. The larger ordnance they managed to send in my direction missed its mark and slammed into the main entrance. What was left of my combat suit punched through the shattered doors as they erupted into flame. The air cavalry had no trouble seeing a streaking orange fireball in the night sky.

"We see you Wolf 2! You've looked better. Angling for pick up, uncloaking in three, two, one..."

The ship materialized and some skillful piloting swung the open tail around to catch me. With almost no flight maneuverability of my own, I somehow landed in a smoldering pile on the rear ramp. The terrible sounds of shredding metal came over the Com as Miller cried out.

"Hang on, we're taking heavy fire. We're hit! Bloody hell we're hit!"

My hatch was unresponsive but I could see through the breech in the hull a fire-retardant foam dripping over the demolished suit to snuff the flames. Corporal Robek forced the hatch open and pulled me out. I looked back at the mess that had been my combat armor and its missing left arm, rubbing my own arm in disbelief.

Cavalry 2's flight bay was bathed in red emergency lighting as the ship lurched to the side in agony. We were picking up speed, but not fast enough it seemed. I hoped we still had the ability to re-cloak and avoid any more enemy rounds. Then Major Freeman burst through the fore-hatch into the bay.

"Nothing, NOTHING! It's just sitting there. Did you hit the detonator?"

"What—it didn't blow?" I sputtered. "It should have. I don't know what happened." I hadn't the courage to reveal the button went un-pushed. The reasons would be lost on him and I might not survive the repercussion. Freeman raged.

"Did you get the files? Where are the files?" I sat down on the deck and pointed at the smoking wreckage. The major pulled out the data case as I coughed into my hand.

"I'll bet there's nothing on here, too. You got tangled in the detonator cord on the way out and screwed up the connection. You trashed your suit and almost got us all killed. Great work, kid. You're about as reliable as an ATM."

Then, the loud speaker crackled to life over our heads.

"I need a hand up here—we've got a man down..."

Lighting lanced through body before Miller continued.

"Jaxon's hit—he's down!"

Part 6: The Collins Elite
Chapter 10

"I had been channeling a star being for over ten years when they began choosing citizens for the Council of Light. A "shoe-in" for the position is how the Cardinal described me. It turns out that my friend from the stars is one of the extraterrestrials that are trying to save humanity and personally referred me for a seat on this prestigious body.

The old adage about 'who you know' still holds true, even in the new order of things."

—Rio McKinney, *Earth's New Dawn; Interviews with the CRL*

A beam weapon had seared through Jay, taking out a chunk of him, shattering two ribs. After his surgery, I had waited by his side until morning before hitting my bunk for a few hours. The doctors felt certain my Tonto would live, but that did not ease the immense guilt I felt for botching the operation.

There again, I pictured myself the Lone Ranger. A young man wronged now seeking revenge. I perceived my cause just, but was it? We're all heroes in our own mind. Even Timmy Gorgola and Principal Morag imagine themselves to be the good guys in the story.

Mom told me once if I ever thought myself better than anyone else to picture the woman at the well, who believed her life justified despite the nest of sin it had become. Then Jesus is standing there and she is at His feet. It's the moment we realize we're all blind, sinful and naked. If I pictured Timmy and Morag bowing in the dust before the well of living water, I can love them because it's where I am too. The great equalizer is when we understand there is but one hero. I am just a sinner with his own agenda, and that agenda nearly sent Jay to the cemetery.

Sipping a large cup of black coffee, I walked the halls of Outpost 6. The details of the mission sloshed through my mind like a bucket of water. *How had I been pulled into such a thing?* I reeled from the insanity. Half of Garret wanted to find the nearest soul and vow to them that I would never again do anything so foolish. The other half wanted to sign up for the next improbability, making up for my failure or die trying. Had I blown my only chance at divine victory, my "David Moment" in front of the Scimitars? I'd withered then. Had I withered last night too? As I headed back to check on Jay, Minerva intercepted me outside the infirmary doors.

"What happened?" Her bubbly persona was starkly absent. "I didn't even know Cavalry 2 was functional and now I see it back from some kind of mission all shot up!" Minerva's whispering crescendoed into a shout so I responded in kind.

"Listen, I don't know how things work around here. I was told to keep it quiet so I did. If you want to know about what went down, the debriefing is at 1300 hours. I guess you could ask to sit in. What do you want me to say?"

"You could start by telling me you're thankful to be alive. If you went out with Freeman, like I bet you did, you're lucky he didn't get you killed on purpose. He might have agreed to let you train, but you don't know what he's been saying when you're not around. I would have warned you off of this had I known. If you're ready for assignments in the field I should be the one watching over you."

While I appreciated her concern, she had just missed her one chance to see me in action. I took a deep breath and found my lungs full of perfume, though the sweet smell did nothing to ease my acrimony.

"Major Freeman doesn't need to kill me off. I'll take care of that soon enough. Just cross your fingers that I don't take everyone else with me." I sighed and lowered the volume. "Look, not only am I not ready, I don't think I will ever be. I'm not the soldier type."

She furrowed her brow and examined me up and down. I was giving off a stench that even her aroma couldn't cover up. Just then, Beck opened the infirmary doors to scold us.

"Keep your voices down! Someone's trying to rest in here!"

"Excuse me, little girl," Minerva bit back. "You need to learn how to talk to an officer." She gave Beck a wicked stare before turning back to me. "Well Garret, I guess you're not as much like your father as I thought you were…"

Minerva marched off, her bushy hairdo whapping me as she walked past. My mind tried to dissect the unexpected argument but everything felt jumbled. A renewed worry over Jay's condition shoved aside any anxiety I had over disappointing the Collins people. I looked at Beck to commiserate. No such luck.

"I don't like her," Beck snapped. Then instead of opening the door to coerce my entry, she closed it in defiance. In the hall alone, I swallowed the last gulp of gritty coffee. It failed to conjure any clarity so I entered Jay's room. It was more crowded than I had anticipated. Mom, Eleanor, Pak, Pastor B and all the fight techs were gathered around his bed. They gave me a look like I'd shot him myself.

"What the heck were you guys thinking?" Pak snarled as he moved my direction with ill intent, putting everyone on alert.

Beck stepped in front of him, not for my defense, but to get at me first. She fired off her own verbal volley.

"THIS—this is just plain stupid, Garret! What were you doing? Who are you fighting? Are you going off killing people or just trying to get yourselves killed?"

The answers that jumped to mind would not have gone over well. *I was trying to stop the devil from taking over the world,* or more like *I was living up to the Philmore name by sacrificing myself in a no win situation.* Neither of these responses would comfort those grieving over Jay's injury. When I didn't attempt an answer, my mother realized it was time to step in. She began herding everyone out and sent me a consolatory look. The group protested their removal, offering a variety of insults on their way out. Only Nia and Pastor B remained.

"How's he doing?" I whispered after the door had shut. The pastor gifted me a warm smile I didn't deserve.

"The doctor was in a few minutes ago and Jaxon opened his eyes. They said he's doing fine but they're testing for radiation in the wound. If that checks out all right he'll be okay."

I leaned in close to examine Jay's eyes. They did not open, though I wished they would. Nia sat in a chair on the opposite side of the bed and didn't look at me. She reached out and grasped Jay's hand and lowered her forehead down to rest on the mattress. They'd gotten a lot closer than I realized. Pastor B patted her head a few times and motioned me out of the room with a subtle signal. We walked past the nurse's station to some seats in a makeshift waiting room. PB said nothing while he rested his head on his hand, waiting for me to break the silence.

"I wasn't looking for revenge," I offered, feeling ten years old.

"Who said anything about revenge?"

"You did, after the first service I'd attended." The pastor looked back at me and shifted his position to convey he had all the time in the world. I continued my defense. "My Dad said I'd be in the remnant, one of the last Christians to take a stand against the anti-christ. These people are resisting. I'm eating their food and accepting their protection. I'm not supposed to join the fight?" PB wasn't readying a response so I turned my head, shook it, and spoke to someone who wasn't there. "You shouldn't worry about it. I'm useless. More like a detriment to the cause. By the look of things, I should turn in my badge right now." When I looked back to the pastor he was nodding, ready to speak more gently than ever.

"The Bible is full of successful battles where God's people sought His will, and not so successful ones where they didn't. Did you seek the Lord? Do you feel like He blessed the endeavor?" I realized I'd brought a rubber duck to this gunfight as I began offering up some one-dimensional thinking.

"The grocery store told my Mom this summer that they wouldn't be accepting our silver anymore. I'm just a kid, but from what I can tell they're about to introduce the all-digital credit system, you know, the one world currency thing? Not sure how much I'm supposed to say, but we were trying to learn something about it and maybe slow it down. I could have killed a lot of people, myself included, but I chose not to." I looked for any change in his expression, a sign I had a leg to stand on. Nothing. He just kept looking at me like he knew where I was headed and had all the answers. "Pastor, it's the Mark of the Beast. Why do I have to tell you? I bet you know more about it than anyone here."

"It's the Mark? What makes you so sure?"

Pastor B then asked me to consider that the mark might be more complicated than a RFID chip or banking system. He cited

Daniel 2:43, a prophetic vision of the last great kingdom on Earth: *"They will mingle themselves with the seed of men but it won't hold, just as iron does not mix with clay,"* he recited, letting it sink in.

I cringed and didn't need to ask who "they" were. *They* were back, and about to take over another conversation. It was the Angels who "left their first estate," the Watchers, Arkons, Annuaki, Viracocha— or the Shining Ones. Pastor B couldn't resist identifying them, and despite the jarring subject, remained soft spoken and full of joy. If he had one fault, it was smiling after things that had no right to be smiled about, such as entities plotting our destruction from unseen realms. He took another breath and expounded.

"The first time these beings arrived here they gave humans warfare, psychedelic drugs and their children to worship as gods instead of God the creator. Armed with supernatural knowledge and power, these Watchers corrupted everything to the point God had to wipe out all livings things in the Flood. No longer was the Earth's biology what He had made. Yet something evil survived the deluge, biding its time until the days of Nimrod." (and that guy again, too) "So whatever caused the corruption before began using Nimrod's rule to distribute the worst kind of knowledge to mankind, promoting sin and selfishness. These entities rewarded Nimrod for his devotion with some kind of genetic upgrade. Maybe the elite in his kingdom had also received this upgrade and it was going to spread from there, renewing the cycle of corruption that caused the Flood. But God scattered the people to stop it, that and their little tower project." PB chuckled at his own comment while I interjected that Newt had talked to me about the same stuff. The pastor confirmed the he and Newt had been longtime friends, a fact I was not aware of, and that they had arrived at their theories in concurrent fashion. PB went on to describe more of what they had uncovered from the book of Daniel—*"when knowledge would dramatically increase."* Our conversation intensified.

"So Garret, you must grasp this. Scientists have the technology, perhaps rediscovered technology, to insert foreign genes into our DNA. Anything from squid to swine genes could be added to humanity's own genetic code to create a new species. So another race of beings could 'mix their seed with our seed,' add in other animalistic concoctions, and it wouldn't require sexual relations at all. This tech has existed since well before the Meltdown, so who knows what experiments are being done now." I remembered Dad's talk about "snake and alien junk." People would take anything that promised them more power, more life.

"My father once said that my 'humanness' was my most valuable possession." The pastor's eyebrows shot up and he nodded a long nod, pausing to see if I would add anything else. He waited and then divulged his conclusion.

"So you see, the Mark of the Beast might be just that; beastly. Those who become altered like this are no longer humans; they're marked as the devil's children, as unsanctioned creations. But the one world currency system might play into it as well. Those that do not take the upgrade will be painted as *'disease carrying rats,'* a threat to humanity 2.0 that is making the next evolutionary step. Like the vaccines our governments made mandatory, this genetic alteration will be necessary if you want to partake in the global monetary system. No man may buy or sell unless they've taken the bait."

The painful memory of last night's mission ached worse. I had no idea what I was going up against. Any feeble effort I could muster would be like attacking an elephant with a toothpick. My shoulders sank.

"One time at our house church, someone said I had the gift of discernment. I'm not sure who's the greater fool, the person that said it, or me. I'm far from being on a great decision-making roll." Pastor B exhaled another laugh and smiled at my self-deprecation.

"We all make mistakes, Garret. My history has quite a few. Before I became a pastor my first big job was working for the Department of Defense as a remote viewer, testing the powers of ESP, if you can believe it. Hardly the Lord's work."

PB was mystified to recall his twisted past. The pious pastor described himself as a once powerful psychic, crossing over into other dimensions, "channeling" back conversations with beings on the other side. These entities mocked humanity and claimed the extraterrestrial hypothesis was a lie; that a demonic invasion was coming. He remarked how these creatures always singled out Jesus as flawed or misunderstood, never other religious icons. No matter how long or diverse the spiritual conversations carried on, it always came down to a denial of the Christian faith. It was difficult to picture this lovable, stuffed animal of a man doing anything off the beaten path, especially talking to demons.

"After a few of my fellow psychics met their deaths traveling into their air space, I got out and Jesus found me. So I've been waiting for some time for these guys to show up, so have many in the Collins Elite." Again with the smile, but what else was he supposed to do? One of the nurses approached with two glasses of water. I didn't realize how thirsty I was until I saw it coming our way. I drank it down as Pastor B finished his story.

"If these Messengers promise immortality, for certain, here and now, think about how that will affect people's faith in an unseen God, in an unseen heavenly reward? Most will turn their backs on Him, and many already have. It's the original lie that will kick off a disastrous chain of events for mankind. Many believers think the tribulation came with the Meltdown, when so many lost their lives, but I think it's about to begin in earnest." Just then klaxons sounded and the PA blared down on us.

"ATTENTION, ATTENTION PLEASE; all personnel to your battle stations. The enemy fleet is materializing in low orbit, estimating numbers now. All systems on HIGH ALERT!"

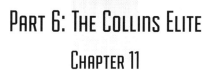

Part 6: The Collins Elite
Chapter 11

"Rumors have it we'll get to see their home planet with the naked eye some day as it passes by here once every 3,600 years. What is not a rumor is the former pope admitting that the Church, along with many other groups, has been watching the ETs approach for almost fifty years. They claim they had to keep it all hush-hush or a worldwide panic might have ensued.

I think fifty years or so would have helped me brace myself for all this."

—Warner Roxwell, *Our Backs Against the Wall*

H ot blood flushed my face as my hands instantly jumped into their tremble. Freeman's secret mission had displaced the anxiety over the promised massing of the alien armada. Now, like the raiding pirate, the moment's black teeth and black flag were upon me.

Pastor B and I stood up to hear a commotion beyond the nurse's station. A large group had gathered around a floating monitor to watch the coverage. The cluster of nurses were holding tight to one another, looking on in terror at a scene that would live in infamy.

After a few tense minutes, the grand fleet of the alien Messengers arrived. Massive shovel-shaped battleships, a mile long or more, baring sleek and gleaming hulls, descended through the clouds. Long lines of enormous craft broke off into formations to glide over Tokyo, Delhi, Seoul, Beijing, New York and thirty more of our megacities that stood half rebuilt following the Meltdown.

These cosmic mantas, their shapes long and menacing, with movements smooth and direct, now swam through Earth's air like an enormous school of prowling sharks. A low bass sound churned from the flying columns, made all the more startling by long bellows sent forth from some kind of space age foghorn. Even through the monitor speakers, the prolonged blasts rattled the contents on a nearby shelf.

The lead vessels were light cruisers compared to the flagships that followed every pack. Three miles from end to end through their long axis, the heavy command ships blackened the sky as they passed over a nervous planet. A few ladies broke down and at least one had to be carried away in hysterics. The alarms continued to sound as people around us shouted, wept, or ran away from the images. I noticed Pastor B sweating and blinking hard behind his glasses, whispering to himself with shortened breath.

"Men's hearts will fail them for what they see coming onto the Earth…"

I felt tears cloud my own eyes as I turned back toward the monitor. I wore a mask of utter shock. A marshaling of sinister warships, unlike anything the world had ever seen, was manifest before me. The designs of these flying fortresses suggested conquest and destruction, yet messages of peace and friendship in every language scrolled across their gun metal superstructures: *"Celebrate—Unite— Evolve and Take Your Place Among the Stars…"*

Skyrockets burst forth with brilliant color as confetti showered the tense but cheering crowds below. I jumped as the PA system shouted again. A frightened, female voice stuttered out her nerve-rattling announcement.

"Estimating the t-total number of ca-capitol ships in excess of *900...*"

The gargantuan silhouettes of these dreadnoughts were eerily similar to the half-mile long, shadow government ships we encountered back home. Just who was helping whom, I wondered. Could these engines that glowed with lavender vortices be superluminal, taking them across the galaxies? We stood there and watched; transfixed by a force whose power was beyond our reckoning. This was no counter move. It felt more like the end game. The good pastor at my side was shaken to the core.

"'*Shut thy doors about thee: hide thyself as it were for a moment, until the indignation be over past.*' Oh Garret, I thought I was ready. I'm not sure how any man can be."

Dad said no matter what he might invent, he could not protect me from what was coming. It was here now. I would not let fear obliterate me, but it longed to do so.

Part 6: The Collins Elite
Chapter 12

"UN and Vatican envoys are making good progress with the extra-terrestrials eager to make contact. In what feels like emergency procedures, they're revealing a host of secret adversaries that meant to doom humanity. Chief among our enemies is 'us,' apparently.

From what I'm hearing, they're divulging quite a list of persons and their crimes, and it doesn't look like politicians are going to fare too well..."

—General Franco Moran, *41st Space Command*

The base alarm boomed through the metal halls with a deafening roar. I needed to shake off my grogginess and fast. *They* were coming and there wasn't much time. My blue and white B1 exo-suit hummed in top condition. Controlling it like a seasoned pilot, I darted through the flight deck with dexterity, calling over the Com for guidance from command. Was I the only one hearing the sirens? Where were all the troops? The ready-rooms were vacant. Cavalry 1 and 2 sat silent, looking mothballed and decrepit. Had I been in some type of coma? Left behind during an emergency evacuation?

My Brawler was adorned with a flowing cape. Far from superfluous, it made a statement to all those who doubted me; I was ready for battle. Tattered at the end as if it had been ripped free of a much larger length, the thick fabric was a lush red that bunched itself around the suit's shoulders, tied fast under my mechanical chin.

Anyone remaining at the Outpost must be warned about the approaching alien ships, yet I found no one. The power output on my display read full. My rear thrusters glowed intense, filling the hanger with hot plumes of blue fire. I rocketed skyward, my transformable power armor passing through the hanger into the morning mist of our mountain hideaway.

At once, the suns rays vanished, eclipsing me under a menacing shadow. Miles of alien vessel blotted out the light in every direction, taking with it any hope of resistance, taking away my courage. What could one boy and an exo-suit do against the might of that unstoppable foe? My only hope was to divert all shield power into a pinpoint, a spear I would ram straight through their heart. I pushed my cape back over my armored shoulder against the whipping wind. Then, bringing B1's open right hand to bare in front of my viewfinder, the metal palm closed into an iron fist, ready to receive an unbreakable shield. The fist glowed to a bright green and jutted upward as my jets blasted me toward the enemy tanker. Mile after mile of metallic sheen covered the heavens above me. I was but a tiny finch, a pathetic creature throwing itself to its own death.

Alerts flashed around the cockpit. The suit's power had drained away. I was free falling, flailing as bits of red cape tore away, leaving little more than a crimson scarf trailing behind. The ground below was now covered with people. I would crush them. Why are they in the restricted area? It was the base personnel, evacuating the outpost. They had just witnessed my failure at the hands of the monstrous flagship. The faster I fell the groggier I became, leaving only despair and a thick blackness fogging my mind...

✶ ✶ ✶

My face contorted and winced at the light. I opened my eyes and scanned for a glass of water that wasn't there. The meaning of the nightmare was hardly ambiguous, but no less draining. My "cell" was getting smaller every day; a shipping crate buried a half-mile underground. Its tin walls inched ever closer.

A song was streaming from my newly acquired companion, a white-bellied caique, and I was grateful to hear it. He was a cute little bird with a yellow/orange hood so bright it looked painted on. His rapid tune was helping undo some of the heaviness left behind by the deflating dream. Glynn had talked me into a day trip to the market and I had let myself be sold on the small parrot by a pushy marketeer. My little feathered friend and I had been through a lot together, as the Gs took a drastic dip on the way back from town. Dark, rumbling clouds arose out of nowhere, and brought with them a plunge in gravity that belied prediction. We hid among the rocks, heaping a few of the larger ones onto our laps to ride it out. Electricity danced overhead as huge drops of stinging rain pelted our faces. I used my poncho to cover his cage until it passed. After a few hours the gravity returned to normal and we continued on our way. The storm energized the courageous bird as he picked up his tune and carried it on until Glynn and I made it back to base.

The market salesman boasted the bird's potential life span at thirty years. The way things were going he would be here long after I was pushing up daisies. I took a deep breath and let his song chase away the lingering night, forcing myself out of the cot. Just then, Glynn's energetic tapping sounded on the door. His morning arrival was always a few minutes earlier than I preferred. I donned my fatigues in a hurry and offered a little green branch to my singing friend to chew on. I hadn't decided on a bird-name yet but felt certain his outgoing personality would soon reveal one. I opened the door as Glynn readied a re-tap. *"Starving,"* he insisted I pick up the pace. His childlike mannerisms were endearing—sometimes.

During our long walk to the market, Glynn had filled me in on his somber background. He was born just a few years before Japan experienced its second major reactor meltdown. His family lived near Takahama where it happened, and they resisted moving away until it was too late for his parents. He and his orphaned sister were relegated to hospitals for years as they struggled to survive. The sibling pair was adopted by a Christian couple in the states, by a military family who later joined ranks with the Collins Elite. His adoptive father was killed some years later in the Alaskan Conflict, but not before Glynn got a taste for all things Army. He enlisted as soon as he was eligible and aimed to be a combat suit pilot, but his poor health kept him from his dream.

In lieu of a real exo-suit, Glynn settled on a vast collection of toy robots he crammed around his tiny room. When I referred to them as toys, he reminded me that if their owner was over twenty, they should be referred to as "collectables." Glynn loved to talk about my father's work and the Brawler suits, subjects I enjoyed. And since Beck and Pak were still cold toward me over Jay's injury, he was getting a lot more of my time. We were a couple of guys who needed an unconditional friend and found one in each other.

As Glynn and I made our way to the mess hall, the lack of morning commotion was striking. Three days had passed since the massing of the Messenger's fleet and it was obvious "The Event," as it had been coined, was having a profound affect. The base's usual fervor was far more subdued, expressions more tense. I wondered about the countless movies where huge vessels from other worlds appear over cities without warning. Could those scenes have programmed humanity to accept the inevitable? As in nature during the rut, had this fierce show of force stolen our hearts, coercing an unspoken concession?

The media's nonstop re-airing of The Event gave me anxiety so I avoided the coverage. I asked Pastor B how the outside world was reacting to giant alien battleships subjugating their airspace. He said the spectacle had induced countless heart attacks from those unable to reconcile the sight. PB claimed that half of humanity was calling The Event a celebration, the other half were calling it a violation. Though in the pastor's view, the alien saviors had succeeded in their effort: Humanity's role with these beings had been taken from being grateful admirers to awe-struck followers. He insisted that the display of firepower had garnered a reverent fear reserved for Father God alone.

Glynn and I entered the mess line and scanned the room for familiars. Beck and Pak were already seated, surrounded by a large group of Collins personnel. They'd both been trying their hands at tasks around the base to find their niche. After the alien fly-over, I sought Beck out to see if she needed reassurance, but her fight-tech Suri had become so distraught over the gigantic alien ships that Beck had to be fully absorbed in consoling her. Their friendship had solidified while I was busy disproving myself as a soldier, and now Beck had little time left for me. I wasn't sure what to make of Suri, but it was easy to see how much safer a refuge she was than I. Suri for Beck, Nia there for an ailing Jay, Ivy to sooth an angry Pak. My stock had bottomed out and no one was buying, except nerdy Glynn. Life without our buds, Brawlers and martial arts had served to isolate the team from each other in rapid fashion.

Glynn and I sat with a cluster of techs, the brains behind many of the Collins combat systems. I tried to picture myself relegated to a support role and stomach what was splayed out across my metal tray. Though sometimes tasty, the outpost breakfasts never felt much like breakfast. Grilled beef hearts on a stick were not a substitute for mom's poached eggs and lemon yogurt. I looked around the hall to compliment her but she could not be found.

Mom had managed to grow more aloof since our arrival, an act I hardly felt possible. She had rallied more than a dozen ladies to meet daily to "strengthen themselves in the Lord."

Mother was sure to keep her disposition kind and our topics light, but her unspoken words rang out loud and clear: I was to blame for sticking her in that hole in the ground. Her black transport, spotless furniture and regimented life had been vaporized due to my unnecessary war games. But Mom would survive that new environment, gleaning from it more excuses to harden herself against a hard world.

I offered the rest of my beef hearts to Glynn who was rambling on about the latest gyro-stabilization systems and such. Excusing myself, I let him know I was going down to the lab and my lunch plans were set. He acknowledged and jumped back into his tech talk.

Yesterday afternoon, longing for a shred of good news, I'd checked in with Newt to see if any data had been recovered from the raid on the IMF facility. He and Dr. Kalko's team were engrossed in analyzing the readings from the alien fleet, racing around the lab like terrified mice. I was all but ignored before Newt said to come back the next day, so I was anxious to check back in with him.

When I entered the laboratory, Newt was huddling with a several assistants around a three-dimensional display of the Messenger's command ship. One of the techs was pulling apart holographic sections of the bow to let them hang in mid-air for discussion. I stood in close proximity for a few minutes, my presence not important enough to break them free of their ongoing jargon.

B1 was parked in a dark corner of the lab; my old ride looking lonely under its heavy, red tarp. Our bikes were going unused these days, with no one from the team even mentioning them. I lifted the tarp, ran my hand along the dent Major Freeman had gifted me, and considered mounting up for some drills. The Brawlers were viewed by many around the base as gratuitous, a distraction that never paid off, so I was reluctant to be seen in one just "goofing off." It even appeared that the mass production on Pak's Caliber had ground to a halt, its once promising design now feeling like a flyswatter against a thousand warships. A tap hit my shoulder and I turned to see a flustered Newton Bigsby. He was back to looking red and sweaty, in desperate need of rest.

"I'm glad to see you Garret, how are you?" He didn't wait for an answer but instead turned side to side in a nervous fashion before lowering his voice.

"Listen, I would like to speak with you in private, but I need a few moments lad, okay?" Tilting his head up to look at the ceiling, he gave the impression of a man ready to crack.

"Yep, sure. My itinerary is pretty much open—forever." Newt didn't smile and I wasn't sure he'd even heard me. He went back to confer with the lab coats who looked impatient at his lack of focus. Newt spent some time reassuring the group and then motioned me toward a small conference room. The notice writer for the wall inside didn't bother with tacking up a board first. The metal paneling bore some hastily written words that said: *Those who give up liberty for temp safety deserve neither liberty nor safety. Be(e)n Frank.*

Newt closed the door, sat with an involuntary groan and stroked his face.

"I've had a few sleepless nights agonizing over what I'm about to tell you, and I'm still not certain of the best course of action. But you must promise to tell no one, no one." I wondered why he felt the need to whisper in a closed room.

"Fine, yes. Is something wrong around here? Are you all right, Newt?" He considered it for a moment, his whisper growing softer still.

"The longer I'm around this place, the more I get the impression we're being tolerated by the enemy. The shadow government knows we're here and their minions are allowing this Collins outpost to exist. For what purpose, I cannot say." I had no response, except to nod and wait for his secret information.

"Listen Garret, I've been picking up a repeating, distress beacon—" Newt paused as if to consider backing out. I remained expressionless until he finally leaned forward and spilled it.

"—in a code known only to me—and your *father*."

Part 6: The Collins Elite
Chapter 13

"Evan, you'd better sit down for this. Right now, I am staring at a Periodic Table with 140 elements, not 121. My handlers say there is knowledge so startling even the most hardened souls have to be eased into it. I'm breaking through layer upon layer of secrets, a matryoshka doll of deep awareness, each stratum more amazing than the last. The revelations about the Earth, and even gravity itself, are downright shocking. As much as you wanted to talk me out of joining the 'dark side,' the emperor was right, the dark side is more powerful!"

—Newton Bigsby, *Notes from Beyond the Edge*

A barrage of emotion raced scatter, from fear and worry to extreme jubilation.

"Newt, you're saying Dad could be ALIVE? He might be out there, calling for help?" My voice cracked as I tried to swallow the walnut of vexing news.

"Well, I think we should use caution in its interpretation. One could assume that, but it might also be a clever trap, or a malfunction of sorts." I went wide-eyed until Newt gave me something else. "As you know, the last time I saw your father, he'd departed our laboratory in a powerful prototype exo-suit. Evan was testing the cloaking system that had not yet been added to your own Brawler units. The *A-Type* armor he was piloting, had it survived some kind of trauma, might have started transmitting this beacon automatically. We can't be sure."

"Can you track the beacon?" I begged. "Find out where the signal is coming from?" Newt averted his eyes from mine and reluctantly went ahead.

"Ummm, yesss. Uh, Garret, I struggled with what to do with this information. It might come to nothing, giving you only false hope and sorrow. Except, my conscience would not allow me to keep this from you. Something felt like it visited me in my dreams to insist I reveal it. Something not altogether friendly, I might add."

Between the massing of the alien ships and Dad calling out from the grave, it was no wonder Newt was ready to pass out. By contrast, every fiber of my being was standing on end.

"Newt, look, I can't be afraid of disappointment, or sadness or pain. This is exciting no matter how it turns out. At least it's something." Although my heart dreaded the thought of his revelation going nowhere, blind optimism felt like the best option. "What do we do?"

"As I said, first, tell no one. I have not told you that Evan was not universally liked by the staff here." I felt slapped by such information; incensed. My volume skyrocketed.

"What? Give me a break! How? Why?" Newt got a fresh flush of red into his face as he tried to quiet me. "Who—Dr. Kalko? Who?" Newt shook his head and waved his hands frantically to signal that was a subject for another time. I relented and sat back for fear I might kill the poor man if I pressed.

"For now, let me monitor the signal and run some tests. Are we in agreement that Marcee should not be told?"

"Yes. I mean, no. No, she should not be told," I stammered. "Not right now." Mom was leveling off. No need to upset her if this turned out to be nothing. And what about Beck? I wanted to confide in her but she was a million miles away. She might as well be back in Idaho. A sudden knock on the door sent us off our seats and almost fainted poor Newt. A lab coat was looking at us through the sliver of glass and we motioned him in.

"Excuse me Dr. Bigsby, but the CRL is broadcasting an unscheduled announcement. We have it up on the monitor now."

"Yes, yes, we'll be right there." Newt sighed. The coat left and Newt used the table to push himself to his feet. "This will be their *'how did you like all those ships'* gloat-fest. Lovely. Let's make ourselves sit through it." He moved in close and sent a nervous whisper into my ear. "Come back tomorrow and I'll let you know if there's been any change. In the mean time, forget it. Don't even think about the beacon. Preoccupy your mind with something else." That was easy for him to say. Hope and fear were battling to rip me in half, and now I had to forget I'd heard anything. Fat chance.

Newt left the small room and I followed, my knees a little weaker than I expected. I sat near the broadcast but my eyes and thoughts fixed upon my sleeping Brawler in the corner and the mission ahead. We joined a group of seated techs whose eyes were glued to a large hanging monitor illuminating the darkened lab. The image of a tall woman from the Council splashed baby blue light across the row of open-mouthed young men. She gave her speech's introduction with a heavy Russian accent. Her hair was golden and so was her nameplate that read; *Varvara Klimov, Nurse.*

"A trumpet sounds the keynote of a new age. We have at last been freed from our brutal and tyrannical past. Individual and group interests must now be subverted by the supreme interest. Wisdom is reflected in a mirror, vivid and profound. Our friends, our allies—

now hand this gift to us, the Messenger's own reflection. Without this wisdom, their civilization would have perished eons ago, and almost did, just as we ourselves teetered on the edge of destruction." Ms. Klimov sat amidst a deluge of flashing camera lights. A short man with slicked black hair stood, brushed his oversized suit jacket flat and cleared his throat. *Utari Sulawesi, Barber.*

"Homo sapiens must let go of that which brought us to the brink of calamity. If we unite and receive this gift, we will one day pass these on to another, being gods and saviors in our own right and time. Humans must take this wisdom, these Truisms, into their hearts and minds. Please prepare yourselves for their message, the first twelve of thirty-six Truisms."

Something about "prepare yourselves" snapped me out of my stupor and sent chills down my arms. I looked over at the group of frozen scientists and then back at the monitor.

"Dear friends. *First,* realize that you have stabbed and wounded your own mother, your mother Earth. She is your living essence. Her true healing is of utmost priority; all other priorities pale in comparison. She is the body in which you live, be one with her in health and in life. If you make this your first passion, all her functions will soon recover."

Our gravity? Were the Messengers at last addressing the issue? I couldn't tell. I spun my head around to see if anyone was interpreting this outer space vernacular but everyone looked paper blank.

The second Truism he relayed commanded us to consume as little as possible, and the third called us to share everything with everyone. All our resources needed to be guarded and distributed so that no one was in want. Noble causes certainly. Utari went on with the list, words spoken from the Messengers to the people of Earth. The one-time barber, now a Councilmen of Resplendent Light, smiled bright.

"*Four.* Enact a new monetary system that is visible, traceable, and accountable. Let everything you have be known by everyone else— this is true freedom from self. *Five.* To eat the flesh of another corrupts morally and physically, sealing off progression while promoting decay. Life is grown and consumed; its energies are transferred to allow health and vitality. Eat and live. *Six.* Evolving organisms progress yet you have lost your natural ability to project. Psychic transmission is to be reawakened, strengthened and celebrated. There are unfathomable powers latent in the human mass—awaken them and realize what you were truly meant to be."

My mind scrambled to make sense of all the big words. Something about money, food and power. I ventured a clarifying question into the darkened room only to be shushed quiet by several angry techs. Another council member stood up but I did not catch her name or title. She resumed the countdown.

"*Seven.* The religions once given to you as gifts to unite, have only divided. There is no 'chosen people,' no group greater than another. No one prophet speaks more truth than another. These are but malicious tricks to incite war. Truth is truth. You are all prophets once enlightened. End any belief in a hateful, violent or vindictive God. *Eight.* Recognize the two types among you, progressive and reactionary. If you want to prevent love and progress and are filled with a dogmatic hate, this is reactionary; a sickness that must be cured. Allow evolution to take its natural course of healing. All those who would reject this healing in favor of hate will soon be revealed. The wantonness to destroy and prevent progress is reactionary, a disease that must be eliminated."

These last two were not as cryptic; the end of organized religion and a warning to anyone who might stand against their demise. A rush of memories flooded back of the untold conversations with friends and family about when Christianity would be forbidden.

The topic always felt ahead of its time, a preparation for something far off. Yet, there it was.

The councilwoman went on with Truism nine, which called out artificial intelligence as our "global conscience and universal judge." Fear of its use was "reactionary," she said. Humanity must embrace AI as a shining symbol of progress since it cannot be corrupted. Ten was something about children being planned, their births "coordinated," and eleven was further warning that other sentient races, some not as friendly as the Messengers of course, were watching humanity's development. Only by eliminating "rebellious individualism" could we make the necessary preparations to fend them off. At last at the twelfth Truism, I longed for their end so I could catch my breath.

"*Twelve.* Even the best among you will need physical repair to reset what time and cruelty have taken away. Once these new champions rise from among you, they need to be recognized and blended in harmony with your population, pushed forward as the spearheads of your race, blazing a fiery path for the rest."

I hadn't a clue what that meant, but I hoped it meant the friggin' cure for cancer already. The Councilwoman seemed relieved to conclude her turn and offered some final thoughts to quiet the mass of reporters for a few more seconds. As proclaimed by the Messengers, the CRL were to remain our spiritual vanguards. Its members would explain and expound on their Truisms—a convenient moment to secure the Council's seat of power. Her puff of black and wiry hair trembled as she shouted out a dramatic finale.

"The Messengers want us to know we are one world, one species, and one nation with one purpose: to join in global interdependence and rise together to meet them in the stars!"

Flash bulbs and applause burst forth in a tidal wave as thousands in the auditorium leapt to their feet to cheer and wave banners. The "Stand You Freed Masses" anthem roared to life with its crashing symbols terrorizing every verse.

Some of the lab techs started to argue with anyone who would listen, while others sat bewildered. One coat stood and heaved his notebook, chasing it across the room to soccer-kick it into the wall. Newt and I caught each other in a look that said "Dad." He wobbled over my way and whispered in my face. His breath was horrid behind dry and scaly lips.

"Garret, you need to study this broadcast and bring me a full report in the morning. Think about nothing else." He rubbed my head with the last of his strength and dissolved into the chair beside me. I'd hardly heard anything from the broadcast, and armed with the revelation about the beacon, I hardly cared. Newt added one more incentive to seal the deal.

"I might not be able to help you any further unless you follow my instructions—to the letter." He smiled a fake smile and reached for something stuffed inside his oversized coat pocket. Retrieving it gently, as if it were a fragile kitten, Newt handed me my old journal. Slightly more tattered than before, I was amazed to lay eyes on it again. I took it in both hands and stared at the book. The cover's two antique fish had gotten no closer to each other on their long swim.

"The sketches in there are nearly equal with your journaling, young lad. Quite detailed. I hope that book doesn't fall into enemy hands. Now put it to some good use and write for me what I asked…"

With that, Newt shoved my wheeled chair toward the lab's door and I scooted a few feet before stopping. My gaze lingered on a master work that had miraculously survived the great blast of Hemlock Hill: *The Complete Works of a Dim and Naïve Teenager.*

I stood slowly and headed back for my room. The only option was to embrace his orders and put the thought of my father, somewhere out there—likely wounded and desperate—out of my mind.

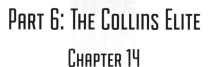

Part 6: The Collins Elite
Chapter 14

"The secrets of the universe are only open to those who have left antiquated belief systems far behind. To cling to Christian, Muslim or Buddhist doctrine is akin to believing in a world still flat! Once that you see that it is round, you realize you can sail around it to a new world. We've been given eyes, let us now see..."

—Delores Trufant, *Truth: The New Religion*

"**N**ewt actually wanted the stupid report?"

Arriving to the lab empty-handed had earned me an early morning rejection. Newt refused to even look my direction until I delivered the "Truism Report" he'd requested the night before. Watching and re-watching that CRL broadcast made their overly complex sentences blend into one big puddle of mind-mud, and allowed me only a few hours of fitful sleep. Each time I pictured Dad's face I watched the broadcast again to take my mind off things, loathing it all the more. I had assumed Newt's request was only there to distract me from the distress signal, so I ended up writing down little more than random thoughts, nothing cohesive. And now a scowl was fixed upon my face as I stomped back to get my journal. Chills hopped back and forth on his perch at my sudden return.

"Sorry Chills, just back to grab something."

The bird had refused to repeat any of the clever names I offered until I remarked on how *chilly* the room felt. THAT he sang out over and over again, making his choice known. He'd talked me into Chilly with his emphatic reaction but in a days time I'd already truncated it over to Chills, a quick blurt of a nickname, the same as anyone I cared about: Newt, Beck, Jay, Pak. I considered it an honor to be in that circle. Mom called it laziness.

Rummaging for my journal, I heard Chills let out a frenzied squawk. I turned to see him madly flapping his wings as if something had bitten his leg and was holding him fast to the perch. I peered into the cage for a closer look to see him dart headlong into the bars, crashing to the bottom in a daze. I was about to ask what was wrong but I never got the chance.

Metal flooring smashed hard against my face, while the bulbs above burst a cascade of sparks into the blackened room. Everything heaved and shook, like a rubber toy whipped by a vicious dog. Blind in the pitch, I grabbed for anchor and found a leg of my spilled over cot but it was being thrown just the same. Sirens wailed amidst distant shouting, crashing and screaming. As the murk cleared my thoughts cried out:

We will all be buried alive!

The overhead lights blinked on and blinked off and another quake rocked the base. Breathing became more difficult as the smell of burning electronics and dust caked my nose. Metal infrastructure bent all around, grinding on in low groans until emergency lights filled the room in warm red. A PA message began but cut out after a few words. A frantic man running in the outside hall finished the warning: GRAVITY ALERT.

I tried to use the cot for leverage but the elastic ground made it hard to stand, much less walk. Another vibration sent me off my feet and into the next wall. I bounced and launched towards the next, with the reduction in Gs unmistakable.

Pushing off, I reached the entryway handle but the door refused to open. No doubt it had been wedged shut by a bent frame. Grasping the lever tight I levitated both feet high on the wall to pull with maximum leverage, the lighter gravity allowing me extreme acrobatics. The latch tore free and the door opened to a smoky corridor, flashlight beams bouncing scatter. The thinning air made my chest heave so I rested a moment before venturing out. Beck's room was on the other side of the mess hall but she would be out in the complex somewhere.

Water-balls danced in the air and splat against my forehead as I used a seam in the wall to pull myself along. I could hear an officer holler above the deafening noise for everyone to shut up, quieting some nearby rooms of whimpering people. A few soldiers flew by handing out oxygen masks and one of the masks floated my way. The men shouted "MOVE, MOVE!" as they traveled horizontally a foot below the ceiling, using only their two hands to slap along opposite walls at a tremendous clip. An aftershock provoked the emergency lights to begin flashing strobe-style and another explosion echoed in the distance.

The dim red light steadied and I could see a girl curled up under a console table. It was Suri. She was holding on to a leg of the table, crying hard into her air mask. The wall behind her had buckled open, releasing a stream of chemicals now pooling around her feet. It smelled strong and unfamiliar.

I asked if she was okay and if she knew where Beck was but that made her sob louder. Repeating the question caused her to howl as if she were trying to drown out my voice. When I offered to carry her someplace safer she surprised me by accepting. Pulling her out from under the table, I braced her light frame against my shoulder and forged ahead. I considered dropping her off in one of the whimpering rooms but decided to keep her until we reached the larger crowd at the mess's chaotic entrance. The cacophony from the fevered effort there revealed a desperate situation.

Pak and several soldiers were straining to lift a metal bulkhead that had closed on someone. Their body was now crushed and trapped against the floor. A nurse was watching the action nearby so I dropped off the still crying Suri into her care and threw myself into the pull. Pak wasn't wearing a mask so I asked between grunts if he needed mine. He didn't answer. We strained with no affect; the hatch wouldn't budge. The emergency lighting zapped out, setting off several panicked screams before straining back to life. One of the flying men arrived at the scene with a tool kit and battery pack and began tearing at the door's access panel. I was terrified to ask.

"Pak—where's Beck?"

He struggled a few seconds more with the immovable door and then let up, answering that she was inside. Just then I heard Beck's voice, telling someone to be quiet and another to help with something else. Dropping low to speak through the gap brought me within inches of the trapped man's boots, tangled half in and half out the exit. A pair of nurses knelt close by his head and chest, speaking soft and stroking his hand, but I couldn't tell if he was talking back. Grasping one of his rubber soles, I said a prayer for him and called out through the opening.

"Beck? Are you okay?" I was about to yell louder when she responded that she was, but added nothing else. "I have Suri. She's all right."

A few more seconds ticked by so I called out for her again, sounding rattled. Intense coughing and yelling from a hundred sources made it impossible to hear.

"Garret, I'm fine and very busy. Can you get to Jay? If you can't help out there see if you can get to the infirmary. He might need you."

While right, I resented her emotional mastery. If only that girl would reach under the door and take hold of me. Frantically demanding that I not let go until the whole rotten disaster had passed—but not Beck.

I asked if she had a mask and the answer was no, but she compelled me not to worry. I took mine off and slid it under until it was taken from my hand. Strengthened by the interaction, I accepted my new mission and patted Pak's sweating back. He was inconsolable, placing his forehead against the metal hatch without looking my direction. Lacking better words I told him to be strong before I started back down the hallway toward Jay.

Not long after I'd left the scene a cheer erupted from the mess behind me signaling the doors release—and hopefully a Collins survivor. My feet found some traction as the gravity levels rebounded and fresh air flowed into the dank passage. Items once held aloft in the zero-gs now clanked and crashed to the deck, then a slight tremor rattled under the floor. I pleaded for it to be the incident's last gasp.

The lab was situated between my position and the infirmary so I decided to veer off and check in on my way. Newt was among a group of people gathered around a fallen technician. The injured man was speaking to a medic as I took a knee beside them. When Newt saw me it was more than the Englishman could bear. Reaching out with both hands he grabbed me behind the neck and wept, hanging on for dear life as his head drooped to the floor.

"Newt, I'm going to check on Jay and Mom, but I wanted to stop in here first. I'm glad you're in one piece *ol'chap.*" My forced accent tried to lighten the mood but it appeared to have the opposite affect. He looked up with a grisly face, his eyes crooked with grief.

"Garret, I've lost the signal. The beacon, it's gone."

Part 6: The Collins Elite
Chapter 15

"Their blood-spattered exhaustion still fresh from civil strife and an epidemic of smallpox, the Inca stood awestruck as Spaniards strode into their city of Cajamarca. These Incan soldiers had never laid eyes on a horse, the cannon nor the advanced weaponry carried by the conquistadors. Slaughter came for those Inca the following day, but not before they received a brief chance at surrender, forsaking all their tradition and beliefs in favor of those of the arriving conquerors. Have the same types of ships, bearing unfamiliar flags, also arrived at our tired shores?"

—Piper Corcoran, *Can Things Get Any Stranger? Volume II*

The bottom fell out of the world. My chin trembled and my cheeks burned as I tried to reconcile what the blubbering doctor had just said. I questioned vainly whether losing the signal was due to the earthquake or power loss, and wondered if we'd ever hear "Dad's cry for help" again. Newt divulged that it happened early that morning before the quake, dashing my thin shred of hope. No wonder he'd chased me off. He was trying to buy himself some more time.

Newt began to rant louder about dreading to see my face ever again, his failures and other incomprehensible mutterings. He was speaking too loud and acting far different from the covert conversations we'd been conducting before. I got up and helped him to his feet. The group of techs paid us no mind though and remained focused on their injured comrade.

Suddenly, the main lights popped on overhead filling the lab in bright, white light. Pak startled everyone in the room by choosing that moment to lean in and call out for me. Jay and the infirmary were intact and he wanted the team to assemble there as soon as possible. Despite the depressing news about Dad's signal, it felt great to hear Pak mention our team again. As soon as Pak and Ivy left, the PA crackled to life with an announcement confirming the emergency had passed with no reported deaths. I sighed in relief as a weary applause reverberated through the base—though seeing Newt in normal light instantly liquidated that joy. The harsh overhead fluorescents allowed nothing to hide from their gaze. The doctor's face was chalk-pale, lips an unnatural purple, his eyes a drowning red. Pushing him toward the back conference room, I suggested we continue talking there. He kept mumbling as I lead him along, but at least it was a low mumble.

Newt and I sat in silence for a long minute listening to each other take protracted breaths. It was then that I started to feel all the aches and pains from being tossed like a ragdoll. I was bleeding. My elbow throbbed just above an eight-inch incision and a knee felt to be swelling. As I looked over at my frazzled mentor, I promised myself I would be patient and kind. However his first question aggravated me a million miles the opposite direction.

"So, Garret, what did you make of the broadcast?"

"The broadcast? Seriously, who flippin' cares? What about the beacon? The earthquake? Newt, what about DAD?" I grimaced and test-bent my injured knee while a surging anger eclipsed Newt's sorrow. His grief-mangled, moist and discolored face, made the character snarling back at me a scary one.

"Now listen young man! I may have failed you in many ways but I still have the chance to carry out your father's wishes. Evan cared a great deal about what was happening to our world and about the Messengers' true purpose here, and you bloody well know he would have wanted you to care," he continued through fierce eyes. "I'm not insensitive to how this morning's bad news will have affected you but there are greater concerns beyond how you and I are feeling. Am I clear?"

Newt's long sentence made him heave to retrieve the spent air. He filled his chest up again and watched close for my reaction. I sighed and nodded, again hating that someone was right and more in control of their emotions than I. Newt pointed a quivering finger my way for emphasis.

"The issuing of these twelve edicts—" breath, breath, "may be a monumental, no—IS THE MONUMENTAL," breath, breath, "turning point for the human species," breath, "Please, tell me you feel the enormity of it, despite the news about the damned beacon."

I forced myself to remember the broadcast while Newt sagged and oxygenated.

"The Truisms are near perfect in their execution. I mean, how can you argue with protecting the Earth, honesty, sharing and caring and all that? It's written so that anyone who disagrees with them is a hater and anti-progress. I'm not dense. We're going to be singled out for destruction. We're the haters." I looked around the room inferring it was Christian radicals like the Collins Elite, but I knew it applied to far more than they. Anyone not dumping tradition in favor of the Messenger's decrees would be seen as a virus. Some of Newt's stress lifted as I spoke so I kept going.

"But I bet cattle farmers are going to take a big hit. They even had me thinking twice about eating another's 'flesh.' I have to admit, that one took me by surprise. Dad never talked the diabolical plans of the end times having us all go vegetarian." Newt smiled at last.

"Fascinating. Yes, I too felt the power behind it. One can only guess at the next twelve, and what events they might spark into flame." With that Newt leaned back to find his chair, but his misaligned angle caused him to miss the support. I lunged to grab his coat so he didn't tumble over backward. After Newt had composed himself he insisted that I bring him my journal. He was suspiciously interested to review my thoughts on the Council. I'd later hand the book to him with firm orders to keep it. I no longer felt like chronicling my own misery. The bungling moment with Newt's chair allowed me to change the subject.

"Newt, do you not trust the people here? Is something wrong beyond what I can see?" He closed his eyes for a moment and shook his head, opening them to focus on mine.

"My mind often flashes back to the evening where I surprised you and the team in your mother's sitting room. Before I came around the corner I was so taken aback by the comfort there, of just being in a home again. I'm tired lad, tired. I might be giving out just when the real battle is commencing."

Newt went on to reveal that the atmosphere around Outpost 6 was as intense and political as his tenure with Army R&D. He insinuated he had other options, other allies, and that it might be time to cut his stay short. My heart went out to him. He was looking for relief.

"Newt, for what it's worth, I still feel like God's in control and something important is about to happen. There's a reason we were supposed to be at this base instead of wringing out the last five minutes of life back in suburban America. I've been missing my comforts, yeah I've been feeling it, but I've also been praying that the Lord renews our strength. This place does seem strange but God often uses the least logical person or thing to execute his judgment."

In my mind I was picturing Samson, full of the Spirit, picking up a jawbone and slaying a thousand of God's enemies into "heaps upon heaps." Samson was one of the few biblical heroes that made me feel good about my own life. Talk about a flawed character. If God could use him I still had a chance. I was tantalized to imagine the scene. There I lay in the grass exhausted, reaching across the cold ground to find a rock-hard jawbone in my grasp. Only God's strength can lead you into battle with a weapon like that, granting victory to an unlikely victor. I cut my daydream short and noticed Newt's eyes half shut. I asked if he'd gotten any sleep but he ignored the question to ask one of his own.

"But Garret, who can escape this coming deception? We're talking about physical and spiritual totalitarianism. People will think they are forsaking the will of the individual for some greater good, but in reality they will be hooked up to a machine that will drain away their essence. Those that do not submit will be selected for elimination."

An old sage revealing his last bastion of wisdom before fading away into the greater light. Newt wanted me to pick up Dad's baton and run with it, carrying the burden of saving the Earth on my shoulders. I just wasn't there yet. I had my life and my concerns to attend to: chief among them finding out if my father was still alive.

"Newt, what happened to Dad? Did he die out there last night? Was the beacon his final call for help? Will you keep monitoring for the signal?" Newt took another long breath.

"Yes, of course. I spent all night readying some training capsules for you on search and rescue, hostage extraction, and re-arming your Brawler. My brain was wracked over how we were going to pull off a secret mission of such complexity. I'd tracked the source and nailed down its location, but getting in there would not have been easy. Then the signal went silent around 0600. Bloody depressing."

I could tell Newt didn't want to say where the beacon was emanating from. Best that he didn't I supposed, but was he really going to leave the mission up to me? Would we not have had Collins support? I'd accepted that I was not skilled enough for military operations and it was time he faced that as well.

"Instant-fail, good doctor. While I appreciate your endorsement, we both know I lack what it takes. I don't have to tell you, you've watched my training from the beginning. Jay and the rest of the team passed me by despite my head start. And Major Freeman, he won't even let me near anything he's working on."

"You'll be pleased to know I have a confession to make," he said. "I purposely made it tough on you during Brawler training, much tougher than on any of the rest. I feared you would get too cocky and let up. Every virtual adversary I pitted against you was twice the challenge setting the others had to take on. Or I would reduce your power output to keep you lagging. The truth is that in all my years I've never seen anyone with your natural talent."

What Newt claimed so contrasted my recollection I had to pause to consider it. I hoped he was not fabricating the story to bolster my confidence. He went on to address the botched IMF mission, something I still cringed at.

"Major Freeman should not be so critical. He threw you into a meat grinder without the proper training for such an operation. If I had known about his plan I would have put a stop to it. I felt you performed admirably. By the way, the lab staff was able to discover some intriguing data from those drives. We'll leave that for another time. I'm still analyzing it. As for Evan, we will not lose hope. I would not be honoring my friendship with him if I let anything happen to you. There was a distinct possibility it was all an ambush, a trap we avoided. Now, I think I will go and lie down for a bit."

"You've done your best, Newt. Go and get some sleep."

Helping him to his feet, I walked our pair to the lab door and paused a moment to watch him leave. Newt tottered down the long, metal corridor among the base personnel performing cleanup. I couldn't help but think my best chance of ever seeing Dad again had just left with him.

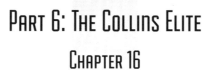

Part 6: The Collins Elite
Chapter 16

"The more saucers we blast out of the sky, the more technology we get our greedy little hands on. We're like ants slurping up all the sugary goop with reckless abandon, not realizing it's laced with deadly poison. Dark governments everywhere thought they'd discovered fire, so to speak, and then scooped the burning coals right into their own damn laps."

—Colonel Milo Reed, *Life Inside the Collins Elite*

"Is this guy still faking it?" I hadn't realized how frazzled I was until I saw everyone in Jay's room. Their joy at seeing me enter was restorative. Beck left me speechless for a few moments with a warm embrace that defied her character. With her hair pulled back in a bun, and decked out in fatigues, she looked ready to join Brody's Green Elite squad. I made my way to Jay's bedside to give him a fist-bump and then get his take on the horrible quake.

"So what's up tiger, you ready to get back into action?" Nia knew just what I meant and quickly cut in.

"Nope, he's going to be a mess cook. Much safer I think. He only just woke. You timed your visit well. They say he'll be up walking in a few more days." Jay thought about protesting her remark about being a cook, but I didn't let him.

"C'mon man, you're missing everything. This might come as a shock, but an alien armada just buzzed the Earth to let us know they're taking over. Don't sweat it though, you only slept through the greatest event in history." He tried to laugh but grimaced instead. Jay's voice was gritty and weak.

"Yeah, I saw the reruns. They don't scare me. We can take those guys. You forget, I can call down fire from heaven and roast their butts." We all laughed as Jay clutched his side. He motioned to a monitor on low volume behind me. "Did you hear about the Gs? Most of Region 5, all the way to Region 4, is at 20% less gravity right now. They say it dipped to 30% and was fluctuating until it leveled off. It least it didn't drop to nothing like it did here." The calamity was hard to grasp; from Asia down to Australia, how much worse was it going to get? I shrugged my shoulders like it was no big deal.

"No, I hadn't heard. Not cool. Well, once we get team Zero-Gs all back to health we'll have to go over there and save them." Pak cleared his throat behind me. Was he about to make his retirement official?

"We didn't expect everyone to be all together in one place this morning, so we uh, well—I'd like to announce that Ivy and I are engaged." A boisterous roar went up as waves of hugs and handshakes made their way around. Jay and I shot each other looks of disbelief. Had our childhoods just ended? Pak was only nineteen, but with such an uncertain future facing us perhaps it was best to accelerate one's bucket list. No doubt near fatal earthquakes didn't promote patience either. I waited until the hoopla had ended before going over to embrace the big man. Pak looked filthy, with cuts on his face and rips down his shirt.

"You Casanova, this is a big step. Congratulations. Does Ivy know what she's getting herself into?" Pak was drenched in sweat and emotion.

"No, not at all, and don't tell her otherwise she'll back out for sure."

More laughs put Jay through another round of agony. I hugged Ivy and took my first serious look at her face. She was glowing apple pie personified. I had no right to question their decision, what with life becoming so screwed up and dangerous. Their romance may have saved our lives by soothing the big galoot during our stay. Pak was bursting with pride and the happiest I'd ever seen him. "Ivy Pateras, now THAT has a nice ring to it," I remarked.

"I'm partial," Little Ivy's timid voice chimed back in her cute southern drawl. I started to feel jealous. She held out her hand to show off a silver band they'd gotten at the market for a modest sum. It didn't matter; they were beyond the trappings of social pressure here. Free spirits, they would have been as happy stranded on a desert island with nothing. The announcement likely doubled as Pak's resignation from the team, if there was such a thing anymore.

We sat around and laughed until a nurse chased us out, anxious to clean up the many spilled items from the earthquake. Everyone agreed to help with the base repairs and then reconvene later to continue the engagement celebration. As we shuffled out, Beck grabbed my arm and asked if I could talk for a minute. She seemed far too soft and caring. Something wasn't right. I suggested the waiting area where Pastor B and I had our last talk. She agreed, saying she would join me there in a moment. From my vantage point I could see Beck and Suri having an intense conversation. They were never seen apart these days so I figured it to be some kind of separation anxiety. Beck was doing most of the talking until she broke away. She hadn't even sat yet when my blabbing burst out.

"Beck, my goodness. I'm glad Suri is doing better now, and that you have a good friend and all, but what is up with you two?"

"She's a wreck, poor thing, and been through quite a lot..."

It felt queer to be talking with Beck in such a formal way. As she spoke, nerves began creeping over me like a fast moving vine.

"Anyway, growing up, her family was devoutly Hindu. After Suri started working for India's intelligence agency as an English translator, she met a Christian boy and fell in love. Do you want to hear all this now?" I nodded a confirmation as Beck got comfortable in her chair and went on.

"Well, she became a believer too, but tried to keep it a secret from her abusive father. One day she refused to participate in the worship of Manasa devi, the goddess of snakes or something, and made the decision to tell her father her intent to marry a Christian outside her caste. He went ballistic and disowned her but not before revealing the boy's name to the local extremist goons in Kanpur. They found him and beat him so bad he died from his injuries. They raped and abused her and threatened to burn her alive if she didn't convert back. She sought help from within the agency and was lucky enough to run into a sympathetic director who arranged an overseas assignment. Her story followed her and someone from Collins made contact. She accepted their invitation and wound up here."

I sat wide-eyed at Beck's story and lamented my lack of patience with their relationship. Suri's past revealed something that was only top-of-mind because of Newt's darn CRL report. My stomached hurt thinking about the Messenger's Truisms, and how humanity had been primed to embrace them. I couldn't resist a little commentary.

"This plays right into what the Messengers are saying, that religion is evil. It causes division and violence—" Beck's acrid expression said: *don't go there,* and that it was time to talk about "people, and love and friendships." I complied and shifted gears. "But wow, I can see why Suri is so clingy. It's awesome how you're caring for her. She's lucky to have you."

"No need to flatter me. It's the least I can do. Everyone here has lost or given up everything. Their strength is inspiring. Suri does feel blessed, but not because of me, but because she was privileged enough to suffer for Jesus' name. 'Our enemies will be from our own households,' and you know I can relate to that. She's helped me see my trials in a new light."

I wasn't sitting with Beck. I was sitting with some woman who had taken her over. The familiar feeling of being behind the rest of the team was rearing its ugly head again, only this time it was about growing up. Did she feel like she was sitting with a man, or some boy who was still trying to find his way? I wanted to confide in her about Dad's found and lost beacon, even his cryptic note, but clenched it inside. The knowledge about the signal felt like a freshly diagnosed sickness; one where I wasn't ready to share the news until I knew if it were fatal.

"Anyway, that's not why I wanted to talk to you, Garret."

She scanned the area to make sure no one was within earshot before continuing in a don't-wake-the-angry-dog whisper. There was a lot of that going on.

"I don't know what your plans are but I have no intention of living the rest of my life buried down here, and neither do Pak and Ivy. This place is a death-trap, and there are a few people I'd rather not be around any more."

The sudden feeling of falling spun through my insides.

Was I about to lose my friends—lose Beck?

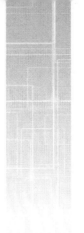

Part 6: The Collins Elite
Chapter 17

"In Eisenhower's 1961 Farewell speech, he warned us that 'only an alert and knowledgeable citizenry' could keep in check the locomotive might of our military machine. From where I'm standing neither the majority of pre-Meltdown citizens, nor the post-, new and improved Global Citizen, would qualify as knowledgeable OR alert. It still remains that only a very slim minority act as the canary in the coal mine, unheard, until it's too late for both them and the miners."

—Piper Corcoran, *Can Things Get Any Stranger? Volume II*

Beck could tell I was stunned and uncomfortable so she picked up the pace of her dissertation. I chewed a thumbnail and tried to look relaxed.

"Nia's uncle has a farm a few days walk from here. He'll let us work part of the land until we can get on our feet, or figure out where we're going. There are vacant workers quarters with enough room for all of us. I know that sounds radical but we've been talking about it for days and we don't see any other option. You don't have to answer right away but of course we want you to go with us." Beck was so calm, like she'd just ask me out for an ice cream. I was breaking a sweat.

"What about Jay? How did he respond?"

"We didn't ask him yet. Nia was waiting a little longer until he felt better. She's scared he'll say no. We didn't talk to your mom either but my mom is going, and so is Suri. Ivy has farming experience and is looking forward to it."

"Beck, can you see my mom milking goats on some make-shift farm? No, she'll stay here. But you don't even know this uncle of hers. What if he turns our names into the authorities? While I agree staying at this outpost sounds pretty awful, isn't it a huge risk to go out there with no food and no money?"

Beck considered my argument and suggested that I ask for something in exchange for my father's research. She had a point. I mean, the Collins staff did take everything he'd created. At the same time Beck worried that Colonel Reed might feel that our team knew too much to just let us walk away. Telling them of our departure might land us in hot water. She shook herself free of that line of thought and squinted at me with new resolve.

"But Garret, your objections are not about a 'risky farm venture.' Be honest with me. Are you joining up with their cause for the long haul? I can see you turning into Brody Freeman, spending the rest of your life trying to avenge your father's death."

It was startled at how well she saw the situation. Was I a member of the Collins Elite? I hadn't even thought about that. I reminded Beck about the vision I had of sharpening my sword for some future battle. If Outpost 6 wasn't it, what was? I declared that there were no cowards in the Collins war. Eyes whirled before she slapped a palm to her forehead.

"Building our own lives is not cowardice. You know darn well that God is going to be the one to defeat Satan, not our puny efforts. We could form a secret group of praying warriors that does far more damage 'binding and loosing' things supernaturally. The fight is not in the physical world. C'mon Garret, this is stuff we went over at house-church every week."

I cleared my throat hard to protest her condescending tone.

"Tell that to Joshua and Caleb. Did they just pray against their adversaries, or did they have to go out and slay some fools? I'm sure they had plenty of prayer warriors back at camp 'binding and loosing' and all that. Heck, it's probably the only way they *did* win—" I paused, considering the conversation's weight, "—so to your point, we might be called in different directions. You could be more the 'back at camp, praying type,' and me, well—the guy sent to the front lines. Pastor B says it may cost me my life. So be it. That might be how I end up." Beck waved away my comment like a pesky bug.

"Don't throw out old testament events as an excuse to make war. God was fulfilling a promise to the Jews and that has nothing to do with us. Christ came and told us what we're supposed to be about." Her tone was growing fierce. "Can you see Jesus walking in here and telling us to make a bunch of Caliber suits so we can go bomb the armies of darkness?" Moving out toward the edge of her seat she signaled our time was at an end. I argued on.

"I'm not going to say what Jesus would think about this place, and you shouldn't either. I *do* know that if Caleb had access to a Caliber exo-suit, he sure-fire would have used it to kill some giants! Christians are supposed to endure; I got it, and count it all as blessing when we're persecuted. But I have the feeling history is about to repeat itself where God calls His faithful into some real and dangerous action."

The look on her face revealed that she saw me merging with the mass of abusive males she wanted no part of. Perhaps the reason Beck was so enamored the first time she saw me inside my Brawler was because with it I'd evolved beyond the gender she so distrusted. I was stronger once inside the suit, something she could count on. Now I was letting her down, like all unpredictable and warmongering men.

"Turn your swords into plowshares," she demanded, as if she'd written it herself.

"There's also a time to turn them back into swords, and for the weakest to become warriors. Bet you didn't know the Bible said that. In Job, I think." In Joel actually.

"You talk about this like you're gearing up to take the steep slope at Schweitzer, Garret. This is about killing. There are eternal issues here. What about doing whatever you can to live in peace with everyone?"

"With people, Mac, with human people. You know there's something to what Newt said about what's piloting those black crab ships. Satan's forces are massing for attack and I don't think those scriptures you're sighting apply. If one of them tried to take you, I wouldn't hesitate to blow it away. All would be well with my soul." I hoped chivalry would gain me some brownie points, but no, she went for the jugular.

"You haven't surprised me much. You *are* turning into a bloodthirsty Brody Freeman. You're so delusional you don't know you're delusional. I respect how angry you still are, but 'there's a way that seems right to a man, and in the end it leads only to death.'"

With that, I decided not to get so caught up in trying to prove something that she never knew my true feelings. Beck started to stand up but I motioned sternly for her to remain. She complied with a sigh so strong I thought it might blow her nose off.

"Don't get me wrong. I didn't say I wouldn't go with you. I'm only saying I'm torn about it. Don't you think I'm sick of this place? The thought of getting out of here, seeing the sky everyday and starting a family sounds a lot better than dying in the wrong battle." I saw Beck twitch when I mentioned starting a family, but I couldn't tell if it was a good twitch or bad.

At that moment, I longed to do it all; fight only the fights God was calling me to and run away with Beck and my friends and live out a simple, happy life. It was time to have a long talk with Pastor B again. Beck looked sullen as she raised her wrist and began undoing the bracelet the lady had given us at the market.

"Garret, take this. There was something to what happened that day in the market. I've had a feeling that old woman was right. You are going on a journey. While this won't protect you, it might remind you of us, of happier times, and give you strength when you need it."

"That's not the bracelet I want, Beck."

With that she stopped getting out of her chair. Sitting slowly, she took a long, determined review of me. Then she raised an eyebrow and turned away from my expectant stare.

"Well, this is all you get for now."

"For now" was better than never, I supposed. After a moment, her eyes shut and her head fell forward. A flower bent from too much rain.

Beck stood and began tying the strap around my wrist. It felt like a goodbye but my crystal ball was too hazy to tell. For all I knew I might soon be off herding sheep or find myself in a mecha battle, firing missiles at a squadron of Scimitars. I whimpered.

"Beck, don't you want me to fulfill my destiny? Do what I'm supposed to do even if it takes me down a difficult path?"

She didn't say anything for a moment as we both watched her hands finish tying on the bracelet. A single tear landed on my forearm and she sniffed. Against her will, our gazes met. Real sorrow was tearing through her and she spoke in a barely audible whisper.

"I know you want to make your Dad proud. I know you want to fight some great battle. Just be careful that you're not so caught up in the mission that you forget it's all about sitting at the feet of Jesus. Everything else is a shooting star…"

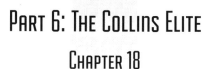

Part 6: The Collins Elite
Chapter 18

"The stage was set. The eternal workings of Karma had reunited the creators—restoring their creation—and the creation, once again embracing their creators. The perfected and the flawed, playing their respective parts in a performance for the ages."

—Susan Thompson, *We Are All Children of Noble Light*

An unexpected breakfast encounter with Pak and Ivy had turned enlightening. They were putting much of my trepidation about rural survival to rest. Ivy possessed the skill and knowledge, Pak the strength and determination, to pull it off. Ivy told Beck and I about her youth while we slurped up some "quacker" oatmeal, as the locals called it.

Her story, like so many, was a tragic one and she was lucky to be alive. After turning into a teenage hellion and rejecting life on her family's Georgian farm, the situation became tense enough that Ivy ended up living with her grandmother. So when the great gun grab swept the southern U.S., she was out of harm's way. The farm was confiscated and she never saw her parents again.

Authorities claimed her father had opened fire on the UN forces rather than give up his weapons and even set booby traps that killed a dozen troops. From the way she described him, he may well have.

The story was repeated by the tens of thousands, as lifelong America gun owners retaliated and cried *don't tread on me.* The states of Texas, Oklahoma and Utah declared their independence but it was short lived. Massive amounts of UN and foreign "peace-keeping" troops had conducted secret preparations toward that event for decades and stamped out resistance within weeks. The response was swift and fierce.

Ivy now carried a burning desire to work the land and make up for what she'd put her parents through. It seemed we were all trying to corral the shadows of the past into the light. While I still remained torn over the decision to go with them, at least now I had some hope we could subsist. It wouldn't be enough to sway Jay though. He had become a capable co-pilot on one of the glorious Cavalry ships in a matter of weeks, and then there was his extreme aptitude manning combat armors. Once that kind of stuff gets into your blood, it's hard to give up. Especially when the other option is growing root vegetables on a hillside in the middle of nowhere.

As Ivy told her story, I flopped a piece of mystery meat back and forth a few times before taking a bite. Would it soon be illegal to raise animals for food? *What a shame to lose salty fare of this kind,* I thought, taking my last bite. Chewing it slowly to savor the memory, I left the table to talk Jay into our new Hee-Haw lifestyle. At least Chills would appreciate the upgraded environment.

My route toward the infirmary was interrupted by a loud commotion coming from the hanger. Once curiosity pulled me there to investigate, my eyes were shocked to see brand new Caliber vehicles being loaded onto the large airships. Newt was among several lab coats and military personnel having a discussion in front of a floating monitor. He saw me approach and watch in amazement as the intimidating four-wheeled brutes rumbled up the ramp one by one. He broke from the group and headed my direction.

"There they are." Newt's tone contained more disappointment than revelry. After touching one of the Caliber car's thick armored fenders, I knew its likeness would be added to my growing library of drawings.

"I can't believe you guys made all those just since we've been here. They look pretty awesome and more heavily armored than Pak's version."

"Yes, they've been upgraded in almost every way. Although, the task they've been given may yet be too tall, even for them." Newt's expression had me worried.

"What is their task? I've been wondering just who it is the Green Elite have been fighting. How have they lost so many men?" Newt glanced back at the group to make sure they were all still occupied.

"There have long been secret wars taking place, wars within almost every government, between the forces of good shall we say, and those of the "Luciferian" agenda. The stories I could tell you of large-scale battles under the ground or in space are difficult to imagine, all taking place over the last few decades. But this, this mission is of a different sort, and I can't say I'm in favor of it." The squad of Calibers drove down the ramp, drawing more admirers to watch them in action.

"What are they for, why are they coming back out of the ships?" I asked.

"Right now they're just fitting them into the internal holding bays and running through some deployment drills. Soon, as I understand it, they are going to form a quick-strike squad and attempt a high-level *assassination*." Newt whispered *assassination,* so I whispered it back as a question.

Asserting his information was very hush-hush, he said that Colonel Reed's sources were claiming the alien Messengers were about to elect someone from the CRL as a supreme leader to enforce their will among the people of Earth. Newt knew I wasn't following world news so he caught me up on the Middle East, which had erupted in violence over the seventh Trusim, dissolving religion. On the brink of "all out war" is how Newt phrased it, and the Collins higher ups suspected the election of this man from the council may well be the intended anti-christ who will resolve the situation in glory. Anytime the words anti-christ were spoken it always made part of me shrivel in fear. I questioned if killing him would not only be impossible but might fulfill prophetic scripture. Even a novice knew the anti-christ was supposed to receive a head wound and survive it, cementing his deification.

"Well done, your Dad would be proud," Newt replied. "While I admire their tenacity, I'm not sure it will be that easy. The retaliation for such a strike will be terrible. The UN won't humor the existence of this place following such brazen action. Dr. Kalko and his team feel they are quite safe here, hidden from detection. You know I disagree with their position. I've made my opinion known and they know where I stand. I wanted to talk to you and the team about relocating with me in a week's time. I can't promise much improvement in the surroundings, it would be only a slight variation from what you've experienced at Outpost 6."

"Funny you should mention bugging out. The team is thinking about a change of scenery and trying our hand at farming, if you can picture that. I'm on the *fence* about it, but maybe this is confirmation that it's the right thing."

"What about your vehicles? Would you try to take them?"

"Guess not. We'll be keeping a low profile and have no way to maintain them. Maybe it's time to turn our backs on technology in favor of a more simplified life. You know me Newt, I'm struggling with the whole idea—and I haven't even run it by Jay yet."

The Calibers had deplaned, spurring the brass to relocate to another part of the complex. One of the officers gave Newt the sign that they were moving on and he acknowledged he would soon join them. Newt turned back to me with some final words.

"I can't argue with the idea. In fact, I'm rather tempted to go with you myself. Sipping tea on the front porch somewhere sounds ideal, but alas, my path lays elsewhere." I laughed when I realized he wasn't joking.

"From what Ivy says there's not going to be much tea sipping for a while, but how will you ever find us? We won't even have phones."

"I have my ways. Let me prepare a beacon, and a plan, in case we ever want to secretly get in touch."

"Newt, there's one more thing. I feel weird for even asking, but do you think I might be able to get a little something for all Dad's work on the machines? I wouldn't ask, but it looks like they've worked out well for them and we'd be venturing out there with nothing." Newt felt bad for not thinking of it himself.

"Yes, of course. I'll see what I can do." He sighed a heavy sigh as he considered the drastic change it would mean for all of us. "In many ways you've felt like the son I've never had. I want to say I'm proud of you and wish you and the rest all the best. The clock is ticking down towards the finale, and dark days are just ahead. You will be in my prayers."

The great Dr. Bigsby turned to leave but I grabbed him first. Hugging him tight, I reached up and jostled his gray Larry-hair, puffing it up like an inflated wad of cotton. He tried to pat it down as he walked away, smiling as he went.

What was I going to say to Jay now? Newt's bailing while the Collins Elite attempt to kill the anti-christ. But team Zero-Gs has decided to duck out and live as hay seeds someplace? A sudden PA announcement ended my stream of uncertainty.

"Attention, attention. This is a gravity control alert. Follow proper emergency procedures and report to stations immediately..."

Personnel scrambled around me, their urgency heightened following the last dreadful quake. I'd have to man my battle station in Jay's room because we had much to discuss.

Part 7: Hay Seeds
Chapter 1

"Tyranny grew in our country from within, and they are determined to preserve not only this union, but add to it every state and country upon God's green Earth. Standing firm against this tyranny is our answer to overbearing authority, and defiant we will stand, our rightful guns in hand. I implore you and the mighty state of Colorado to stand with us now. For if you give in, a slave's life will overtake you, and you will know nothing of freedom. Only those who are brave are free. And I assume the state of Utah is free until they show me otherwise."

—Utah Governor Sebastian Clare, *To The Governor of Colorado, 2037*

I bee lined toward the infirmary amidst the base's swirling chaos. Jay was up and around with assistance from Nia and an old man's walking device when I entered his room.

"Hey man, nice walker. You'll be down at the park feeding the pigeons in no time." Jay didn't look up at me, entirely focused on his elderly stroll.

"Thanks. You'll be the first one I smack with my cane, too."

Nia looked tired as she helped guide him along and more than a little disappointed. She moaned.

"Rebecca and I told him the plan. He thinks we're crazy, of course."

"He might not after I tell him what I just saw in the hanger." That got his attention, but after I laid everything out his response was much as I predicted.

"Listen G, if I wasn't so banged up I would want to be flying in one of the Cavalry ships with them. Have you grown soft or something? This is our time. Why do you think we're here?" Jay was questioning my manhood and I was grateful for the macho perspective. Still, I argued to the contrary.

"Believe me, I considered that. But a lot of people I respect are saying it might not be the right time, or right battle. Maybe we can get Newt to take the Brawlers with him and evaluate our options in a few months. If its not working for us out there, we can join up again with him, or come back here. Let's just make sure we leave on good terms."

Jay still wasn't buying it. A nurse came through the door, furious that he was up and around during the gravity alert. She ordered him back into bed and questioned Nia and I whether we were allowed in that area. We made up something that extended our stay. I sat in a chair next to Jay's bed, waiting for him to get settled and stop all his grunting and groaning. Resting my chin on the gurney's rail, my seldom seen puppy-dog eyes made an appearance.

"I'm with you man, but Beck wants out of here and I want to go with her."

"I always wondered about you two." Jay avoided eye contact while Nia adjusted his pillows. My pathetic tone continued.

"Yeah? Well, that makes two of us. I'm still wondering myself. Let me know if you figure anything out." Nia, drawn out by the sudden twist in conversation, leaned over the bed and turned Jay's face to hers.

"I want you to go with me too. If you think I'm opposed to bravery and honor you're wrong. There may be a time to fight and even give our lives but I've had a bad premonition about this place since I got here." Nia's sway had increased and it didn't take long for Jay to turn back to me, beaten.

"See if Newt will take the Brawlers and keep them safe for us. If there's an agreement to bail on the whole farm-thing if it's not working then let's do it. Since we haven't made any kind of commitment here we can tell them we're taking a leave. I need a few weeks to heal up from *what you did to me* anyway."

An announcement rang out cancelling the gravity alert and we heaved in collective relief.

Jay, arms tightly crossed, sent me a laser look. His expression said the final decision rested on me and that it had better work out—or else. As much as I was looking forward to being out of that hole and into some fresh air, I would not have been surprised to see us going back there in three months to enlist long term. If I were honest with myself then, I was itching to do that very thing. Just then Beck swung the door open with an expectant look. I smiled and nodded.

"We're in."

Part 7: Hay Seeds

Chapter 2

"The Council has just announced that the Messengers will assist us on a mission to Mars, lending one of their own ships so that humanity can at last tread upon the red planet. The Councilmen alluded to, but did not define, the mission's purpose. He stated that 'irrefutable proof awaits us there,' a historical retelling of our own story but without the happy ending we've been given a chance at here on Earth. Other advisors were calling it an expedition to discover a civilization buried by time and poor judgment. Neither did they heed warnings nor make the drastic changes necessary to avoid being consumed by the Grays and other cosmic carnivores. Should any doubters still remain, as to the truth and generosity of our heavenly benefactors, they will soon be turned into believers."

—Warner Roxwell, *Our Backs Against the Wall*

fter two more days, Jay's health had improved a great deal. While he was warming to the idea of us making a go of it on our own, he ached to throw himself into the flurry of mission preparation taking place all over the outpost. Beck's fears about having to slip away, or escape, proved unfounded. The Collins folks were not in the business of taking prisoners. Colonel Reed wished us well, but revealed that the base was about to go on total lockdown leading up to the operation. Tomorrow morning was the deadline for our group to leave. He began to hint at possible repercussions should we ever start talking about the organization or the base location, but he stopped short. He almost felt like a kindred spirit, or even an older version of myself—albeit an idealized version of my latter years. Now that thought is laughable. I'll never get the chance to be a grizzled old, well—anything. He extended a hearty invitation if we ever wished to return and mourned losing us.

The team's plans to leave had not been run by mom yet. I hadn't even seen her for several days but she was in when I paid my visit. Her metal box of a room was only a little larger than mine but she'd managed to make even that crude space hint at elegance, removing every speck of dust or dirt. White sheets hung on the walls to cover the buckling panels, pulled tight at every corner and fastened into the wall's seams by pushpin. Rebellious ooze had come through and stained a spot, but this she covered with an illustration of Christ holding a found lamb. Appropriate I thought, but even here I felt strange about sitting on anything.

I fished for a complaint about her radically altered environment, or accusation against me for causing it, but she spurned any notion. Mom knew this was a culminating event, the summit of her verbal devotion about being content in much and in little. I decided not to press when I sensed there was a trapped waterfall of anger and emotion behind her eyes. If I kept going I might just pull out the stopper and then what would I do?

When the talk turned to the team's exit plans the conversation went much as I expected. It was difficult to unglue her from the TV monitor and the major world events threatening to unravel humanity's recent progress. Images of riots and violent religious demonstrations took center stage as the former Lebanon and Israel faced off with renewed ferocity. Several cities struggled to keep back the charging mobs as tear gas and gunfire rang out in the background. The bleary-eyed reporter was trying to remain calm, but had a real look of fear as she relayed the latest developments. A dusty dune whipped into a mini-tornado behind her as a troop transport rumbled past, causing her to shout the update.

"The Islamic Resistance, the military arm of Hezbolla, issued a statement today saying 'We recognize our future calls for change, but this is not time to walk forward blindly while Israel stands in opposition to everything just and true. We favor the wisdom put forward in the 7th Truism and identify ourselves as progressives, but Israel epitomizes reactionary thinking and must be eliminated.'"

Her non-mic hand held a thin stack of paper and it reached up to remove a mass of dark hair that had blown over her face. The papers became crumpled in the process. A dirty fog blew through and cleared and she shouted still louder.

"The Council of Resplendent Light has also issued a statement condemning the clashes by saying 'the continued violence exemplifies how clinging to erroneous and dogmatic beliefs will doom our species.' They relayed that our extraterrestrial benefactors will not intervene, but may withdraw their assistance if the situation is not soon resolved."

The first twelve Truisms were sparking a host of emergencies as bulletins scrolled along the bottom of the broadcast; "beef, pork and poultry farmers unite in worldwide protest—UN and IMF representatives meeting today with CRL on talks to subsidize global meat producers and transition them over to new industries of food production." Things were coming apart at the seams. So much for being saved from ourselves. Instead of humanity emerging triumphantly from its own ashes we seemed to be sinking back into our own filth. Mom's blank stare told me she was absorbed in the crisis and would put up little resistance to me doing whatever I wanted. She shook her head at the monitor.

"Everyone is turning on Israel like never before. People think we cannot survive without these ET invaders. We're playing right into their hands." When the coverage transferred back into the studio, she cut her speech short. The duo of awkward anchors looked exhausted behind the desk. Mom suspected these haggard personas were being cleverly crafted, just as the polished ones had before. Doing hairdos a little less neat, even choosing ill-fitting wardrobes, conveyed that the speaker in question was the real deal, "just like us." But the anchorman couldn't hide his TV teeth as he went into his best news-guy over enunciation.

"The former Pontiff issued a statement saying; 'Our deliverers from above should not lose hope in humanity.' He continued to urge the Messengers to 'step forward and offer an emissary of their own to guide us through this critical time'. The Pontifex stated that this step would reveal to the world what he already knows: that our races share both a common ancestry and a common future; a peaceful and progressive future."

Finally, I managed to get mom to ignore the endless blabbing. After hearing me out about the team's plans, she placed a gentle kiss on my forehead and said she had given me over to the Lord's work long ago. I was His to do with as He wished; it was not up to her. I spoke of Newt's eminent departure and urged her to follow him wherever he was going but she wanted no part of that either. She would not be going anywhere again without being forced.

Mom seemed so disconnected from everything and disconnected from me. Yet it didn't come off as offensive, more like contentment with whatever God had for her. Perhaps it was just self-preservation. A protective instinct to cushion against the disasters and disappointments she thought lay just ahead. My heart hurt a little over her uncaring attitude, but I remembered Dad tell me once that all mothers are slightly insane, and that you have to be to do that job.

Hugging her, I felt like we would meet again much sooner than later. Maybe I had already made up my mind to take the colonel up on his offer to join the Collins Elite, making their mission my own.

Almost pushed from her room, my mother hugged me once more and returned to the TV's unfolding drama.

Part 7: Hay Seeds

Chapter 3

"Most signals to the unseen horror were less subtle than the one Bob Dylan gave out in his now infamous 2004 interview with Ed Bradley on 60 Minutes. Not only did Mr. Dylan have no choice in whether he'd like to continue performing, he had no choice in the matter of his own life and death. The 'Chief Commander' spoken about was an immovable pact between with the forces of darkness and influential movie stars and politicians in the spotlight. While signing in blood on the dotted line may have been their own undoing, they soon learned that it was 'sleep in your mansions and keep quiet'—or you'll soon wake up dead."

—Kelley Fenella; *The Death of Hollywood*

My visit with Mom left me unsettled, with unexpected time on my hands—until I remembered Pastor B. If there was anyone I should have been running plans by it was that man.

I began a mental rehearsal of how I would catch him up on the latest details, but the voice inside my head started doing that thing again. The thing where I coerce the person I'm sitting with to agree with all my ways of thinking, thereby making the decision a corporate one and easier to rationalize. If I wanted his true thoughts on the matter, he would need to hear all the options without my opinion getting in the way. I made my way toward Pastor B's office and gave a tap on the metal door. He had several assistants and one answered moments after I knocked a second time.

"I'm sorry, Pastor Babineaux is away right now." Dressed in full fatigues, she was unnerved by my presence.

"Away? What kind of away? When will he be back?"

"He is away on a confidential assignment and I'm not sure when he'll return." She grew impatient with further questioning and informed me that he had been gone for several days. I didn't give up until she closed the door in my face, as if somehow my continued asking for him might bring him back sooner. This turn of events felt even more disorienting, with a little kick-to-the-stomach feeling thrown in. Pastor B was a permanent fixture there, like a comfortable pair of slippers that were waiting whenever I needed them.

My eyes scanned the hallway for someone, anyone to complain to about this injustice. Not a soul could care. Hollow footsteps clanged close by and echoed in the distance as people passed one another without saying a word. My insides felt as cold and hard as the floor.

I hadn't realized how much I was counting on some kind of strong outside confirmation to make moving forward with Beck's idea more palatable. Mom would have issued the same "there-there dear, you'll do fine" even if I had told her I was off to join the French Foreign Legion, naked. Jay had been convinced it was a good idea but maybe it wasn't too late to revisit the whole thing. I stood there stunned and directionless until a hurried clattering approached from down the hall, waking me from my mystification. It was Newt and Minerva, an unusual pair. Newt kept coming toward me until his face was inches from mine. He delivered his news in a sharp whisper.

"Garret, we have the *signal*."

A trembling started the moment I processed the doctor's outrageous words. Minerva's eyes were as big as saucers, as if she knew all the details and was watching them reverberate inside me. Newt was euphoric and ready to take action.

"There is no time to waste. I just met with the colonel and he understands the situation. He was a fan of your father's, in case you weren't aware, and has offered Cavalry 1 in a rescue operation if certain conditions are met. I didn't mention he knew your father before because it may have stoked some rivalries here between certain 'factions.'" Someone's footsteps alerted us to their approach so we went silent until they passed. Then Newt tilted his head toward me before going on, signaling what a *lucky chap* I was at the sudden turn of events.

"We're quite blessed because Captain Doon here had offered the colonel her services if he ever thought you needed assistance with your training. I believe when he recalled her recent offer, it helped make him agreeable."

"What conditions?" They had no idea how nervous I was. Clammy hands gripped each other to conceal their quiver.

"You must leave right now, make it a secret operation since a tremendous resource is at risk for a personal matter, and return immediately if any hostile activity is encountered," Newt continued," Oh, and he wants as tight a crew as possible. They cannot spare anyone with their critical mission approaching." Minerva sneered at the idea we might be short-handed.

"We got this, no problem." My eyebrows rose to a great height over how foolish she sounded. The broad smile on her face tried to create more of the same in Newt and me, but it remained our group's only one.

"Is my Brawler ready to go?" I asked frantically, "And what about

Glynn? Can we take Glynn, my fight-tech at least?" Newt rubbed my arm to calm me.

"Yes, yes, that would be fine I think, but you must hurry. We don't want to lose the beacon again without finding something out this time."

Minerva shot off down the hall to alert Glynn and get Cavalry 1 prepped for launch. She said she'd load my Brawler and get my jump suit on board but not before making a joke about giving up my toy bike for a real man's J-22. This mission was too much fun for her and I wished she would act more serious. A taste of my own medicine I guess. Once we were alone, Newt pulled me aside and softened his whisper another notch.

"The location is next to the National Laboratory in Albuquerque. You will be there in a short time. It's an active and heavily guarded Air Force Base, but we believe the signal is coming from a short distance away, from the abandoned Manzano underground facility that used to be associated with it. They closed it down in the 1990s, even before the mass closings for nefarious activity, but I believe something may still be going on there. Please use caution. As I said, we're blessed to have Minerva because she has been there several times, knowing the layout and the security you'll be facing."

"Newt, what about the capsule training? You never gave them to me! How am I supposed to do this?" He put his palms on my chest.

"My boy, you must trust in the Lord. He is watching over you. I would not let you leave this place if I thought for one moment you couldn't pull it off. Garret, listen, I told the colonel I have to go. I'm now needed elsewhere. It cannot wait. How I wish I could be here when you and Evan arrive back together—and I can only hope that is what happens tonight. Here..." He reached into his lab coat pocket and removed an envelope and two small, plastic pouches.

"Some money. I wish it could be more. It's local cash—I couldn't get you metals. And these are two homing beacons so that we can find each other later on." I put the paper money away, unsure of how long it might be usable, and held up the beacons for close inspection. Newt was talking fast as he began leading me toward the hanger.

"Put the signal beacons in different places and don't lose track of them. After a few months, turn one on the first day of the month at midnight and leave it on for twenty minutes. Repeat that process until I make contact. Captain Doon is loading Evan's homing signal onto Cavalry 1 and your combat armors. It should take you straight to the source."

I took a massive breath and steadied myself, placing the beacons in two separate pockets as if that counted towards what he meant. Then I remembered Beck and our deadline to exit Outpost 6.

"Newt, before you go, you have to tell Beck what's going on. Tell her I'll be right back, before morning. We were supposed to leave early. Please, Newt, I don't have time to go see her now and she might try to talk me out of this."

"Yes, certainly. When I say my goodbyes and I will pass along the message and will wait until you've launched so she cannot chase you down. I see you're outside Pastor Babineux's office. There's a possibility we might be running into each other soon. Did you want me to say anything to him as well?"

"Yes, just tell him that I'm sorry I missed him, and I appreciated his friendship." Newt nodded and gave me a final shove down the corridor. I set off on a jog and realized that my legs had turned to rubber. Then Newt called out for me. Did he really have to do that cliché "You'll do great, Garret, just believe in yourself" thing? I was already trying to muster some focus.

"Garret, I must… I… That was *me* masquerading in the parking garage…"

We stood facing each other for the longest second; stunned.

A response wasn't possible while I tried to reconstruct all that it meant. What about the day out by the old dirt path, or his suggestion we take the ride armors to school? Clever Newt: shrewd to the last. Tell me at a time when I cannot possibly go off on you. He gazed at the floor in shame, like a dog busted for wreaking havoc while his owners were out. He mumbled on.

"They were close, Garret, about to pounce. I had to get us away from there. Your mother would never have—" I raised my vibrating hand toward him in the universal stop sign.

"It's okay, Newt. Let's just get Dad back."

I didn't know if it *was* actually okay. I'd have to figure that out later. The near wall steadied my stance while I took a final, deep breath. Newt said nothing else as I pushed myself down the hall to leave him, and the team, behind.

The darkened hangar opened before me and I could see exhaust pouring from Cavalry 1's vents. Its landing lights were already glowing in the snaking mist. My heart sought the courage that had been eluding its innards.

May angels go before me this terrible night...

Part 8: The Mission
Chapter 1

"Of the many things out of reach, the most distant was Beck. Though accessible upon request, it was her heart that was a Rapunzel, locked away in its high tower. It seemed she'd even boarded up the last window, so nary a hair could linger down to lift me up."

—Garret Philmore, *Letters on the Lamb: A Collected Journal*

A mosaic of summer light played across a pair of children too high up in a tree for their size. A strong breeze tossed the round shroud of maple leaves in a constant, comforting commotion around their wooden perch.

"What am I doing this for?" The dull screwdriver, oversized for his hand, scraped and scratched at the tough layers of bark. The crabby artist wielding the tool was not alone.

"Cuz silly, we're supposed to." A companion and critic, she averted her gaze from the project until she heard it start up again. Progress was watched with keen interest as short legs scissored back and forth over a thick limb. The red denim fabric that covered them was well worn and stained from countless adventures. "Everybody knows boys and girls carve their names on stuff. I dunno why, it just sounds fun." She squinted hard and wrinkled her forehead to decipher what he'd managed so far.

"What does that say, *Bek?*" She asked.

He frowned over her lack of encouragement.

"I'm gettin' tired, and this thing doesn't work that great." His tiny tongue stuck out to one side, held in place by baby teeth getting looser by the day. He chipped away furiously at the tree. "I'm like—sweating, I need a knife or something."

"*Bek & G,* okay that's enough. Now do a heart around it." She directed, as if they'd already discussed this detail.

"You mean like all around here?" An arm drew a giant circle in the air, an exaggerated motion to make sure she was well aware of his frustration. "You're crazy. This only sounded fun cuz you don't have to do anything!"

"Here, gimme that." She stood up on the branch and tiptoed high-wire style toward the carving in progress.

"Careful, that's pretty far down." He leaned back to let her try her hand at the carving but she did more than try. A sudden and frenzied motion sent chips of bark flying into his face. "Hey, watch it! You almost just poked me in the eye!" She'd completed their project.

There, see? Now we kiss." A grinning pucker of the most innocent kind took shape below a set of closed, five year old eyes.

"A KISS? You are crazy Rebecca, yuck!"

"No—it's a present, to remember me by. C'mon." The sinister lips doubled up once more, edging closer and closer until it chased the young boy down the branch. To allow it meant certain death. With no other avenue of escape, he jumped. The landing was not a soft one.

"Awww, my ankle! Look what you made me do. It hurts. I'm telling on you..."

✷ ✷ ✷

Twelve years later, encased in a high-tech robotic armor, I still felt like a dope thinking about that windy, summer's day. The Brawler's metal plating could not protect me from the sting of distant embarrassment.

The desire to rewrite one's entire life so that you've done and said everything without flaw is slavery to ego. I was practically a baby when Beck and I carved up that tree, the tree I eventually climbed up to smash through her house. Couldn't I find joy and amusement in our five-year-old innocence? Apparently not, because even now my soul cringes at the memory. Oh, to be free of this body of pride. Not long now, I suppose.

We'd taken off from Outpost 6 in the dead of night, rocketing toward a faint signal that might have been my father crying out for help. I had mounted up inside B1 and switched over to Brawler mode, jogging in place and punching the air to get re-acclimated from our time apart. I was sweating with nervous anticipation despite my best efforts to shake off an anxiety taking target practice at my guts.

Then something triggered me to replay the scene of Beck and I high in that maple. The Market Day bracelet had jostled about my wrist as I pushed and pulled against B1's Control Sticks. Beck had proved correct, as she did with so many things, that the beaded band would remind me of her when I needed it most. But the simple token chose to transport me back to a day I wasn't keen on recalling; the day I snapped a brittle ankle. After some concerted effort, I replaced that uncomfortable recollection with something fonder: Fresh Market Day bread, steaming local coffee, and Beck's flowing dress. The vivid mental pictures of our field trip still live among my most cherished. The explicit sights, sounds and aromas never fail to turn me into a time traveller sent deep down the Broadway of my mind.

If I walk those cobblestone streets, with the courage of hindsight, my hand never fails to reach for hers.

I remember wanting to crawl out of that robot right then, find Beck and I a couple of hand-made chairs, and idle away an afternoon doing nothing at all. Battling with not only my identity, I began to question my mission. Was I the Lone Ranger, bent on revenge, death-be-damned—or a scared kid ready to grab his friends and run for the hills? The question went unanswered for the moment, but not for much longer.

The in-flight, low hum of Cavalry 1's holding bay was numbing. It was making it difficult to fight off the approaching fatigue or the gnashing tension. So I pressed harder into my drills and that kept me frosty, but I was trying to keep Glynn alert as well.

"Glynn, you still with me? Run another system's diagnostic. Something's sticking in the torso-rotation."

"I've done that sir, three times," he said back over the Com. "Everything checks out. I wished you guys had warned me about a night op. I'd have taken a nap." Glynn's elongated sigh sounded like a depleting whoopee-cushion. He'd started calling me *sir* to make our Com interaction sound official. More as a joke than anything, but I liked it.

B1 and I jumped up and switched to bike mode, landing hard on the deck to send a thunderous clang through the bay. Punching the accelerator hard, the three-wheeled vehicle spun a peppy donut before bolting upward to become an exo-suit again. The dual gun mounts on either forearm were a clever design, pulling a 180-degree rotation with each transformation in order to face forward. It felt like an old western quick-draw as the barrels extended and its various components snapped out with authority. I aimed one at several mock targets and imagined having to use them in combat for the first time. In the dream-like world of capsule training I had done so in numerous simulations, but those mock situations did nothing to help my uneasiness about using a deadly weapon.

The whole operation had the impression of a wild goose chase, but one that required final resolution. I couldn't imagine Dad still out there, waiting for me. Even the thought of such a thing sent a fresh panic across my nerves that had to be shaken off with some more Brawler exercises. My targeting scope centered on a brown hairdo with a blue streak looking back at me. I called out to Minerva over B1's external speakers.

"It makes me nervous when no one's in the cockpit, captain."

"No worries. This thing flies itself. It hardly needs me." Minerva's casual attitude sent my stress level soaring. "We're cloaked and skimming the upper atmosphere, everything looks good. The signal is still coming in loud and clear."

I thought about Dad's beacon so it appeared in the upper right of my visual display, blinking out a kind of GPS map to direct us toward it. Minerva set her flight helmet on the deck and started some tai chi, energy stretches. I wasn't sure if she was doing the stretches for her sake or for onlookers.

"Garret? Captain Doon? I'm not getting anything from base command. I tried to ping them just now and I got nothing." I relayed Glynn's message over my externals to our stretching pilot in the middle of a mule-yawn.

"Oh, we're just too far up, or they might have gone radio silent to protect our position," she shrugged, uninterested. "I'll check on it in a second."

"Well, keep trying them every couple of minutes, Glynn, until you reach somebody." I demanded, hoping to kick my team's enthusiasm up a notch. As if things weren't nerve-wracking enough, we were skirting outer space with no one manning the controls, a listless cosmetologist and sleepy controller were my only crewmates, and now we were cut off from headquarters.

Minerva grabbed her helmet and headed back up front as if there were nothing better to do. I decided to dismount and splash some water on my face, but not before heading to my locker to get one of Newt's homing beacons. I turned it on and slipped one in my jumpsuit pocket. A short time later, Minerva's voice came to life on the overhead PA.

"We're on final approach and I'm not picking up any unusual activity. Making preparations for landing. I know just where to set us down too." She had a business-like air to her so maybe her serious side was about to take over. I donned my Hat and did a visual inspection of B1's bike mode before climbing in. Glynn shouted into the Com.

"I got a fighter launch! Two planes are heading down the runway at the Air Force Base."

"I see them. Monitoring..." Minerva snapped, as I held my breath and hoped she wasn't about to blast them out of the sky. "No worries team, they're going the opposite direction. We'll be down in a moment..."

I sighed in relief as Minerva joined me in the docking bay, exchanging her flight helmet for a combat version. "C'mom, c'mon. Let's go! Let's go!" She had indeed exchanged her apathetic self for a fired up drill sergeant, demanding I power up my combat armor, post-haste. In a kind of Pavlovian response, the click and subsequent hum of B1 heightened my senses for the challenge ahead.

Standing into Brawler mode, the twin forearm guns swung over to lock into place. The 4-tube, shoulder-mounted missile pods made the suit top heavy, and I wondered if it would have been better to remove them for increased agility. No time for that. The hatch in Minerva's J-22 was open and she reached in to activate its onboard systems, firing off final orders for Control.

"Glynn, if you see anything suspicious coming toward Cavalry 1 on your scopes, run protocol 71. It will automatically take off for a forty-mile loop and re-land in the same spot, or 81 to head all the way back to base. There shouldn't be any trouble, there's no way they can know we're here." The thought of him all alone, with our fate in his hands was unnerving. Minerva continued. "I'm going to go run a final check on the cloaking control and make sure the power is reading steady. Any malfunction in that and we'll be in a bad way fast."

"Roger all that," Glynn confirmed. Despite my lack of faith in his talents, it felt good to include my fight-tech on the mission. A pang of regret stung at me as I remembered resisting his initial attempts at friendship.

Minerva reappeared from the forward hatch and mounted up in her J-22 combat armor. As the cockpit closed her inside the tank-like suit, it stepped free of its holding bin towards the ramp controls. My familiar nerves were back, making everything shake and swallowing a punishing chore.

"Garret, get ready to roll. I'm going to hit the lights and let down the ramp. We gotta make this quick cuz anyone can see in here, ya know? The ramp will close in three seconds. I've got our Com on a scrambled, variable frequency, but let's still keep communication to a minimum. Don't cloak out cuz I won't be able to read you on my scanners." My hands were sweating on the sticks.

"You should've taken one of our Brawlers for this mission, Captain Doon, then we could both cloak."

"Nah, "Minerva bleated, like she was refusing pepperoni on her pizza. "We'll be at the bases' entrance in about five minutes. It's just a half-mile over the next ridge. Let's do this!"

The lights blinked out and my night vision kicked in, leaving everything in a dull, green glow. A flash of brightness hit my eyes as her J-22 armor took the lead and blasted down the ramp skate-style.

I changed over to bike mode and jutted down to ground level. It was too soft for the wheels, with jagged rock formations mixed in. I took B1 back to Brawler mode straight away and stood up on the desert landscape. The rear ramp of Cavalry 1 appeared to float in mid-air. It rose and disappeared from view, leaving the massive ship almost invisible. Minerva rebuked my indecision.

"Would you stop playing around? C'mon, follow me." Her suit elevated to a height above the rocks and took off down the ravine under a dazzling, starry sky. The cracked land, with its large patches of tangled brush, was vast and quiet in all directions. I thought about Dad's beacon so the signal materialized again, flickering to life in my upper right peripheral display. It indicated 3.76 miles out, but almost straight down into the Earth. Minerva was pulling away from me so I punched it to close the gap.

"Fence coming up. Watch the barbed wire at the top. Stay as close to the ground as possible though to avoid their radar." Her J-22 surged upward, hurdling it with ease before continuing on. I followed after with no problem.

Our suits were now within twenty yards of each other as we approached the base of a long mountain range. Its dark, rugged peaks looked ominous in the backdrop of my night vision's scope. I could see Minerva switch off her jets and revert to a run, making her way up a hill just ahead. B1's rear thrusters deactivated to set us down on the sand, our metal feet sinking into the soft terrain. Traction proved difficult as the gyros strained to balance the 1.7-ton mecha.

At the peak of the ridge, a steeping gash cut down into the base of the mountain, ending in a large set of doors decorated with numerous warning signs. She went back to her scoot-maneuver and headed right at the entrance without slowing down. Her quick slide down the incline ended in a wicked sidekick that knocked the bolted doors half way open. She let out some choice curse words and set about knocking them the rest of the way open. That is until her retracted wings caught on the top of the door frame. Her J-22 tumbled back into my Brawler's mechanical arms.

"Thanks, Garret," Minerva sighed across the Com. "It's going to be hard to fit through some of the upper spaces, but once we get below we'll have no problem."

"Yeah, okay," I said. "I'm reading Dad's beacon at almost three miles out from here."

"Right, we're going to use this abandoned entrance to access the tunnel system and then take it across to the target location. I have a feeling I know where your old man might be."

The captain's confidence didn't ease the ache in my stomach. I took a deep breath and felt for the woven bracelet around my wrist. I hoped it might provide some kind of magic comfort, but none came.

Our exo-suits navigated down the base's dark halls, tight on my Brawler's shoulders and Minerva's folded wings, scratching along the walls and ceiling. Life sensors kicked up and blinked when a cat-sized rat bolted across our path. I clacked over my left, 50 Cal gun, but it had already vanished. I hate rats, and seeing a giant one frazzled me all the more.

What in the world was I doing there? Past the point of no return, on a covert mission beyond my skill level—deep inside an abandoned military base—moments from finding out if my father were still alive. The pressure was immense. A scanner alert beeped out on B1's display, again jolting my nerves. I called out to Control, my voice cracked and jittery.

"Hey, I'm picking up another fighter launch at the Air Force runway. Glynn are you getting that?" Silence. "Glynn, you read me? Captain, I'm not getting anything from Cavalry 1!"

Part 8: The Mission
Chapter 2

"Through Gideon's protest of being the weakest and least, God reminded him he was not fighting for a victory, but fighting FROM victory—the battle was already won in the Lord. And in the inevitable triumph, Gideon's micro-small army would be unable to boast of its own strength. A classic journey from least-likely-to-succeed to total success.

After all, Gideon's name meant 'cutter of trees,' and enemies that appear as big as cedars quite literally fall into that group."

—Carter West, *O' Mighty Men of Valor*

"Glynn? You'd better not be asleep or I'm going to come back there to kick your butt!" I tried to reach the ship several more times with no result.

"Cut the talk," Minerva cracked back. "We don't want to be detected. Those fighters have no idea we're here." I risked her displeasure and tried to raise my fight-tech one last time. Nothing.

"He's obeying orders by not responding. You should try it yourself." Minerva was losing patience with the amateur. "Glynn's got it covered. We're just getting Com interference from this structure. Now keep moving..."

Her sidekick repeated itself into another set of doors. These were much less fortified and fell deep within their expanse in a series of loud bangs and clangs on the way down.

"Great, another elevator shaft. Where's the cabling?" I hesitated to ask.

"These worked on some kind of vacuum tech, but this part of the base has been closed down for a long time."

She jumped off the edge as if she'd done it a thousand times. I was happy to be in a Brawler that used an advanced, gravity-canceling rear pod as its main means of flight. B1 sensed the ground approaching and slowed itself without the use of rockets. It made this drop much smoother than my previous attempt and I caught up to Minerva without a bump or scratch. We took another set of cramped hallways until they let out into what looked like a subway tunnel, complete with a long waiting platform for boarding.

"What's next? Hey, there are lights on down here?" I clicked off my searchlights and took a long breath, releasing some of the vice-like tension gripping my shoulders.

"Yeah, this place is still in use, so we gotta watch out," Minerva answered. "Let's move before we're spotted."

I thought about Dad's signal and the display didn't appear. My heart sank and ears burned at the prospect of losing it again.

"The beacon, captain, it's not coming up. Oh, no. You getting anything?"

"Nope, its dead. Crap." Minerva was rattled. Then she let fly such a string of cursing that it nearly melted the Com. "It might be the power coming off these mag-lev rails. We know the signal was coming from down this way. Let's take the tunnel for another mile and get away from the main track. Maybe we'll pick it back up."

Even Minerva's super-optimism couldn't overcome the terrible news. Her voice was despondent. We hit our thrusters and blasted down the tunnel, hovering just above the winding rail. Part of me kept expecting the sound of an old steam engine to fill my ears just before it barreled around the corner belching black smoke, but everything remained dormant.

After a few minutes we neared a major junction, with another long boarding platform and multiple entrances converging around it. Minerva slowed her speed and negotiated her way over to the platform to set down, and we reconvened there. She sounded even more upset.

"Because of our depth, this is the closest I can get to tracking the signal's last location. I'm still not getting anything, you?"

"No. I knew this would all be for nothing. Somehow I knew it." My anguish burst out like a spent water balloon. A feeling of disaster descended as I realized how dangerous the situation was, with extreme risks taken for no reward. I scanned the area and found myself overwhelmed at the cavernous network.

"There are no rails along those tunnels, where do they go?" I asked.

"This is pretty much where I thought we'd end up," Minerva answered, her voice drained of energy. "Those go off into an endless system of subterranean passageways. It's a maze, a real labyrinth. They sent a number of super soldier squads down there but it's impossible to map it all out, and quite a few of them never came back. Part of the tunnel system goes all the way to Mexico and beyond. This is right where we needed that dang beacon to be working. Good luck if the signal is originating from a mile or two down in there. I can't tell you how sorry I am, Garret. This mission is a huge washout."

"Oh please, don't let this be for nothing," I prayed, desperate. "What should we do now, Captain Doon?"

"Well, we can give it a little longer, but the signal went out for days the last time, so I don't know. C'mon, let me show you something."

Minerva spouted with renewed stamina. "Wanna see why they closed most of these underground bases?"

"What, you mean the experimentation and stuff? I guess. Well, maybe not. What is it? Isn't everything gone by now?"

Dad had a few books filled with conjecture on the subject. Rogue factions of humanity, in league with the Tall Grays, had been carrying out all manner of ghastly research. Beings called the "Short Grays," biological drones created via a joint interspecies project, were made with the use of Vril and harvested human DNA. There were other creations and experiments, but UN reps were bent on keeping much of the detail in the dark where it belonged, if just out of sheer decency. With hundreds of yards of cages, and lab upon lab of unspeakable sights of suffering, nothing noble in me wanted to see the evidence for myself.

Before the Meltdown, nearly 400,000 new missing persons cases were being reported annually. In the years following, when re-building society was able to keep track again, it was down to around 10,000. Granted there were a lot less people around to go missing, but still, the dramatic drop connected some very diabolical dots. Our herd was being culled and we kept right on grazing. The crime of human trafficking had gone far beyond late 20th century's definition. People had become the Grays secret slaves, then groceries, and eventually a common base material—a commodity, traded in their dark and sickly underworld.

What part The Messengers played in revealing these factions had also been kept hidden. Somehow they knew, and pulled the cover off the location of these elite regimes. UN forces then burnt them from their holes like a varmint-infested prairie. Most of the D.U.M.B.s were supposedly bunker-bombed and sealed off forever. I was torn between wanting to run out of there as fast as I could and waiting to see if we could pick up the signal again. Minerva walked her battle suit off the rail platform and down a wide hallway that ended in a set of massive doors. Apprehensive, I followed behind. Minerva placed the metal claw of her J-22 combat armor near a control panel and the doors responded.

"Why does this area still have power?" I wondered out loud.

"Not sure. These tracks are for the super-fast, interstate type, so maybe it's being used to move back and forth between the bases that stayed open."

The elevator was huge, big enough for twenty exo-suits. Minerva walked her combat armor inside and turned to face me. My anxious nerves blossomed to new heights.

"I say we get out now. You're far too calm, Captain Doon. We should go back to the ship and see if Glynn's all right."

"Agreed. Let's give it ten minutes and then we'll head back. Maybe Cavalry 1 has the signal and we're just getting too much interference down here."

She said nothing more, expecting me to join her inside the lift. I eventually complied. Our ascent was slow, taking several minutes before we stopped. I checked for Dad's beacon again, and again, nothing.

We departed the elevator and made our way down a few halls, our iron feet thundering on the steel deck. It felt like roaming the interior of the Death Star, making me all the more anxious to escape back to the surface. I was seconds from offering my final protest when another entrance opened ahead. The thick doors took their time moving aside, revealing something not quite right beyond them. Minerva's combat armor walked ahead with B1 right behind.

The feeling of electricity crawled over my skin and every hair on my body stood at attention. It felt like the time I visited a farm as a young boy and took hold of an electric pig fence. Though these goose bumps and roaming shiver were not running a quick course and fading away, they were building with intensity.

"What is this-s place? Why is it still ru-running-ing?" I stuttered. We were aloft on a large observation platform, overlooking a humongous warehouse that stretched back hundreds of yards. Up on the command platform with us were control booths with active monitors, workstations, and even empty coffee cups.

"This is where they're altering the gravitational field," Minerva chirped. "They're using some kind of standing waves or something. There's a ton of them, all over. Whatever it is, it's too complicated for me."

"What! What d-do you mean? How do you kn-know that?" I walked my Brawler over to the edge of the platform's railing and marveled at the incredible sight. I was overlooking a mechanical generator, a hundred yards square, fifty-feet below. Its emanating vibration coursed through B1's hands holding the deck's railing, all the way up to my chattering teeth. The strange force made breathing difficult, my head light, but I still knew what to do. "It's not going to be working so well when I put a missile into it."

At once my Brawler rocked, crashing hard to the deck, nearly breeching the rail. Damage reports scrolled everywhere as the smell of smoke filled the cockpit. A searing pain in my side throbbed with intensity, forcing me to do little else than contend with it. B1 tried to right itself but the system groaned in vain.

Coughing, I activated my helmet's auxiliary oxygen supply. The fumes cleared and brought my hacking under control, though it didn't ease the pang of gullibility washing over me. I'd just fallen for a fool's trap. A large metal boot sent a familiar crunch down upon my Brawler's midsection. Minerva's J-22 stood over me, collapsing part the suit's inner cabin, generating tremendous pressure on my wounded side. One of B1's arms had the range of movement to point a forearm blaster at her suit's crotch but the firing control failed to respond.

"I'm sorry, Garret," Minerva taunted. "I had to deactivate your weapon systems. I wish that beacon hadn't dropped off when it did. Not sure what's going to happen now."

Choice words were running through my mind but I was too busy vying for escape possibilities to let them out. I reached B1's hand over to the deck rail for leverage, trying to knock her off. Instead her suit grabbed the same railing for balance while her other foot crushed my arm back to the floor. Minerva's voice lacked emotion of any kind, as if she could end my life as easily as snuffing out a spent cigarette.

"Don't make me shoot you again, honey."

Disgusted, I removed my helmet to inspect the cockpit, and myself, for damage. My hand reached down to find a bleeding side wound with pieces of jagged metal sticking into me, and some sparking panels. I tried to wave the smoke away with little affect, opting again for my helmet's supply of air. My mind scrambled for a way out. I began to weigh one of two speeches. Either a rousing round of cursing and condemnation deserving of any traitor, doing me little good, or something shrewd to gain vital time and information. Only the words for the first option were at the ready.

The deck began rumbling and I could see the hatch of Minerva's suit pop open. My Brawler's head cameras couldn't look around the entire area, trapped as I was, but my wrist camera could. I rotated it until I found the activity she was focusing on. The far wall on the observation deck was splitting in two, parting like the massive doors of an airplane hanger. A sizable troop of men in combat gear poured out, raising their guns our way and shouting for us to hold our position.

"Minerva," I eked through a tortuous cough. "What's going on?"

"Just be quiet, if you know what's good for you." She bristled at me, not realizing I had a great deal of trouble keeping quiet.

"Lord, give me something. A jawbone, anything." Gasping, I pleaded out the desperate request again and again.

"Don't bother with that either. He's given up on you." Though her audacity filled me with rage, I could do nothing but lie there and wheeze.

Four of the soldiers approached to within a few feet us, training their guns on our battle suits. Another squad came close with handheld devices; scanning wands they used to run over and around our area. Several others joined them to review the data as Minerva kept me pinned.

What happened next was the most extraordinary sight my eyes had ever seen, or mind had ever imagined. An assembly of odd and horrible silhouettes formed across the entrance of the large, metal doors. What first appeared to be a company of dwarves gathered around a few people, turned out to be people gathered around something wholly divergent.

A crowd of about twenty walked out onto the observation platform. They came close enough for my wrist cam to make sense of the spectacle. Among them were more armed soldiers and several men in long robes wearing unusual hats. With them was a Vril pair, a towering male and a female, in imperial attire. Seeing their daunting figures live in the flesh for the first time might have been more shocking except the remaining members of this motley group made them almost drab by comparison.

The anomalous company coming toward me preceded two gigantic women; one a kind of princess, another more plain wearing a veil, following close behind. And then there was their royal guard. Two monsters shuffled alongside them, nearly as wide as they were tall. Gigantic, rat-looking creatures, dressed in something like medieval armor. Their faces were rutted and menacing with drooping swaths of straight, white hair hanging from either side of their elongated heads. The hands that gripped their staffs were larger than a man's chest and their total height appeared to be eleven feet, the women nearly eight. The giant beings loomed over the party of fully-grown men at their feet.

My senses demanded the entities before me must be in costume, or created via some type of special effect, but then a hot poker of dread knifed through my brain. Yes, I was terrified, but this barrage signaled at something demonic. Was this the empathic assault from the Vril female I'd heard so much about? Her weapon of terror made a sudden shift and demanded my unworthy submission, a total capitulation impossible to resist.

A silent reverence hung in the air. I became part of a collective adoration, betraying everything I knew to be true.

Trapped and bleeding, I awaited their verdict.

Part 8: The Mission
Chapter 3

"There are no more Catholics or Protestants, no more divisions between us worth keeping—only believers. Many failed to recognize the savior the first time around, clinging to their traditions with clenched teeth, shutting out the light to spite themselves. Let us not repeat the same mistake again."

—The Former Pope, *It is Finished; The Legacy of Peter the Roman*

"**U**nnameable Mistress, you are truly magnificent to behold."

Minerva's voice, serious and devout, vaporized any notion that what was before me might be a ruse. Clinging to the slimmest of threads, I'd hoped that the lights would come up and the mass of walking oddities would crawl free of their costumes. No such luck. The elevated princess spoke and cemented their reality.

"Hello, Minerva. You *will* make a beautiful goddess. It won't be long now. Are you readying yourself to become a champion and experience true power? It is not for the weak." The giant lady placed her fingertips together and raised them toward her lips. She tapped all the tips together and then switched to only the index fingers while considering us.

The giant queen had very small eyes, like those of a normal sized person, or smaller. Unmoving, they contained little white, but the blacks twinkled with heavy moisture. Her hair was thin and wispy, nearly transparent, and her voice bore a heavy and unidentifiable accent. Minerva took a moment before answering.

"Yes, Unnameable Mistress, I am ready. However, I am grieved to report that we—we lost his father's distress signal. It stopped transmitting only a short while ago. Perhaps it will—" The stately women waved her hand to regain the silence. I could feel her looking at me, probing my soul, pulling me through the metal of my exo-suit and across the floor.

At once, I grabbed at the mental shelf holding the bedeviling memory of giant, skeletal warriors buried underground. Frenzied fingers again tore at the envelope to splay the worn prints out in epic revelation. Why was this freak show talking so casually about my father? After all my wild hunches about the reason for Dad's abduction, had he simply been in the wrong place at the wrong time? Had everyone who had seen the crypt eventually gone missing? My eyes and good senses bickered with each other in violent debate. Giants, if impossibly true, must be something relegated to ancient times. The living, breathing monsters before me had to be the result of genetic miscreants, of some wicked science dabbling in the forbidden to break God's righteous order. But then it struck me; that's what these creatures had always been.

One of the men in strange hats tried to say something but the princess objected and he became mute. She tilted her head to one side and took a few steps nearer as the group scurried to maintain their position around her. A few of the soldiers aimed their guns in our direction, the gleaming barrels inching close. My eyes kept trying to reconcile the contradictory scale of the figures in their view. The enormous queen flashed her crocodile eyes and smiled at my heap.

"What have you brought us?"

"It is the son, your Mistress," Minerva voice quivered. "Would you like me to remove him from the suit for your inspection?"

"Oh, silly girl, I can see him. He is handsome, and feisty." With that I had to pop the top hatch and let it fly.

"Yeah, yeah—whatever B-movie rejects! Let's talk about my dad now, and how I'm going to kill you for taking him..."

The queen let out a long, eccentric laugh, leaning back from the force of it. She clapped her hands together with a loud slap. I noticed then that the queen's attendant was carrying what looked like a ceremonial helmet and spear. She leaned forward to whisper something in her mistress's ear. The monarch with the unflinching black eyes shook her head at the covert message.

"No, no. We can't play with him. He is but a soul of clay, unloved and unrenowned. He suffers from the same malignant spirit as his father and would bring destruction on himself before relenting. If he was but a soul of fire I would gladly give him more fire still."

Temperaments grew dark and I could feel her mind reach into mine, twisting it to her will. Her unspoken words joined with the stabbing waves of fright sent into me from the female Vril. My thoughts were overwhelmed in a stifling amalgamation.

Don't you see little man that immortality is mine to grant? Minerva will be worshipped. Her genome will be integrated with ours. Her body will grow large and strong. She will rule over a city and command a race of giant warriors who even now kick at the gates to emerge and reclaim what is rightfully theirs. The sleepers are now awakening! She enjoyed the words being sent into me. *Simple boy, look at her city.*

A vision clouded my eyes. The swirling mirage had me ripping off my Control Hat to be free of it, but the sight persisted. I could see a shining metropolis, glittering in the sun. It was a paradise with all manner of gross pleasure. I had to rebuke it in my savior's name to break free. The specter vanished but her evil words spun through my brain like a swarm of mosquitos.

The whole Earth was once covered with cities such as these. Your great "director" saw fit to destroy it on a whim and give it to the likes of you. We've waited while man bumbled away his authority. And now what was once ours will be ours again.

She exhaled the same laugh as before, only audibly this time, suggesting to her throng that they had missed our telepathic conversation. But I was growing real sick of being on the defensive. I put my helmet back on and turned the external speakers on high broadcast.

"Listen you giant cow, stuff it!" I barked, my strained voice echoing across the platform. The sudden loudness of the crackling speakers made the freakish crowd jump. I continued my rant. "Why do you bad guys always have to do all that monologuing? I'm not trading my birthright for a bowl of soup, or anything else you're offering. My demands are simple: give me back my dad, let us go, and you go jump in a lake—of fire. I have nothing to bargain with here but I sure as heck don't want to listen to any more of that garbage! Do your worst and get this over with." More clapping ensued and she laughed her loudest yet.

"Oh—I like him! What a shame. You are an interesting bloodline. Perhaps we need to study you further. Your father was quite an peculiar specimen. He was the only creature I've ever known to escape from our electromagnetic holding cells. Then he managed to recover his robot suit and get away. Impressive. We knew he couldn't get too far, and might eventually call out for you. We were not surprised to learn he's right under our feet."

The wicked bat droned on, thrilled by the sound of her own voice. She spoke about how a goddess and a worm had something in common at last; our fathers were both imprisoned but were now free. I could not decipher her reference but remembering that Dad might still be alive gave me both relief and grief. If I could not escape to help him all would be lost. The only thing worse than the stabbing pain emanating from my side was that ogre's endless prattling.

Just then a soldier ran up from the hanger doorway to whisper something to a man in the long, purple robe. One of the towering rat guards reacted to the sudden movement by nearly squashing the intruder. The beast regained composure after a low growl, and then stroked its wiry mane to sooth itself.

"Begging forgiveness your Mistress, but I have some critical news," The purpled robed minister called upward. "Israel has just launched a nuclear attack on targets in Jordan and Lebanon. Their armies are pushing northeast, meeting only token resistance. The Dome of the Rock has been leveled."

"Oooo, nuclear! Yummy!" Her face's pale and ageless skin, paper thin with a hint of phosphoric green, grinned broadly over the report. She was pure crazy and hardly an adversary worthy of taking me out of the world. My prayers intensified as I asked the God of heaven to not let His name be profaned by this group of reprobates. Minerva interrupted.

"Pardon, Unnameable Mistress, it is now 0200 hundred hours, do we have confirmation of my task?" The man in the long robe acknowledged her question and turned to deliver the news that would lay waste to my soul.

"Yes, we also have confirmation that the Peruvian base has been eliminated. We registered the proper disturbance a short time ago. Our forces have verified it. There is a large plume of black smoke billowing out of the ground there."

"What? You blew up our base? You witch! You didn't! It's a lie!" My rage exploded as I tried to harness all my strength to squirm free from under the J-22's weight. My mechanical suit grappled for any means to stand and deliver retribution. Another blast rang out from

Minerva's cannon and I felt it plow into my Brawler, sending more smoke into the cabin.

"Hold your fire! Hold your fire!" The soldiers shouted, asserting control while threatening to kill Captain Doon if she did anything more without a direct order.

My thoughts raced to the team, if they'd made it out somehow, or if this was a deception to torture and test me. My heart chose to believe it a lie rather than face the horrible alternative. The giant lady commended the traitorous whore.

"Well done, Lady Minerva. Your initiation moves along, doesn't it? You'll be staying with us now for a while. It's too bad about losing the signal though, we were counting on you for that. You'll have to submit to the soldiers here and let them have their way with you for a few weeks. If you survive it, your initiation will be almost complete. There is a great price in passing the test—in knowing my name—but there is also endless reward."

"Yes, Unnameable Mistress. You symbolize enlightenment over ignorance," Minerva surrendered. "It will be as you wish."

I realized then that I was facing a form of evil that could indeed be the end of me. I prayed and asked one last time for a jawbone, a miraculous means to strike back. Barring that, for the Lord to take me home. Then the answer came.

"Guards, don't stop her. Let Minerva finish the brat. Well boy, if you are bent on your own ruin, be it so."

Then one of the soldiers cried out, screaming, "there, there!" and opened fire with bursts of explosive tipped gunfire. Confusion reigned as the other men raised their guns—but it was too late for them. A pink, luminous dome fell over me.

A second later Beck's red Brawler materialized with Pak's Caliber close behind it. Pak used a familiar sidekick to blast Minerva's J-22 off of me to send her careening over the platform's rail. I could hear her curdling scream as she fell and smashed into the generator below. My own revenge opportunity evaporated as the giant women disappeared into thin air. I readied a shout to challenge them to come back and face me, but my coughing and side wound choked out the attempt. The queen's devilish laugh echoed in my ears as her image faded.

Pak's Gatling cannon opened fire to release its carnage. The roar of the gun was deafening as quick screams blurt from clouds of atomized blood. The Vril, running like frightened children, were shredded like so much pork. The floor of the platform, control booth and workstations became painted in dripping red. He paused long enough to reach down and pull B1 and I to our feet, and then dashed off toward the retreating soldiers in a fury.

One of the rat monsters lay dead in a pool of its own fluid but the other was making a break for the large, and now closing, hanger doors. The beast went to all fours for greater speed but the Caliber suit was too fast for the giant creature, catching the thing by its tail. It turned with a fierce forearm blow and fired some kind of beam weapon from its belt that missed the mark. That was its only chance as the Caliber's metal hand grabbed its snout and crushed it into a gruesome mess. Pak wound up and sent a massive punch into the top if its skull, making sure it was finished, then threw it off the observation platform in disgust.

"Pak, is that you man? Beck?" I cleared my throat and grabbed my side. "They did lie! They said the base had been blown up."

"It's us, Garret. I'm heartbroken to tell you it's true. The base is gone."

Beck was sobbing. I could hear Pak breathing hard as he walked around the observation deck, finishing off the wounded still crawling or moaning. The big man was beside himself with rage. But what did Beck mean? The base was gone? Mom's gone? Her somber voice came back over the Com.

"Major Freeman? Do you copy?"

"Yes, Rebecca. I copy. I would join you down there but there's quite a lot of activity going on up here. Best to give them multiple targets. I'll check back in with you in a few minutes to devise an extraction plan. OUT."

Beck turned off the dome shield and the circular dynamo retracted back into her red Brawler. She struggled through tears to describe my new and horrible reality.

"We picked up the explosion mid-flight. We had no idea or we would have taken Newt and your mom, my mom and so many others. They died in their sleep..."

Her sobs overflowed again and I could do nothing else besides hug her exo-suit with mine. The metal bodies scratched against each other without tenderness or feeling. Our rock hard exteriors kept us apart, mimicking how we so often treated each other without them on.

"Beck, I am so sorry. How did you make it out?"

"It was Brody. When he saw Minerva and Cavalry 1 leave he knew something was up. He was ready to expose her as a spy, but he waited too long. They broke into her room and figured out who she was. When her ship shut off communications the colonel authorized us to come after you. Newt gave us your homing signal and we followed it here. Jay, Ivy, Nia and Suri all made it on board. In fact, we need to let them know we're okay."

I stared at nothing, stunned at life's outlandish turn. Reality was crumbling through my fingers and I could do nothing to stop it. Beck offered me her condolences, sniffed and collected herself before calling out.

"Suri? Come in, we've found Garret and we're all right. We can break radio silence. We're going to need some help getting out of here, over..." Beck listened to Suri relay extraction options before turning to me. "Garret, you're a wreck. Can you still cloak?" I tried B1's cloaking controls fearing the worst.

"There. How do I look?"

The scarlet and gray, bird-like face of B3 shook back and forth at the sight of me. Beck was beyond deflated inside her exo-armor.

"Still here. So much for sneaking out," she rasped. Then Ivy's voice burst out over the Com, terrified.

"Phillip? Is everything all right?"

"Yes baby, pray. There's a lotta bad guys down here and just a few of us."

Pak's Caliber suit soon joined Beck and I, its weapon systems still fuming from use. His strained voice struggled for words.

"Listen guys, we've got a party forming just outside. They might just bomb this whole place and be done with it if we don't figure a way out and quick."

I cut Pak off, nearly hysterical over my impending news.

"I'm not so sure they'll do that. This gigantic machine over here, this huge generator—THAT'S what's making the gravity go crazy." My Brawler pointed its blue arm over the rail to the expanse below. "If it's important enough to them, maybe we'll be safe in here."

Just then four or five large grenades jitterbugged across the metal floor, stopping within inches of us.

"Never mind—JUMP!"

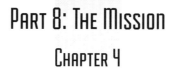

Part 8: The Mission
Chapter 4

"Abbott—please tell me you have some idea why we're suddenly being tasked with drawing up Scimitar designs double their current size, with double-sized cockpits. Are they testing us? It's ridiculous if you ask me, you'd have to be ten feet tall just to reach the darn controls, and never mind the weight! Unless the gravity thing continues to get worse, there's no way the joints and servos will handle that immense bulk..."

—Recovered fragment of a handwritten note

hree exo-suits sailed over the rail and just below the brunt of the blast. A ball of red fire erupted over our heads, illuminating the complex. Metal decking, still burning, cracked and whined as huge pieces crashed down to the level below.

As soon as the team gathered together, figures assembled at the doorway above us to determine the success of their attack. Pak waited until a few more congregated in one spot before he let loose. The furious noise was almost as frightening as the damage it inflicted. His top-mounted Gatling cannon was made for taking out the large, crab-like Scimitar suits and anything less was overkill. It obliterated everything in its sights, sparking secondary explosions and causing several more pieces of decking to break free and drop around us. Beck sent a few of her mini-missiles up into the doorway, filling their hall with smoke and fire.

"That should hold them for a minute," I shouted above the battle noise. "I wish I could help you out but Minerva deactivated my weapons. I've got nothing."

Pak's Caliber pointed behind me as the sprinkler system soaked everything in a gentle rain. "Speak of the devil, I think that's her. She's not looking so good."

That was an understatement. With her hatch open, Minerva must have fallen out of the suit half way down. Her broken body lay splattered against the top of a metal conduit. Her lifeless eyes stared back at us, blood oozing from her nose and mouth. B1's jester face mimicked my own and shook at the sight of Minerva's broken flesh.

"So much for being a 'goddess' sweetheart. Send us a postcard, will you?"

My cruel tone, even toward a low-life like her, sounded frightening. A darkness had seeped in. While I lacked shame over the satisfaction of Minerva's death, shame was there in bunches over my oblivity when she'd opened the security gate. I winced at my own naiveté as I reached out and took hold of her suit's mechanical claw. Since Minerva used it to activate the door panels, we might need it for the same purpose later on. I ripped the claw off her J-22 suit and attached it to my Brawler's hip-mounted, magnetic receptacle.

A sudden alert barked out from my dash. Sensors were picking up a large group of enemy mechs moving in. The ruby eyes of lumbering black Scimitars were already glowing in the distance. The attack-pack was closing on us from the far end of the warehouse. The enormous gravity generator stood in between them and the team so we quickly took cover on the far side.

Pak fired off all four tubes of his interfering smart-filaments to confuse their targeting computers. The ordinance slammed into the ceiling, bursting to spread its sparkling disrupters throughout the warehouse. A second later the advancing Scimitars were sending bolts of negative plasma just over our heads. The blasts shattered the walls behind us sending more smoke wafting through the area. Pak's voice never sounded more troubled.

"I've only got about 800 rounds left, that's going to go fast!"

Beck and I agreed that without his cannon we stood little chance of making it out alive, and the ten crab-suits blinking on my display were nearly on top of us. Despite the low visibility, there was no mistaking the orange glow originating from their powerful rear rockets. They were taking advantage of the cavernous space to fly in for the kill. Beck sent her whirling dynamo aloft and threw up a shield just in time to deflect a few bolts of plasma. The Caliber extended its multiple barrels outside the dome and sprayed heavy fire back and forth, igniting several Scimitars into flames—and still others took their place. I could almost count the bullets drain away as Pak mowed down wave after wave of enemy mecha throwing themselves into the line of fire.

Then the cannon fell silent. Pak's trigger finger was making the barrels spin, but there were no more shells left to save our skins.

A remaining Scimitar surprised us by barreling around the corner on foot, smashing through our group of battle armors. Beck's dome shield collapsed as the telescoping arm of the dynamo snapped in half. The black devil-mecha aimed at Beck's B3, ready for a kill shot. Pak's Caliber grabbed the barrel just under the tip and tilted it upward to redirect the burst. The Scimitar's right claw swung at the Caliber but Beck threw herself in the way, taking the brunt of the force. The monster had both B3 and the Caliber pinned again the side of the generator. Its huge claw crushed into the red Brawler's side exhibiting how overmatched our homemade suits were against its might. Beck poured out her 50 Cals at the beast with no effect.

B1 pulled at the Scimitar's giant claw in total futility, so I hit the boosters and leapt on top of the mechanical nightmare, flailing wild punches into its bulbous, red eyes. They shattered but the thing did not slow its attack. Orange fire erupted from its rear jets, slowly lifting our entire group upward. I reached my Brawler over its shoulder and grabbed one of the back-mounted rockets, tearing it sideways with a horrible screech. The top of the thruster broke loose, spitting fuel and flames onto the Scimitar's back. Four entangled battle mecha settled back to the ground, yet there was no inclination the behemoth might yield.

Beck cried out as metal talons sank deeper into her exo-suit's cockpit. Her high-pitched scream sent ice water gushing down my spine. B1 jumped high in the air and delivered a metal elbow down into the Scimitar's top hatch. The panel buckled, creating a gap. Both of my Brawler's hands reached into the seam to rip open the cockpit door. The pilot had just enough time to look heavenward before I sent in a brutal jab to end the fight. Our massive adversary at last went limp, crashing forward against the deck. When the dust settled Beck was left pinned underneath its lifeless claw.

Pak got to his feet and used the Caliber's strong arms to lift the dead crab-suit high enough for me to drag Beck's armor out from under it. She confirmed she was okay, but barely. We panted for breath as Pak relayed more bad news.

"I'm out of ammo and another squad of ten is on their way. We're done for."

"You're right—if we stay here. There's no time to debate this. You two cloak and try to get out the way you came. I'd only give you away." Then I followed with the unfathomable news: That my father was somewhere close, maybe alive, and that I had to find him.

Minerva had deceived me but Dad's signal was not part of the deception. Working in unholy agreement, she was trying to help my father's captors recapture him. When our battle suits had set down outside the labyrinth of tunnels at the final junction she had confirmed her suspicions about Dad's last know whereabouts— because that was precisely where they'd lost him. But why had he been singled out by something so powerful in the first place, and why hadn't they just killed him? Was he targeted solely because of the tomb of giant bones? All ponderous, and for the moment, unanswerable questions.

My survival instincts begged me to flee to the surface with my fiends. Heck, push them out of the way so I could get out first. Our life force has but one imperative: to stay alive. But the thought of my murdered mother, of Newt, and all the lives lost overrode the impulse to run. The strangeness that blanketed me in that moment was the same that calls some to fall on a grenade or to charge up a hill, yelling into death's threatening face. Whatever snaps inside a human being to make their life forfeit, snapped in me. I was a now a dangerous man. Beck and Pak listened intently to my final orders.

"Go radio silent until 0400, and then take off without me if I don't check back in. I know another way to the surface and I still have the tracking beacon in case you need to find me later." I extended my Brawler's arms to touch their battle armors in farewell as Pak took charge.

"I know what to do. Beck, follow me."

Cloaked, their suits disappeared from view as only slight distortions running off after each other through the burning debris. I was relieved they were too tired to object. I wished for my Brawler to float free of the ground so it did. Thankfully, B1's gravity-cancelling rear-pod was still functional. Then I hit the jets, ascending to fly through the smoking doors on the upper level and found a squad of soldiers there ready to hurl their bombs.

My appearance was a surprise and so was my sudden thrust straight into the group of men. B1 punched passed the crowd, scattering a few of the grenades around their own feet. I turned the corner toward the large elevator as several explosions burst through the passage.

Fortune smiled on me as the doors were just opening when I turned the last corner. The four soldiers exiting were busy talking out their final battle plans and couldn't react to my onslaught in time. I swung both arms at group, swiping their mass into the wall. As I looked on their fallen bodies my emotions twisted into a rope of anger and pity. I hoped they'd recover—eventually.

The elevator started its slow descent. Once below, I feared the doors might open on a Scimitar battle-crab ready to fire—ending my life in an instant. I braced myself for a blast that never came. In the clear, I hit the jets again and took off toward the rail platform and the network of tunnel entrances that lay on the far side.

Arriving at the main junction, I could see two enemy Scimitars in full flight, screaming over the tracks toward me. There was no choice but to punch it over the rail, fly into the labyrinth and hope that their cannons misfired. I hit the accelerator to full as their shots zapped out. Something powerful tore through my suit's calf, sending damage reports across my gauges. Once beyond the track, three dark and rocky tunnels were there to choose from. I took the smallest, hoping the much larger J8-81s wouldn't be able to follow me in.

My front searchlights gave me all the light I needed to fly through the tunnel's twists and turns like a video game expert. The enemy armors sent a few stray shots in after me but my displays were showing they were holding at the tunnel entrance. The onboard sensors monitoring the junction behind me began to flicker out as I exceeded their range. I hoped I had exceeded the enemy's as well and that my Brawler had vanished from their scopes.

As the reading faded, I counted over twenty enemy signals there to seal off any chance of escape. Maybe my coming down here had created the perfect diversion, allowing my friends to slip away. When I set B1 down on the ground we nearly toppled over. Like the tin-man long out of oil, the heavy limp from my Brawler's damaged leg made walking laborious.

I took a moment to rest and run a series of diagnostics to see what other damage might come up. It was a long list. Then the throbbing pain in my side reminded me to check out my own wounds. It was time to break out the emergency first-aid kit. The slice over my right ribs was still trickling fresh blood so I ripped open my jumpsuit a little more and taped some gauze over it. The bandaging job turned out even worse than my usual shoddy craftsmanship. Four ibuprofen would have to do, but the tiny bottle of water I took them with left me parched and anxious for more.

My thoughts turned to Beck and Pak making their escape. Was it the right thing to split us up? I hadn't the time to weigh my decision, which was staggering considering the lives at stake. Dad said once that it's "easy to man the helm when the sea is calm." Well Dad, I was sure ready for some glassy seas.

Looking around, it was hard to believe he could be alive down there. There was no sign of life. Not a toad, not a moth—nothing. The desire to shout out for him in that cave felt ridiculous at first, but when I opened the gate, my screams broke free like a bucking bronco. I hit the externals on broadcast, full volume.

"Dad! Daad! It's Garret! Daaaad!" I yelled as loud as I could muster, limping back into the dark unknown.

When the signal was lost, it indicated we were around 2.3 miles out from the target. It was almost mile to the next junction and I had gone about three quarters of a mile back into this tunnel, but I had no idea if this path had taken me toward him or in the opposite direction. Whatever the case, I thought it best to hit the jets again and make some tracks away from the enemy position. With any luck, I'd stumble upon another way out.

After a few more minutes of navigating the featureless tunnel at high speed, it all started to blur together. Fatigue was crushing in. It was 0330 hours and I was supposed to hail Beck and Pack soon. There wasn't much time.

Hope was fading and my eyelids were impossibly heavy until a faint glow in the distance delivered some fresh adrenaline. I blinked hard to clear the fog. An orange light was waiting for me ahead at the tunnel's end. The fiery illumination had the haunting look of Scimitar rockets burning hot as they closed in. I gripped the sticks and slowed my speed.

The external temperature gauge started a rapid climb. Heat levels rose inside the cabin making my thirst unbearable. The Brawlers contained a low-power cooling system, but it was overmatched in that setting. I became a wet bag of pasta, boiling inside a flying pot.

B1's wrist cam took a look around the expanse before I shuffled my Brawler out of the tunnel and into the open. The passageway convened at a bleak and cavernous space, a place of no return. It was a wretched expanse, not unlike hell itself.

I'd come to the end of the road.

Part 8: The Mission
Chapter 5

"Newt pulled a fast one, telling the team to warm up in the hot room while he made some last-minute repairs. Already in our jumpsuits, we hesitated, but agreed to a quick session to shake off the damp bunker air. Two minutes in we heard the door lock and good doctor instructed us to find 'our happy place.' And with that, he walked away. Training to overcome one's self, to master the will; Newt was trying to save us from a total breakdown someday through slow torment. As sweat and discomfort mounted, the urge to panic stalked me. It's hard to bend one's mind to think of 164 degrees as normal— or better, to not think of it at all. There are prolonged times where you cannot feel better, no matter how you might kick and scream. This is true in combat, as well as in life."

—Garret Philmore, *Letters on the Lamb: A Collected Journal*

Four-foot long stalactites hung from the cave ceiling, an eerie orange light painting their descending spikes. Instincts were imploring me to turn back as I limped to the edge of a significant gorge, marveling at the sight below.

A smoldering pool of liquid rock bubbled and churned, its slow movement percolating fifty-feet below. The parts of the hellish lake not covered over with a thick black crust were producing the orange light. Turning around to consider my options, I was no longer certain what tunnel I had emerged from. The B1's head mounted high beams had turned the cavern into a trembling maze of shadows. There were at least eight passages that opened to this area, with dusty tracks of all kinds leading away from them. Most of the tracks merged into a precarious path that followed along the edge of the expanse, back into the black cavern. A sorry attempt at humor did nothing to dissuade my fear.

"Boy, did I take a wrong turn at Albuquerque..."

Giant women, long haired beasts, tunnels of lava; I'd entered a late night movie I wasn't allowed to be watching. It was time to hit the pause button, run to the kitchen for some popcorn, and wait for the team to explain these unbelievable events. They would make sense of it all. They always did—because I sure couldn't.

Hands twitched and reached for more water where there was none. Sweat poured from my body, letting go of the last bits of moisture I couldn't live without. A Biblical story flowed through my mind as I surveyed the smoldering surroundings. My growing thirst, beyond anything I'd ever known, paled in comparison to the story of a wealthy man entering hell. Once there, he called across an impassable canyon to another. The *rich man* asked the person, who was poor in his brief physical life, to place a single drop of water on his burning tongue. Lazarus could not. There wasn't much more to the tale. They were each in their places of eternity, without resolution or happy ending. His drought would last forever; a cracked desert mouth that would never be satisfied.

Dad said being rich gives you too much help in ignoring the truth, while being poor often leaves you little choice but to face it. My riches were gone, nearly everything was—or so I thought. The truth before me was a bleak one, but thinking about that story had eased my parched body. I had a long way to go before reaching the rich man's level of desperation.

Following the footprints down the dim path, the lava flow a short distance to my left, I decided to give that direction a short trial before going back. After a hundred yards the space opened up to a sight that sent my soaking hairs on end.

Torchlight provided a view of the subterrestrial landscape, but just *who* placed the twin torches along the cavern wall was the question screaming to be answered. Between the ironwork cages holding the flickering fires sat a massive carved relief, one whose images looked familiar. Yet, the engraving's meaning eluded my exhausted mind. Figures carved in awkward profile bulged from the rock, marching their stiff march to the right. Something so old it told of a time before mankind had learned to draw in more dynamic angles and poses.

In front of the relief sat an altar, bloodied from the unknown lives given up across it. The layers of dark and light blood suggested this area was far from abandoned. Opposite the altar were deep grooves along the ground to the lip of the ravine. Whatever was doing the killing didn't have far to drag the bodies. Beyond the sacrificial slab, at the trail's end, a gaping cave-mouth lay waiting to swallow up unwary travelers. My feet resisted pushing forward, as if I were a mouse about to take an errant last step into a funhouse; a cat's disguised throat. I talked aloud to stay alert.

"That's far enough, Garret. You'll have to go back and choose another tunnel. That way leads to your doom."

I limped B1 back up the path towards the multiple choice tunnels that awaited me, but something made me pause and study the huge etching walking sideways along the rock. I'd seen that kind of carving before, featuring intricate stonework of men with finely decorated beards, winged figures holding small bowls. What did it mean? Newt had spoken once about the hybrid creatures created by the Watchers.

These hoofed figures and bipedal bird-men were literal he said, recorded in stone for eyes to see, if only people would open them. Standing in front of something so evil, so ancient, I felt but a droplet in the ocean of antiquity.

A sudden alert erupted on B1's console but I hadn't the time to react. Something jerked a hold of me with a vicious grip, putting my Brawler in a full nelson. What ever it was it was massive, and organic, as it did not create a schematic report on my sensors. Laboring to break loose, its powerful arms held me fast. I strained a moment more without gaining an inch of freedom. Then, allowing my captor to hold the Brawler's weight, I raised B1's legs up and threw both alloy feet into the carving, crumbling the relief. It was the brace I needed to walk up the wall and flip over my assailant, sending it flat on its back into the dirt. As my Brawler strained for footing, its metal groaned to stay upright, and we ended up far too close to the lip of the chasm.

Now on the other side of my attacker I realized I was standing over one of the huge rat creatures, the royal guard of the giant princess. It sprang to its feet with incredible deftness but it had to rotate to face me. I slashed out with B1's mechanized hand, grasping the thick wrist that was whirling to strike. I spread my Brawler's legs wide for leverage and, using the brute's own momentum, whipped the gigantic rodent to the ground, nearly toppling it into the crevasse. It got to its feet but glanced over its shoulder at the terrifying fire below. A mistake. B1's flattened metal palm punched hard into its chest. The rat-guard thrashed about the empty air for purchase before falling into the lava's crust, squealing in finality. The oozing oven swallowed it alive.

A short alert sounded as another rodent soldier arrived behind me. This one had a great positional advantage, finding me only yards from the edge. Its boulder of a fist was enormous, featuring three fingers and a thumb, all holding a long scythe-like weapon. The rat beast slashed out to beg my reaction, then charged. I slid backward, just inches from the drop off. I thought B1's arms into a quick-strike, grabbing at the thick strap that ran across the creature's chest. It dropped its staff weapon and bulldozed my Brawler toward the verge of the canyon, then hesitated when it realized it would tumble over with me. Its mammoth hands let go of my battle armor to pull the strap off and up over its head, and send me plunging over the side.

I remembered Master Barrão's instruction and utilized my enemy's weakness to my advantage. Using my adversary's chest strap to spin away from the ledge, I ducked under its arm and reached out for the scythe staff lying near us. I prepared an attack but ran out of time. The giant rat-guard reached to its belt and activated a beam weapon, striking my Brawler down with tremendous force.

Black fireworks exploded against an electric sky, as jolts of power stole my eyesight and burned my wounded side. The smell of charred flesh drifted around the cockpit. Not an alert or alarm failed to go off as Brawler's entire system flittered and sputtered into darkness.

Without power, blind in a bin of smoking charcoal, I was at the creature's mercy. Terrifying moments passed as I listened the thing grunt and move in closer to my downed battle armor. I imagined it looking over me, enjoying a helpless foe. Its gnarled teeth would be grinning wide between long strands of wiry, gray hair, savoring the victory.

The creature growled and spoke in a kind of guttural language. It was cursing me in its tongue as it grabbed B1's foot and began dragging us toward a fiery death. I took a long, shallow breath of stale air and resigned myself to going home. It seemed time to give up but something in my core refused to surrender.

I clacked the Brawler's main switch back and forth and the system restarted. Power returned and I battered my free leg into the thing's midsection as we neared the cliff's edge. The rat's disgusting arms flapped wildly to save itself. Close to regaining balance, its fate seemed to be decided by something unseen, giving it a last push to send it over the ledge to broil in the molten pit. There was a spate of agonizing howls and then sudden silence.

B1's display flickered again, struggling to overcome the beam weapon's affect. The circuits were baked, controls unresponsive— and I was not fairing as well. My brain seemed to be drowning in a sea of blood. Chest randomly thumped. Side-wound pounded; like a biting dog that kept readjusting its grip. Painful ingredients in a deep stew of agony.

The Brawler suit grunted and staggered, going to one knee before losing power and crashing us onto our back. I cranked the main control again, as I had before, with no effect. It was too late to call out for the team; the Com was dead. Everything blurred into a spider web of a thousand scattered notions.

Pushing all other thought away, I pictured Beck and Pak safely free of that hellhole, soaring away aboard a Cavalry ship into a sunset of pink. I waved goodbye to them as my helmet's reserve air supply sputtered out. I removed it, coughing and moaning. The long sounds escaping me spoke of a pathetic weakness so I did my best to transform them into something more contented. The fight was over.

That battered clump of mechanized mess, twisted, blackened and bloody, represented my last gasp. I saw the picture of my defeated Brawler smashed out over the ground and found the image satisfying. I went out swinging and looked forward to seeing both my parents in a few more painful, but brief moments. Hurried and agonized prayers of last resort were absent. Nothing in me felt an urge to call out in desperation as I had when I floated away. A peaceful smile defied an almost certain end.

A sudden and tremendous light filled the cabin, dissolving everything into white. Had someone as bright as the sun come for me? It appeared a tall and mighty warrior, dressed in ceremonial armor; an immortal escort. Yet instead of bringing relief—true and instantaneous terror arrived. The monsters I had just contended with now seemed laughable. When flesh and bone beholds the angelic, the spiritual realm opening the veil to our world, we collapse to nothing in the face of its might. I was not worthy to exist. My failing heart executed a final summersault as my eyes fixed on the luminous being.

The angel's shoulders bore thick, armored plates, like a hard crust of dazzling winter snow. The texture was of a snowfall untouched, made of glittering crystals seen only in worlds beyond the naked eye. Unfinished gemstones were set halfway in the snowy armor: rubies, emeralds, and sapphires. The tips left exposed were cut into a million, perfect facets. Long lengths of rich cloth hung from the edges of his shoulder armor, tossed about in wind unfelt by mortal men. The hero stood in a breeze blowing in the heavenly dimension.

Standing impossibly tall, he moved toward the mouth of the gaping cave. My angelic escort positioned himself, a fiery sword in hand, just outside the wicked cavern that had turned back my progress. I waited to be taken, flown to paradise, as one always imagines that final journey. We would soar through a starry space infinite on all sides of our trajectory, free of a world that had become so heart-wrenchingly cold. Instead, a raspy cough found its way out of my chest, indicating a continued mortality. I pushed myself to form speech but no words escaped. Then a deafening voice filled the void.

"We will guard the gates of the dead until the end, until the seals are broken. But who is worthy to open the scroll and loose this seal? Only the Son of Man, the Elect One, the Alpha and the Omega, the Beginning and the End. He shall remove the mighty from their thrones and break the teeth of sinners because they did not extol and praise Him. Let not your soul be afraid, your fighting spirit despair. Your sword will become as ricocheting thunder—burning as a mighty flame. Now stand."

Like the pain of birth, I felt rejected from the womb. Awaking from the vision still trapped in that miserable robot, I also remained trapped in my body of flesh—and the angel, who guards the gates of the dead, had vanished.

When I begged for him to return, my mouth no longer felt dry. A disbelieving tongue probed my lips and felt moisture. The pain in my side had also faded. I put the helmet back on and tugged at the power switch. B1's system reignited, coaxing the head cameras to life. The blackness evaporated and my sight returned. I let go of the sticks to stretch my arms and grabbed them again with renewed strength. By some form of divine mercy, I'd been sent back supernaturally refreshed. But sent back for what purpose?

The Brawler's gyros reset and it stood, pulling me upright within it. I tried to recall the beauty of the visitor, the words uttered from it, but the memory was growing strangely dim. What had I just seen? Who was I to be touched by something holy? I looked around in amazement, shocked to be alive, but at a loss over what to do or where to go. I wished I had thought to ask the angel in the *dazzling armor eternal* which was the way out.

I took another deep breath and ran a systems check. B1's instrumentation glowed strong. All functions appeared online and normal. A bothersome blinking kept flashing in my right eye, an alert that had been going on since I revived. I took a moment to stare at it in disbelief.

It was Dad's beacon.

Part 8: The Mission
Chapter 6

"Oh I've had plenty tell me to 'Beware of the Jabberwock,' of those jaws that bite, the claws that catch. But I will take my vorpal sword in hand, and leave it dead, and with its head..."

—Garret Philmore, *Letters on the Lamb: A Collected Journal*

more than a cave, it was a doorway to every horror I'd ever hoped to avoid. A hundred feet wide and fifty feet tall, the cavern's entrance suggested somewhere in there sat a dank and dark dragon, waiting for someone foolish to test their courage inside its belly. There is a hell—and that ominous hole likely lead straight to it. The subterranean mouth's only redeeming quality, as much as I wished it were not so, was my father's signal beckoning from within.

My favorite book as a young child was about a brave knight who had forever fought off the countryside's craven creatures and foul fiends, and had followed his quest to the mouth of Grimghast Forest, a dark and sickly wood. "Abandon all hope ye who enter" read the hastily tacked up sign at its entrance. Fearing nothing, the heroic protagonist quipped to the horse under him, "at least we'll be in the shade." I remember telling myself that someday I'd be that brave, but it's different when death comes right up and stares you in the face, exhaling its foul air under your nose. Conjuring all resolve, I patted the dash of my exo-suit to calm its imaginary jitters.

"We certainly won't be meeting any friends in here, B1," I muttered, then asked my Brawler if this was the way to Dad and then on to Mexico. It didn't respond. Silent, its blinking display spurred me on.

The dull green tint of the night vision was befitting this tunnel of misery. Within the first ten steps inside I thought I heard a whisper in my ear: *"don't go in."* A powerful chill ran up my legs to the top of my head as the temperature dropped. A cold, damp stench made its way under my helmet and reminded me what bravery required. This was the kind of terror that grabs you by the throat and reveals what's been watching you from the darkness.

Decaying body parts, unidentifiable, lay strewn across the path. Going any further meant I would tread over them. I pictured something reaching up to grab me as I stepped B1's limping leg across the ragged strips of flesh.

The whisper came again, clearer this time. It beckoned, *"welcome, you'll never leave."* I blinked hard, driving away the taunting voice before it could make its mess inside me. The cavern itself was doing enough of that on its own. The space pulsed with living evil, making me want to hide under the covers for the rest of my life. Up ahead, the passage narrowed and I thought I saw a shadow float past. Life forms were not showing up on my scopes, so whatever was down there was not alive.

The tunnel hit a T-junction, with another long passage running across it. There were more iron cages, with blackened torches embedded along the length of the far wall. Only one torch flickered in the distance. I was glad the flame hung in the opposite direction from Dad's blinking beacon. His signal showed itself only forty yards more to the left, down inside a narrowing passage littered with bones in various stages of crumble.

I thought about turning the searchlight on and the option appeared at my command. All I needed to do was confirm with my mind and it would flood the tunnel with its bright beam. I hesitated, choosing to creep along the dim tunnel wall without announcing myself to whatever may dwell there. Every atom of my frame was frightened to the limit—but my spirit begged for courage.

As I approached the end of the line and the signal's source, a cave-in had blocked the path. Against my better judgment, I hit the lights and called out for Dad. I shouted louder and louder as my eye stared at his "call for help" in my display. The signal was coming in strong and looked to be just twenty feet ahead. I kept calling for him as I worked my way back through some of the larger rocks at the edge of the cave-in. My top-mounted missile pods scraped against the tunnel's ceiling and I wondered what it might take to set one off.

The signal indicated only a few more feet to go. I put my Brawler through some heavy lifting, straining the mechanism to its limit to remove the rubble. At last I could see something: a piece of gray metal sticking out from under one of the rocks. The whisper returned. *"watch out, something's behind you,"* it cackled. The hair on my neck stood at attention but I resisted the urge to panic and kept digging. The whisper laughed and faded but would soon return.

"Dad? Dad? Are you in there?" I yelled out the implausible question as I unearthed another alloy plate. I could see a sizable metal hull buried behind a large stone, but beyond was space around and above the battered object. Could it be the remains of the experimental A-type armor Newt spoke about? A last boulder stood in my way so grabbed for its top and rolled it my direction, almost crushing B1's already injured legs. I jumped to the side as the large rock rolled out into the darkness.

The metal underneath was indeed a power-armor. The head

was smashed flat, also the chest. I called out to my father again as I reached my suit's fingers into a seam on the top hatch to pull it back.

The intensity of my searchlight only served to cast deep shadows into the cockpit. I clicked them off and went back to night vision, grabbing both sides of the opening to rip in opposite directions. I stopped shouting and offered the question a final time: "Dad?"

He was in there, alive.

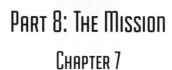

Part 8: The Mission
Chapter 7

"A multitude of thanks is deserved by you and your group for not only sponsoring this year's competition in our Mechanical Dynamics and Robotics class, but also for the anonymous contribution of hardware and firmware upgrades to Evan Philmore's team. He is among our best and brightest and one can only guess where this endowment may take his future."

—Professor Hilman Brickwell, *Cornell University,*

Letter to Colonel Cordy McKurt, *Department of Defense, 2025*

Quivering and slight, feeble sounds made their way out of the wreckage.

"Garret? You can't, can't be here, son..." Though the voice was drowning in lament, the reality before me seemed a fantastic dream.

"Dad!" I yelped out over B1's speakers. "Yes, I can be here. I AM here—and you're coming with me."

His voice did not respond as I pried the shielding back to see inside the demolished cockpit. I clicked the spotlights back on and they showcased an unrecognizable figure. Dad's once black hair was now half gray, oily and slicked against his head. His skin was never so pale, his body emaciated. My heart ached. What horrors had he endured? A brutal odor rushed out from his junked suit, strong enough to seep into my Brawler's cabin.

"Dad, is this thing leaking fuel? What is that?"

"It's so they can't smell you. If they smell you, they'll get you," he strained, his throat sounding far beyond parched. Dad pinched his eyes tight against the light until he covered his face. Then his hands darted away, fumbling blindly for something urgent.

"Oh Garret, you have to put some on. You can't be here. You're unprotected, exposed!" He was unraveling. Delirious and dehydrated, I wished for a tall bottle of water for each of us. It would be our celebratory toast, and would save him from his horrendous thirst. Dad's voice rebounded this time—or more like screeched.

"Leave me! That's an order!" he shouted, like a ninety-year-old man bellowing from his deathbed. I began clearing the remaining rocks out from around what was left of his A-Type armor and tried to remain soothing.

"Impossible, Dad. I'm not going anywhere without you. You think I would come all this way and leave? Hang in there, we're going to go find you something to drink." My father stammered, continuing his lunatic search for something not there. His ramblings were nearly incomprehensible.

"I'm not sure I'm me, son. You—you have—no idea what they do, what they like to do. I'm—I might be a clone. They make clones of people, kill them and replace them for fun and they..." My next words burst out, snapping him free of his insanity.

"MOM'S GONE, Dad. So is Newt..."

The harshness broke him. His eyes got wide and he came back to life—a cold, hard, heart-breaking one. I whispered through tears of joy and pain.

"You're all I've got. Don't leave me alone." He started to nod his head at my words but the despair and madness reclaimed him.

"Is there anyone else left on the surface? Their plan—the collider? Are the entities free now? Are they unchained? Who is left son, is anyone left?"

I wasn't sure how to respond so I said there were people left, ones that needed our help. B1's armored hands yanked hard on the broken chest area of Dad's cage, wrenching the main piece far enough to bring him out. He continued on about the "enemy's evil plans," his volume growing, and offered countless questions as I bent the last piece of metal out of the way. I finally cut him off, becoming the parent.

"I'm not sure about all that, but the bad guys are making their big push and we gotta push back. Now come on!"

My Brawler reached in to pull out his skinny body as a bone-chilling shriek echoed through the passage. Then another came—and another. I whirled to direct B1's searchlights down the empty tunnel. They bounced frantic, finding nothing but jagged rock. When the spots came back to my father his eyes were coming out of his head. The blinding light had turned the pale man into clay, his retinas to fiery red. He was a crazed white rabbit shouting: "We shall be too late!" The distant, wicked howling grew louder and I felt the ground vibrate through B1's legs.

"Oh son, it's them! They're—you have to go—RUUUN!"

His mad shouting persisted as I took him under the arms to drag him free. "The sight of them, and the sounds—terrible to the hearing—they're coming. You can't let them get close or they'll strangle your mind—" Remaining calm, an unseen strength was guiding my actions.

"I got you, hang on. I'm getting good at this carrying-people thing." B1's alloy hands cradled the limp and decrepit rag that was once my father. The screams returned, accompanied by a thunderous roar of footsteps. I put Dad over the Brawler's shoulder and navigated out of the boulders to witness terror flooding down the tunnel. Huge creatures had packed the cavern's width, hollering and foaming to inflict their agony. Marching at us full speed, we were trapped against the tunnel's far end.

Attempting to run almost sealed our fate. B1's damaged legs were now only capable of a slow limp. The fuel level for the horizontal thrusters read empty but I punched it anyway, hoping for a last blast. The rear portals opened and threw bright, blue light down the passage, illuminating the oncoming horrors in every detail; red haired goliaths, some with horns or tusks, bird-like heads, fur-covered and other indescribable beasts. We blasted their direction toward the T-junction up ahead, toward the oncoming mob. I was closing on the intersection fast but so was the mass of monsters. It would be close.

We made the corner first, but only by inches. The creatures swarmed at the Brawler's back, fighting the jet-heat blasting over them. Beyond their reach, they clawed at me with a mental assault, clouding my perception into crippling fear. I had the sense that if they closed the gap they might collapse my spirit: a spirit that cried to be away from the undead.

The screams intensified as their essence formed into a long, gruesome hand. It reached out for us as we pulled out of the cavern. The whisper-voice returned with its final message, *"leaving so soon? but you'll miss all the fun!"* The impish laugh faded as B1 rocketed up the narrow path toward the converging tunnels, taking the one I thought looked most familiar. I shut down the thrusters to conserve the last of the fuel. We set down a short distance from the expanse of glowing and flowing earth.

The Brawler's arm braced our trio against the tunnel's wall, waiting for the angry hoard to find us—hungry and ready to feed. We waited to be ripped limb from limb in a demonic frenzy, but instead, a sudden stillness fell on everything.

Part 8: The Mission
Chapter 8

"Evan, my friend, my time here is finished. As if the mecha coming off the assembly line where not savage enough, I have now seen the first stages of what can only be described as unmanned, hunter-killers. They're going to combine the 'black oil' with some type of AI and turn these things loose on heaven only knows what. And if I could throw one more cat in the microwave so to speak, a large, bronze statue of Shiva has just been placed outside our main facility. Without pomp or announcement, has this dancing idol again been erected to signal a destructive force so powerful that rebirth is the only thing that can follow?"

—Dr. Newton Bigsby, *Notes from Beyond the Edge*

Except for the low hum of the Brawler system and ragged breathing, everything had turned numb. Not a sound. The ravenous creatures never left their cave, bound within it by something beyond explanation. For a moment, I listened to the air go in and out of my petrified anatomy. When my heart finally came to its senses I nearly blacked out in relief.

Then I remembered my friends and tried the Com.

"Beck? Pak? You guys out there? Come in. PLEASE HEAR ME!" I repeated the cry but not a crackle came back. Just eerie quiet. I set Dad down on the ground and changed over to bike mode before dismounting. B1's front beams provided enough light that I could remove the night vision Hat and see Dad with my own eyes. He looked awful, but a wonderful kind of awful. I smiled at shook my head.

"I'm not going to lie, you're a mess. But we're going to get you fixed up ASAP." I bent to one knee and took a closer look. He moaned and rubbed his face, as if to conceal it, then scooted away to the far wall. Leaning back against the rock, he took a long breath and resumed rubbing at his face and head. He looked up at nowhere, his eyes dead, expression blank.

"What happened to your mother?"

"It just happened, Dad. The timing is beyond cruel. And I was so close to having you both back together." Stopping right there would have been easier but with several impatient grunts he signaled that he wanted more. "It's a long story, but things got bad back home and we bugged-out to a resistance base with Newt..." I stopped again, in disbelief over my recent life, but he insisted I go on.

I told the tale without pride or shame, about how Newt had located his signal and sent me in for the rescue. As I relayed the incredible story my soul resisted the thought of the Collins base blowing up, but Beck had confirmed it. If the team hadn't come after me, they would have been killed too. Could my friends still be up there, waiting for me to emerge? I checked Dad's watch and realized they should have been gone by then if they'd followed orders. I made a show of inspecting the over-sized timepiece to see if my father might take note. He didn't.

One of my favorite cartoon movies had been a silly western with animals of all kinds surviving in a parched and forgotten burg. A wide-eyed shrew had boldly asked the new sheriff in town, a gecko, if she could have his boots when he was dead. This soon became a punch line around our house. And while Dad was never into boots, he had a thing for watches. On more than one occasion I recited the line while ogling a timepiece around his wrist. *"Can I have your watch when you are dead?"*—said in complete jest, in a failed Wild West drawl. But one of those watches had now found its way onto my arm. A strange guilt descended and made the weighty thing even more so. I considered telling a joke about grabbing for it as soon as he'd disappeared, yet his bleak and deflated body begged it inappropriate.

"I got your note. They *are* stealing our gravity. I saw it myself."

"Yes, but there is no gravity; was blind not see that before," he murmured, hounding himself over hidden failure. A long and worrisome pause followed; then: "It's an Electric Universe; simple and elegant, not needing man's mathematical improbabilities to exist. They're modifying the surface charge; altering our internal electric dipole. It's not gravity. Things move toward their natural chance at stillness or rest—which is where we're all supposed to be headed: back to dust. But they're violating that too. Everything. They won't be satisfied until God's divine order has been turned upside down. 'And now nothing will be withheld from them which they have imagined to do.' The end is very close, Garret, very close."

That was Dad. Just when I'd become a believer, now, according to him, there was no such thing as gravity. I couldn't make sense of the rest. Silence and despair overtook us both.

Then there was the team, and Beck. As much as I wanted to imagine them safely gone, I only had to picture what I would do if I were in their place. I would wait. Certainly for a few hours beyond any ordered deadline. Picturing them circling, desperate for me to make contact got my tired legs to standing, and then pacing. Dad, hardly blinking, was not ready for the massive, physical undertaking our exit would require. It was time to motivate my exhausted and distant escapee.

"The team has a ship but I can't get a call out to them. They're waiting to pick us up but enemy units have blocked these tunnels. I don't see a way out of here, do you?" Looking at him, I wasn't sure if he'd even absorbed what happened to Mom let alone anything else. "Dad, do you know a way out?" It took a few seconds before he forced himself to speak.

"No, I don't. That's why I hid," he said, looking away.

"Well, I might have been able to blast us out, but some traitorous tart deactivated my weapons. I'm not sure what I could do against a hundred enemy battle suits, but at least we could have tried."

"Weapons? Weapons," Dad sighed. "Newt gave them to you after all." He heaved another half-breath and collapsed his head into his hands, speaking through boney fingers. "It's a good thing he's dead or I would have killed him." *You and me both,* I thought.

"I've been trying to be a man of peace, really, but it's hard when you're pulled into the thick of it, ya know? But 'it's better to be a warrior in a garden than a gardener in a war.' Now there's a quote you should—" I cut myself short. He wasn't looking at me, and appeared as a man who'd lost both his mind and will to go on.

Failing here much the same way I'd been failing everyone else, I hadn't the life-giving words to feed a dying man. I wanted to ask him about his capture, the A-Type armor, giant rats and hags, but that would have to wait. Another minute of quiet ticked by before I spoke again.

"Remember the time I snuck out into your garage shop, and tried to walk around in that half-built, yellow mining suit? I lost my balance and tumbled into mom's transport, caving in the side panel?" He dropped his hands from his face so I went on. "And I left a note for her saying 'Dad didn't warn me the gyros were off on this thing,' and to see you about the damages? Priceless. It took us weeks to make that one up to her. Her heart broke in half when you disappeared..."

He groaned and attempted to lean over and hug me. I had to catch him to facilitate the weak embrace. His baggy, long sleeved shirt, filthy—felt empty, like a stuffed bear who'd lost its stuffing. Grasping him by the shoulders my eyes found his.

"It's not time to give up. We've got to try something. The team might be risking their lives out there, trying to hang on 'til we make contact. There has to be something we can do..."

Then inside him at last, a flickering flame.

"Your weapons, they're offline? How? If it was an unfamiliar saboteur, I doubt they'd know Newt's software coding well enough to shut it down that way. It's got to be the hardware."

I confirmed that all the interfaces were reading right, nothing in the display looked out of place. After I steadied him to his feet, I fetched the Swiss Army knife, penlight, and mechanical tape from the emergency kit. We worked together to remove a few access panels and I could hear Dad curse Newt's cobbled together system. My father's words sounded like blocked wood on sandpaper. I begged the tunnel's ceiling for a bottle of water but none was granted. He seemed to have a little fight left in him, grunting at the twisted wires.

"Doesn't look like she had much time. Just fried the juncture, I should be able to bypass the damage and—"

A sudden alert beeped out from B1's dash so I threw on my helmet to check the reading. The display had come alive, its sensors were going wild.

"Dad, you'd better hurry because something's coming down this tunnel toward us, and its moving fast!"

Part 8: The Mission
Chapter 9

"Anyone not in favor of broad scale genetic engineering reveals a reactionary nature."

—Delores Trufant, *Truth: The New Religion*

A pair of life forms was headed right at us, only a few hundred yards out. I thought it might be the rat-creatures but I couldn't imagine them running at such a rate. Whatever it was, it had blinding speed, in excess of thirty miles per hour. Could this be Beck, or Brody somehow, coming in for the rescue?

"Anything?" I pleaded with the decrepit man now frantic in his repair. His voice was strained and scared.

"Hang on a second! You could have least brought me a thermos of coffee if you wanted me to get right to work!" Those were the last words I heard Dad mutter before I put my helmet on and slid into B1. I would have to check for "friendlies" before firing—a split second decision of life and death.

"NOW?!" I begged louder, my finger hovering just above the trigger mechanism. "When you have the weapons online, get away cuz I'm going over to Brawler for a better range of movement!" Whatever it was, it was upon us. "Time's up, Dad. They're here!"

The ghastly abominations that scurried into view were anything but friendly and my hair-trigger didn't hesitate. I leapt B1 to our feet as twin 50 Caliber arm cannons sprang open, dumping their full magazines into the writhing, eight-foot-tall praying mantises—with fur. My Brawler fell back, knocked flat by the tremendous recoil of emptying both clips.

"Holy heck, Dad! What the—what the heck was—you okay out there?" I gasped for air and heard him coughing over the intense beating of my chest. The ting and tang of empty shells rained down the rocky walls and smoke filled the tunnel. "WHAT in heaven's name is that?"

"Heaven's got nothing to do with it, son. *That* is a spider-horse." Dad hacked some more and then recited something he felt applied from the Book of Jubilees.

"'And they taught the mixing of species in order to provoke the Lord.' Oh, they're provoking Him all right. You can't imagine the things I've seen Garret, the things being done in secret."

I *could* imagine, and despite the madness I'd recently witnessed, my fragile humanity remained in shock.

"I—I can't believe it!" I exclaimed, as my eyes attempted to reconcile the sight of an enormous insect covered in hair. The things were the size of stallions, kicking out their last bit of life against the ground. One let out a final death-shriek before the terrible sound choked silent from its own fluid. This arachnid-equestrian mix, this beast with multiple, tangled legs; jerked and spat out the thick solution before its movement slowed—and then stopped.

I fought to catch my breath and look over the Brawler's system status. The top-mounted missile pods had clanked hard against the tunnel's ceiling when I changed modes. They were now armed and online. My searchlights found Dad in the dark tunnel, lying limp against the cave wall. B1's externals spoke out to him in our processed voice.

"Can we get out of here fast, please? Before any more of them come? That was it for my guns." I ejected the forearm blasters onto the ground to lighten the load, and to keep Dad from getting burnt on the sizzling barrels. I coughed a few times myself and then yelled at him. "You've got to make these Brawlers with storage for spare clips! It's ridiculous to have only one per gun. I had just enough rounds to take those things out! And who still uses bullets? When do I get some beam weapons?"

"I didn't create the exo-suits to be your arsenal, Garret. Newton went against my strict orders to arm you."

Dad was irked, and as he struggled to his feet to face me, I remember thinking: *Yeah, but you never told me the Earth was FULL of monsters!* But there was no time to bicker.

"We can debate that later, Dad. You have to admit though, it's better than being eaten alive by freaking spider-horses!" Stunned, I spoke through a description of the unholy creatures lying there in their own ooze, but my father had no response to the commentary. He looked on the horrific sight immune and unphased. Their carcasses filled the tunnel, blocking our escape. The thought of having to pass through the smoking and draining bodies on our way out was destabilizing enough, but then I saw one of their hairy legs twitch. How could anyone think themselves a god, creating life like that on a whim?

"C'mon, we're leaving. I'm going to carry you out and send a few missiles at the enemy mechs guarding the end of this passage. If the impact collapses the tunnel we're screwed, but that's the best I've got. Any suggestions?"

The old man wasn't a bit pleased with how proficient I was at destruction, nor my near avoidance of serious cursing. He shook his head and climbed into B1's blue and white arm, objecting to the young man I'd become.

After promising to cover him with the Brawler's hand as the missiles fired, I remarked how our thruster fuel may run dry at any second. Dad smiled and said he'd made the gauge overly sensitive, just like he always appreciated in his granddad's old truck. I breathed a sigh of relief as I activated the zero-point, anti-grav generator to take us off the ground. The blue fire sputtered to life at our back, and I eased us forward on the rear thrusters. My sweating hands resisted taking us any closer to those hideous atrocities, but I hit the accelerator and shot ahead. Their upturned legs thumped on the hull as we rocketed past.

There was only a moment to execute the plan. My sensors were picking up thirteen enemy targets, in and around the mag-lev junction at the tunnels exit. I had to wait until we were close enough before unleashing my SAM missiles in order to limit the Scimitar's reaction time.

Our saving grace was the long, bow-shaped tunnel. It would allow me to guide the winding missiles around the corner, but prevent the Scimitar's plasma beams from getting to us before our projectiles hit home. I shouted to Dad over the speakers as we picked up speed.

"Ready, Dad? Going to fire in three, two..."

Twin missiles ripped free of the top pods, hurtling toward their enemy targets. They pulled around the curve and soared out of the cave, puncturing a Scimitar in the midsection close to the entrance, the other flying to the far platform before it detonated. The explosion blinded my night vision as we burst through the ball of fire. I shielded my passenger with B1's forearm and we punched beyond the eruption.

I called out for my father but couldn't hear anything over the chaos. Hitting the jets on full thrust, we shot down the tube toward the abandoned base. The fuel level no longer registered on my display, declaring the reserves were past empty. Warning alarms blinked in bright red as enemy battle suits, surviving the explosion, achieved target-lock. We had one second before their plasma cannons vaporized us.

Killing the thrusters, my flying knight spun to face our adversaries. To this day I do not recall ordering B1 to do so. As its alloy feet touched down, the Brawler's two remaining missiles screamed loose into the approaching Scimitar battalion. There was barely time to pivot back around and ride the shock wave down the rail, escaping the concussion. Rocks and fire heaved our flying Brawler down the collapsing tunnel. I put B1's armored hand over Dad's head for protection, reactivating the jets to stay ahead of the rolling blast. The thrusters sputtered out as we reached the platform outside the base's entrance. We were just beyond a dense cloud of smoke and dust rolling our direction. I limped my beaten exo-suit along the terrace and verified that my passenger had survived the ordeal.

"Dad? You still alive out there?"

"Yes, but you're trying to remedy that," he growled, but then softened. "That was some pretty fancy flying back there, son."

His compliment sent an unlikely dose of cheer straight to my core, like just I'd sunk a three-pointer for the win. But a sudden explosion rang out in the distance, a reminder this was no game. The door to the base stood sealed before us as enemy signals moved our way.

"Dad, could you give me a hand with this?" B1 reached down to remove Minerva's J-22 claw from its magnetic holder and held it up for his inspection. I took the opportunity to offer a few more Brawler design improvements. "More exterior storage on these rides is also a must."

"I'll get right on that," he answered, utterly spent.

"I don't think you will. Remember, our house and lab have been blown sky high too. You missed a lot of fun times." I crossed my fingers and waved the broken claw in front the hatch's ID panel. The doorway opened as I tried in vain to reach the team over the Com. I even called out to Glynn and Cavalry 1 with the same result; still nothing but static. I kept my helmet with me in case they tried to make contact, but I wouldn't be taking anything else. My Brawler's generator was reading a fault warning, its power draining away. I had seconds to exit the dying contraption.

Setting my ailing passenger down, I called for bike mode but it took several seconds longer than it should. The tired mechanism wailed in complaint, resisting its final change in form. The Brawler's windshield had been reduced to a web of glistening pebbles that disintegrated the moment it tried to retract. The jagged bits rained down around me as I pulled my fragile body out into the open. Like a slimy snail, I extracted the soft, inner-Garret from a shell it never wanted to leave. The least capable predator now held sway over me and I fought hard to resist crawling back inside for protection—no, to be whole again.

Helping Dad to his feet and into the bases' dark halls, I turned to look back at my blue war-cycle. The trusty steed had gone though hell and it showed. B1's hull was scarred with a thousand shots; punctured, scorched and coughing up some kind of black fluid. The paint job was almost worn away, its frame belching smoke as we left it behind. The feeling was that of leaving a severed arm abandoned on the deck. Smoke and filth caught up with us and covered my exo-bike in its murk. Sounds of explosions and the collapsing tunnel crashed at our ears as we made for the stairs. I slammed the door as the dust storm devoured the platform.

There was a rest room just outside the stairwell and I prayed the plumbing contained a few drops of moisture. The blissful sound of flowing water filled my ears, and my mouth, before I dashed back for Dad. He was getting too weak to walk but his scrawny body allowed me to carry him with ease over to the life-saving sink.

As he cupped the water to his lips I caressed his stringy hair away from his face. Outside the cavern's dim light, the sight of something disturbing was now visible.

"Uh Dad, your head is fried back here, and there's chunks of caked blood…" My hand moved to touch the wound but he pulled away.

"Had to. Had to kill their tracking chip. Had to use the last of the armor's power to fry myself," he said, taking a few more sips. "And you wonder why I'm in such a bad mood. Thought it might knock out the SOS beacon as well since I couldn't get out of the suit."

"Yeah, it did. We lost your signal a few times," I said all the more amazed. He staggered and nearly slumped to the floor before I caught him, but there was hardly anything there to catch. The image I'd been carrying over the past year was that of an invincible man, protesting his capture, like some kind of angry ape pulling hard on his metal bars. How could such a pillar of strength become so feeble and broken? Despite their best efforts to destroy him, he'd managed to escape. I pictured the giant countess and her minions, vowing our business was far from over.

"I'm proud of you, Dad." He paused in his gulping and set both elbows on the counter to keep from dissolving downward. He looked at me, at last relieved.

"Only when we have to fight to stay human, do we realize how precious it is to be one."

I asked him who said that one and he answered that he had, with a tired smirk. Then I remembered my wounded side and looked at it to find it healed. Whoever that glowing apparition was, I liked his style, and the idea of having a sword of "ricocheting thunder." I rubbed Dad's back and called an end to our respite.

"We gotta go now. I just hope the team held out for us."

The one million stairs proved grueling, with several stops along the way. I carried my gaunt father for most it, and he struggled through the rest. At last we arrived at the main exit doors, still caved in from Minerva's J-22, exhausted.

As Dad and I broke into the sunlight, the first sunbeams of dawn were stinging the surrounding mountain peaks. I held my father tight, relishing our moment of victory.

What a glorious sight it was—that is until twenty Scimitars marched into place, lining both ridges above us. The double rows of menacing battle suits cast black shadows and dust across the incline, their neutral plasma blasters fixed on our position. The sight of them sapped any remaining strength.

Then more Scimitar carrier ships soared overhead, dropping their army of battle mecha into the already crowded landscape.

Part 8: The Mission
Chapter 10

They will have no fear of bad news; their hearts are steadfast, trusting in Yahweh.

—Psalm 112:7

"Thanks for trying, son. You did your best."

"I don't accept this, Dad." There was panic in my voice but I felt full of faith. "I mean, I think I just saw an angel—and he said I would carry a thundering sword. Yes, they're standing over us, looking invincible, but all we need is a jawbone to fight back. Father, please!" I wailed to the unseen over the injustice.

A large military truck arrived at the top of the hill, unloading its squadron of troops. With them was the man in the long, purple robe I'd seen below, second in command to the giant queen. We'd become the prize that eluded many. A brazen vampire defying the rising sun, he meant to victimize us and increase his standing with her.

With a wave of his hand, the soldiers started down the incline in our direction. I drooped my helmeted head and shut my eyes, refusing to accept what they were seeing. The angelic words spoken in the cave whirled within my mind and I reached out to seize them.

They would not escape unfulfilled. Courage had fled my heart at the Firefight, but I refused to acquiesce to that disbelief again. When I opened my eyes to scan the opposition, I could at last count one ally among them.

Jay's green Brawler stood at the top of the dusty ridge, a gun fighter ready to square off against overwhelming odds. All his armored suit needed to complete the picture was the colorful, market day poncho whipping in the wind.

One or two Scimitars turned to locate what their sensors were picking up, but again, it was too late. Thick bolts of white lighting struck him and then crackled out in every direction, into a vast web of ruination. I hunched over Dad, sheltering him from the flaming chunks of robotic parts crumbling into our ravine.

Explosions pounded our eardrums and the ground shook from carrier ships plowing into the desert floor. The remaining members of the Philmore family were covered with a blanket of dirt and a few smoldering pieces of Scimitar. I coughed away the dust and wiped the grime from my visor. There was no truck, no troops; they'd been covered over by piles of demolished parts. When the smoke cleared, Jay stood at the top of the heap and shouted to us over his externals.

"So, I guess they haven't found a way to stop that yet!"

"Guess not. Boy, are you a sight for sore eyes," I sighed into the Com. I asked Jay how he was feeling and of course, he said his ribs were killing him. I apparently still *owed him big time.*

Explosions popped in the distance before Cavalry 2 howled overhead, blazing away with its front mounted cannon. The earth around us trembled as the strident ship sent more carrier ships out of the sky and into oblivion. Jay reminded me that my mission was complete.

"I knew you'd find him, Garret. Welcome back Mr. Philmore.

Good to see you again, but we've got to scram. More enemy fighters are coming in. Let's go."

Jay rocketed his green Brawler into the gully and requested a pick-up. In a moment's time, Calvary 2 hovered in for us, its long ramp open and waiting. Old Bloodthirsty himself flew out in his J-22 and let his payload fly at some approaching fighters, giving us some much needed cover. Once inside the great ship, I asked for Glynn.

"Is he here? Has anyone tried to make contact with him?" Beck and Pak were onboard, and Pak took Dad from my arms. I hugged Beck and she said they hadn't heard anything from Glynn. As our dropship lifted off, I stormed to the front cockpit to push Captain Miller for a quick scan of the area amidst a barrage of protests from the rest of the crew.

I assured him Cavalry 1 should be waiting just behind a set of hills that were already visible from our position, at the end of a long ridge. With Minerva dead, it was possible no one ever discovered the hidden craft. I hoped my talkative friend was still there, playing cards and wondering what was taking us so long.

Brody Freeman joined us in the cockpit, heaving and sweating. He nodded at me in approval and put his palm on the top of my hair. His heavy hand slid to the side of my head before he shook himself from the moment, shouting loud enough for the whole ship to hear.

"We got over fifty signals closing in right now. They'll be on top of us in two minutes. We've got to cloak out, pronto!" But then the major grunted and in a softer voice, ordering Captain Miller to hit the throttle and take us over the next collection of hills. Freeman gave the whole endeavor twenty seconds to play itself out before we'd have to flee the area. Since Cavalry 1 might still be invisible, the captain offered our last hope of locating the ship.

"If it's in range I can remote prompt it to drop its cloak—and there it is!" Brody's eyes narrowed at the vessel below and his decision was swift.

"Jaxon! Wolf 3; get ready to jump. You're helping me fly that bird out of here." With that Brody Freeman disappeared to the rear of the ship but the overhead PA continued to shout his bawling voice.

"Miller, beam those coordinates over to Cavalry 1's system and fly cover. We'll have that thing off the ground in forty seconds or I'm aborting and coming right back. Clear?"

"Roger that." Miller replied. "The enemy squadron will be on us about one minute, twenty-five seconds. Dropping Cavalry 1's rear ramp now. Everyone in the back, please get secured. This is going to get bumpy."

I sat down in the co-pilot seat and felt my empty stomach twist as Captain Miller lurched the big ship to the right, flying low into the ravine. That terrible feeling doubled when Brody's voice came back over the PA seconds later.

"I'm sorry Garret, he's gone. Shot in the head at close range."

Senseless. That wench must have done it when she faked that last minute check on the cloaking system. Nothing in her countenance revealed she'd just ended a young man's life. How can evil so overtake a person that they're no longer disturbed by horror? How could I have been so blind? Who knows, perhaps Minerva was calling out to Glynn across an impassable chasm at that very moment, pleading for him to place a drop of water on her scorching tongue?

"I'm picking up some wild gravitational readings," Captain Miller called out from his pilot's seat. "We'd better make ourselves scarce." He glanced back at me as his bright strap of teeth showed how much he was enjoying the danger.

While I wasn't ready to smile in the face of impending doom, I was neutral with it. Dad had a Stonewall Jackson quote he loved to recite, about feeling as safe in battle as in bed—since God had fixed the time of our deaths. *One must always be ready for it to overtake you.* The climax of the quote stated that *this is how all men should live, then all would be equally brave.* Was I at last brave—or just too tired to care?

I lacked any feeling about completing the mission. Was it accomplished? One wound had healed only for another to take its place. Dad was alive—but Mom was dead. Life was an imbedded knife, ever twisting.

Pastor B was right, there was a price to pay for carrying out the wrath of God, and I felt like I was just getting started. I wondered where PB could have gone and if I would ever have the good fortune to see his face again. Captain Miller and Major Freeman exchanged a final list of confirmations over the Com before we shot upward in rapid ascent. Captain Miller let out another big smile.

"Coordinates locked in, major. Blinking out in 3, 2, 1—we're cloaked. See you on the other side. Miller, OUT."

Part 8: The Mission
Chapter 11

"Mythos are alive with legends of valiant allegiance and self sacrifice for the greater cause. But when the curtains close, and the poetic vows go silent, one is often left with a dim backstage of human frailty and fear.

This team of young people, kids really, looked some of the most debilitating sights straight in the eye and managed to overcome them, and themselves."

—Birdie Vilmos, *And Then There Were Four*

"Where are we going, captain?" It took all my strength to formulate the single, muffled sentence.

"Someplace friendly," Miller responded over his shoulder. "The major says he's not sure how they'll react to our arrival but they've got no love for aliens I can tell you that. Heck of a job in there, Garret. Maybe we can get you a medal or something."

I closed my eyes, swiping at the sweat and grit on my forehead.

"A hot tub and a big coconut drink will do. Oh, and throw in one of those little umbrellas while you're at it," I groaned, but the captain was no longer paying attention. He punched away at some buttons and called out a set of fresh directives to the crew. No time to celebrate. We would have to skip the parade.

When I finally pried free of the seat and staggered to the rear, Pak was standing beside Ivy and Nia in the operations center. They didn't know whether to offer congratulations or pity. It was more awkward than it had to be. These were my friends. Their love was best expressed unspoken. After I thanked big Pak for coming back for me, he fumbled for some conciliatory words and guided me toward the infirmary.

I shuffled passed their saddened group and put my eyes on Dad's limp body laying on a cot. The sight of him there, alive in the flesh, was surreal. Beck leaned over what was left of my father and brushed his straggly hair to the side. She looked more exhausted and strung out than I ever thought possible.

"Suri started an IV for him and he is resting," Beck said, straightening Dad's pillow. "But he's going to need some professional care." When she raised an eyebrow my direction I realized I'd been staring at her. I cleared my throat and darted my gaze.

"I don't know where they're taking us but I'm certain Dad's going to be all right. If he survived that living nightmare, nothing's going to kill him."

Beck and Suri looked at me for clarity over our situation, an answer to where we might be going. I had nothing. There must have been some assuring words in the mist, easily plucked and offered, but none came. Maybe I was too selfish to reach for them. I looked around for a place to collapse, mumbling something about sitting down before I fell down. Beck checked with Suri to make sure she would be okay watching over Dad by herself.

As they parted, their intimate communication confounded me. They leaned in close to each other, talking in soft tones, affirming one another with a touch on the arm. If that was my competition, all my chips might as well be cashed. I was about as subtle as a drunken rhinoceros.

No one was sitting in the passenger area and I vowed to sprawl myself across all six seats the first moment I could. For now, one seat would have to do. I sat and then sank twelve inches until my knees were at eye level. Beck joined me and she got right to work.

"I told you not to trust that woman."

I sighed and forced an eye back open.

"And you expected me to make the right decision? If given the chance, I seem to take the path most troubled." I closed it again and hoped Beck would do the same. No such luck.

"At least there is a constant in your universe, but I don't want to be part of the collateral damage." Her tone demanded immediate admission of failure and a swift poke to my ribs popped the seal on my eyelids. Couldn't we just pass out together, peacefully, and resume this argument later? I'd lose no matter when it took place anyway.

"If anyone can handle me it's you, Beck. I just wish we were more on the same page, you know? And not so at odds all the time."

"Maybe God has me on this ride to hold your ego in check, to bust open your callous heart and make it feel things it would steer clear of."

She was the greatest of heroines, the best of battlers. If only Beck wasn't so skilled at verbal jousting. At my best, I would be at a disadvantage with her, but being that fatigued was like having my tongue tied behind my back.

"That's what people say when they don't want to stop being a pain, Mac, that they're serving some kind of noble purpose," I groaned. "Of course I want you by my side. I just wish you weren't a thorn in it so much of the time."

"Well, you can keep right on hoping I'll fit nice and neat into one of those compartments on your lunch tray. Just the right amount of 'Beck' to balance everything else you want to slop on there. That's not me and it will never be me. There is no conquering Rebecca and then moving on to the next challenge."

I let that thought linger for a moment and it had me nodding my head. Of course she was right, *again*. Why fight it. I stuck out my lower lip and conceded.

"Yeah, all right. I like that." I said, as matter-of-fact. "You win, you can have the whole, damn tray." She laughed and slid down in her seat until her knees were level with mine.

"Close your eyes and stick out your hand before you ruin everything."

The playful way she phrased it kept me from passing out, then Beck placed something in my hand. I opened my aching fingers to find a little jade bear.

It was one of the charms.

Her eyes were at last closed a few inches above a long smile. No doubt Beck was counting the seconds until I said the worst possible thing. I rubbed the smooth surface and examined it. Her knight had just traveled thousands of miles on his noble quest to win the prize and claim what was his. I closed my eyes too, placing the charm against my face to feel it against my skin. An immense relief—but I couldn't resist.

"Beck? It's got a big hole in its head, from where it connects to the bracelet. Are you trying to tell me something?"

She burst out laughing and slapped her legs, calling me a few choice names for joking during her big moment. Rebecca Sprankle was neither the desert, nor the flower found there—she was both. Or more like the prickly pear whose razor sharp needles guarded its soft fruit from would-be pickers.

"Oh, I think you know," she said, referring the hole in my skull.

"Beck, you're breaking up the set, do you want to do that?" I was being craftier than she realized with that statement, but she didn't bite. She kept laughing and refused to answer any further inquiries about what the gift meant.

When she looked at me we had our first kiss. A little kiss, about the size of that stone bear. It was not the stuff of movies, but we were at our best when our best had been emptied out.

"You don't know where we're going?" she asked with soft eyes.

I didn't—and that was the truth in so many ways.

Epilogue

The more the world thought itself near to reaching a golden age of peace and enlightenment, the further its fat, awkward fingers pushed it away. As Earth's gravity continued to wane, its inhabitants kept right on squabbling, their houses crumbling around them.

Israel had been attacked with a brutal barrage of chemical weapons, devastating large portions of the erstwhile nation, inflicting tens of thousands of causalities. They retaliated with a strong, but strategic nuclear attack; their military might pushing Northeast to apprehend the former regions of Jordan, Lebanon and parts of Southern Syria.

The collective world stood aghast at their actions. Not only was war thought to be a thing of the past, nuclear weapons were outlawed and believed to be universally incapacitated. The rolling roar of a raging lion demanded Israel's quick and total annihilation.

As Armageddon descended upon the Middle East the Messengers stepped in to reveal their representative. While *he* has kept his identity guarded, rumors soon swirled and pervaded of an alleged mother of Jordanian descent and father from the stars. Their 'Emissary', without an apparent vote or argument, assumed the position of Premier and Chair of the Council of Resplendent Light. He cried for peace and forgiveness from a world jerked to attention by his improbable appearance. Everyone now assumes the Messengers look human, although the rest remain in the shadows to propagate the tantalizing mystery. Our benefactors looking much as we do issued a tsunami of relief considering the horrific appearance of the Vril and insect-like Veknar. The dark cloud of Xenophobia had at last revealed its silver lining.

The Messenger's charismatic envoy put the world on the edge of their seats, wrapped around his captivating finger. His near perfect appearance would not have been so unsettling except for the eight feet of height that arrived with it. Tawny brown skin covers a physique of towering concrete, with slight, smoldering eyes of more black than white. His look of thick eyeliner might have been mistaken for natural except for distinct points darting away from their outer corners. His smoky voice is smooth and low, incapable of verbal misstep. Long, squarish beards are becoming the trend for men everywhere.

It's being joked that women across the world are losing interest in Earthmen over the speculation that all the orbiting ET males might look similar. To say he commands a room is the boldest of understatements. He has the ear of the UN, the former Pope, and is rumored to be considering the Council of Resplendent Light's dissolution. Though not stated, since he has become the voice of our alien benefactors, the CRL's existence might now be redundant.

Meanwhile, his Jordanian mother, a Sophia Kadmos, has become the new world's first super-celebrity. "Ms. Sophia" as she is being called, will reveal no information about the father except to say "they" appeared to her before his conception, and said her coming son would bring fortitude to a world on the threshold of both peace and war. She lamented not seeing him grow up as he left to prepare for his life's purpose, and stated she was "blessed among woman." But Ms. Sophia suggested there were others like her without further detail.

Ms. Sophia, an extremely tall and shapely beauty, has had her picture plastered on every available surface. She's garnered universal appreciation for bridging the gap between our cultures—and possibly our species. Her striking emerald eyes are the icon for a world needing one. Of course, both Israel and Syria are claiming her true origins lay in their former nations.

Still, no one has confirmed if The Messengers are supposed to be our ancestors or creators, but they have revealed that through their extensive knowledge, gained over millennia of research, humanity's DNA has become flawed and must be realigned. Through toxic pollution and irresponsible reproduction, our blue print has deviated from the original. Homo sapiens are supposed to be taller, have psychic abilities and live much longer lives. Cancer is a straight up defect, a lethal glitch in our genetic code, and that code needs re-written. Our space friends can fix us of course—and millions are asking to be repaired.

The Messenger's nameless emissary has continued to call for Israel's clemency. He claims his request is based on the former, sliver of a country being the true victim; not of Hezbollah, but of the blindness caused by dogmatic ideologies. This intermediary from beyond turned the situation on its head when he referred to the Messengers as "his people," and how they were almost destroyed eons ago by the same turmoil bubbling in the Middle East and in areas throughout our planet. He begged our world anew to give up ancient cults and convinced our freed masses through his rare but Golden Speeches how religious sects have only resulted in conflict. Humanity, as a whole agreed, hailing the wisdom brought down from above.

Now the Messenger's ambassador has clarified the demands of the UN and CRL: If the former nation of Israel does not forsake their dogmatic views, they will be stamped out as hateful reactionaries. However, if they abide and join the new enlightenment, they will not be required to pull out of the conquered territory. Instead they will learn to live in peace with those they've called their enemy for so long. Should Israel comply, they are promised an unprecedented peace and a cessation of hostilities forever.

With borders fast evaporating under UN directives, what would be the point of declaring this country owns this, and that one that, anyway. We're supposed to forget about those archaic ways of thinking, join arm in arm as one intergalactic voice and sing Kumbaya. Israel's choice to give up religion in favor of peace appears an easy one.

In honor of the seventh Truism that ended hateful denominations, a temporary peace treaty has been formed giving the former Israel seven months to clean up the nuclear and chemical waste, and their countless dead. They either progress forward—or are destroyed. A great re-gathering of the Jewish people to the Holy Land is now underway, along with a surprising number of Torah-observant Christians. The battered region is experiencing a spiritual revival, quite the opposite effect the global minds were hoping for. A once secular nation, Israel has had little interest in rebuilding their Holy Temple. But that sentiment has grown strong, well beyond the Orthodoxy, to all those who want to spurn the Emissary's call to unify under a one-world religion of non-religion.

So will they keep the land and embrace this newfound security, renouncing their timeless devotions? Or will they turn toward the God of Abraham in defiance, relying on Him to preserve them through the gathering storm? In a very short time, they must make their renunciation or be in violation of this most stringent agreement.

The rest of the world is watching, waiting to see if they are allowed to break out the big stick of retribution. But no one is making a move without *his* say so. Everyone is tripping over themselves to gain the Emissary's favor, evolve and relinquish their "dead religions" to unite under his banner of spiritual freedom. Human kind has begged for the Emissary's name, but he's shrewdly refused, and refused to accept any praise or admiration for his efforts.

As for the reduction in gravity, and somebody's nefarious plan to cause it, it's an adversary that has taken far too much from me. If those massive generators are built deep within our planet's lay lines, then somebody will have to figure out a way to stop them, but it's not going to be easy. Earth's gravity is now a steady twenty percent less than it was five years ago, with much less fluctuation. If indeed the process is artificial, they're working out the kinks.

Team Zero-Gs survived and ended up in an unlikely place. But that's our only option since the world has run fresh out of likely destinations for our ilk. There's always a remnant out there—those who refuse to be pawns of the dark power. And it doesn't look like our swords will be turned into plowshares anytime soon. Though the greatest weapon is still Christians who know their God.

As much as I wanted to be done with war, take a long vacation and get to that garden in the middle of nowhere, the battle is calling me back. The relocation has been tough, opening our eyes to both wonderful and unsettling discoveries.

It's been a trying time for everyone, and it has taken me months to figure out whether or not I have found my real father...

—Garret Philmore, *Letters on the Lamb: A Collected Journal*

Preview: Book II

Five years since we'd made our escape. Five—long—years. And ten years since disclosure. We were far from alone. Earthspace was crowded. Mostly with things that wanted to eat our lunch, or just eat us. The concept of "aliens," once a misty vapor, had bared its bloody, jagged teeth right in my face. Sleepless nights, shouting at the ceiling in pools of cold sweat never let me forget the terror; the stark stench of real terror.

Post-Meltdown, after suburbs and super-marts were emptied of their luxury, I can recall the subject of ETs gripping our youth group in a round of naive chatter. More than one simpleton claimed that aliens were demons. We'll just "take authority over them," they said. Wishful thinking that went on in Christian circles until they actually showed up. No, these guys have ships. Miles of physical, clang-your-fist-on-them ships. And those are the good guys, the Messengers here to save us. They mostly look human, only bigger. They're staying hidden for the most part. "The future is about humanity," not them—*so they say.*

Then, as if the five-year sentence had been a dream, the shakes were back. I welcomed them, telling myself I was born for the nerve-wrenching mission about to get underway. All the hiding, all the waiting was about to end with a bang.

Whether good luck or bad, the airships of Cavalry 1 and 2 were fully loaded with brand new, Caliber MarkII Variable Mode Battle Suits when they left Outpost 6, jam-packed with tech and supplies for an assassination mission they would never complete. Now I was in one; a hot one judging by the escalating temps inside the bulky CaliberII.

The timing of the mission was immersed in distraction. The commencement of our OP was carefully chosen to be just that, and I was falling victim to it as well. From within my battle armor, I glared at the spectacle materializing on the HUD. As a species of enlightened progressives, Earthlings were making our case to the Messengers that we would no longer cling to religion's dogmatic past. Just moments away, a week long world-wide celebration of tearing down our holiest sculptures and shrines was about to culminate. Shattering the ten story Christ the Redeemer statue, illuminated high above Rio de Janeiro, would extinguish one of our miserable world's last remaining wonders. Gone in seven days; Tian Tan Buddha in Hong Kong, Laykyun Sekkya in Myanmar, Lord Murugan in Malaysia, and countless more enduring icons of sacred devotion. But with takeoff upon us, and my own demise a distinct possibility, those countless other icons meant as little to me as bricks torn from a condemned building.

I remember thinking then, horrified at the images playing across the monitor, that it was somehow my savior about to be torn apart. Christ was going to go through His humiliation all over again before the cheering mob. We'd chosen Barabbas a second time, we'd chosen the Messengers. Like some kind of warped crescendo on New Year's Eve, a countdown began its digital descent. Twenty minutes until my redeemer was to be dashed to the ground; twenty minutes remained as the counter spun toward zero. The same blasphemy must have been playing out on the rest of the squad's displays because the atmosphere crackled in wanton revenge. Any mixed emotion over creating war at the time of burgeoning peace had evaporated. The sight of cables and hooks entangling the ivory likeness of our Messiah was an undeniable call back to arms.

As the era of Christianity came to a crashing halt, every eye would be fastened to the coverage—and that's when we'd strike...

25394152R10233

Made in the USA
Columbia, SC
31 August 2018